INDIA'S GREEN REVOLUTION

Economic Gains and Political Costs

Written under the auspices of
THE CENTER OF INTERNATIONAL STUDIES,
PRINCETON UNIVERSITY

A list of other Center publications appears at the back of the book

INDIA'S GREEN REVOLUTION

Economic Gains
and Political Costs

FRANCINE R. FRANKEL

PRINCETON UNIVERSITY PRESS
PRINCETON, NEW JERSEY
1971

Publication of this book has been aided by a grant from
the Whitney Darrow Publication Reserve Fund
of Princeton University Press

This book has been set in Linotype Caledonia
Printed in the United States of America
by Princeton University Press

Acknowledgments

THE PHRASE "green revolution" has all the qualities of a good slogan. It is catchy; it simplifies a complex reality; and most important, it carries the conviction that fundamental problems are being solved. Agriculture, it suggests, is being peacefully transformed through the quiet workings of science and technology, reaping the economic gains of modernization while avoiding the social costs of mass upheaval and disorder usually associated with rapid change.

Yet, a democratic government does well not to be persuaded by its own slogans. Indeed, there is a strong inducement of self-interest in wanting to discover the truth. Opposition parties will in any case trumpet bad news and seek to use it for their political advantage. The press will give wide publicity to all the details of any disaster.

At the time I arrived in India in February 1969 a growing number of politicians and bureaucrats were persuaded by considerations of prudence to probe behind the slogan to the reality. The program for rapid agricultural modernization formulated in 1965 to concentrate new high-yielding rice and wheat seeds and complementary modern inputs in irrigated areas had shown mixed results. On the one hand, there was strong evidence of a productivity breakthrough in the irrigated wheat areas. On the other, the potential of the new rice varieties was still largely unrealized. At the same time, sample surveys showed that, far from the total transformation of the agricultural economy implied by the slogan of a green revolution, only some 10 percent of the area under crops had been affected. More disturbing, this area was largely accounted for by a minority of large land-owners with capital to invest in costly modern methods. Most alarming, there were reports of a sharp increase in the number of agrarian agitations organized around demands of the landless for distribution of land.

The interest and concern about the social and political consequences of the green revolution was strongest inside the government agencies immediately concerned with the implementation of the new program. The Directorate of Economics and Statistics of the Ministry of Food and Agriculture, always interested in tapping all available sources of information, undertook in this instance to coordinate the arrangements for my field trips to selected districts. My gratitude to J. S. Sarma, Economic and Statistical Advisor, Ram Saran, Special Advisor, and D. V. Reddy, the then Extension Commissioner, cannot be overstated. I also want to express my personal appreciation to Raj Kumar for the careful attention he invariably gave to even the smallest details of scheduling.

I was doubly fortunate in having the assistance of the Planning Commission's Program Evaluation Organization (P.E.O.) headed by Dr. P. K. Mukherjee. The major obstacles involved in carrying out field research over five widely separated areas of India, each having a separate regional language, were overcome by arrangements for the regional Project Evaluation Officer to travel with me and act as interpreter. The value of this assistance was all the greater in view of the P.E.O. officers' specialized training and skills in interviewing informants within a rural setting as part of their responsibility for collecting data used in official progress reports.

I remember with special gratitude the courtesy and cooperation extended to me by local development staff members and the P.E.O. officers in each of the districts visited. I particularly want to express my deep appreciation to

Pritam Singh, Project Officer, Ludhiana; T. V. Thomas, Joint Director, Palghat; P. T. Joseph, Project Evaluation Officer, Calicut; Y. Seshagiri Rao, Project Evaluation Officer, Eluru; and K. N. Ramanujam, Special District Agricultural Officer, Thanjavur.

I have benefited greatly from the willingness of Indian and American scholars and administrators to share their experience with me through informal discussions and comments. I want especially to thank A. S. Atwal, S. S. Johl, J. S. Sarma, P. K. Mukherjee, Tarlok Singh, John P. Lewis, Ralph Cummings, Jr., Wolf Ladejinsky, William W. Lockwood, and Karl von Vorys.

My debt to a number of institutions for support during this period is also very great. The University of Pennsylvania granted me a leave of absence which permitted an extended field trip to India. The costs of travel and living expenses were met by a grant from the American Philosophical Society; and also by the U. S. AID Mission, New Delhi, where I was a Consultant. During the period of preparing this manuscript for publication I was aided by my affiliation as Visiting Fellow at the Center of International Studies, Princeton University, and most particularly, by the superb secretarial assistance of Jane G. McDowall, June Traube, and Mary Merrick.

In sum, I was extremely fortunate in receiving a very wide range of cooperation and support in carrying out this study. Any shortcomings, therefore, are all the more my own.

Contents

Tables

INDIA'S GREEN REVOLUTION

Economic Gains and Political Costs

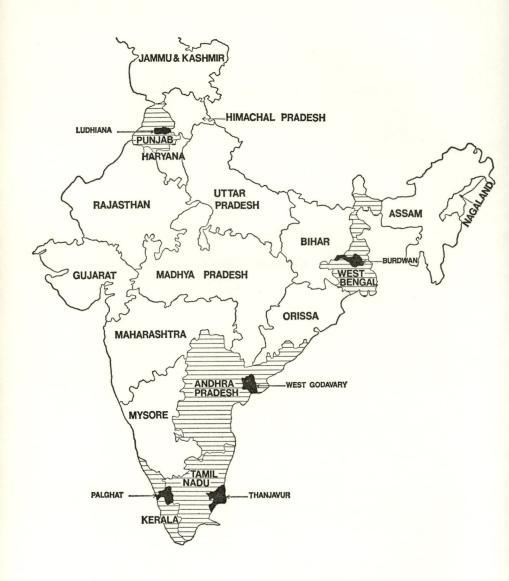

1. Introduction

DURING the first three five-year plans, India's approach to agricultural development was characterized by a commitment to two co-equal, yet often irreconcilable goals: the economic aim of achieving maximum increases in agricultural output to support rapid industrialization; and the social objective of reducing disparities in rural life.

One of the most difficult dilemmas arose from the obvious economic advantage of concentrating scarce inputs of improved seeds, fertilizers, pesticides, and equipment in irrigated areas of the country where they could be expected to bring the greatest returns in output. Indeed, the selection of the first Community Projects in 1952 was guided by this consideration. They were allocated only to districts with assured water from rainfall or irrigation facilities. Almost immediately, however, serious social objection was raised to the practice of "pick[ing] out the best and most favorable spots"[1] for intensive development while the largest part of the rural area was economically backward. Within a year, the principle of selective and intensive development was abandoned. The Planning Commission announced a program for rapid all-India coverage under the National Extension Service and Community Development Program with special attention to backward and less-favored regions.

The social goal of reducing disparities also influenced the selection of methods of agricultural development. The planners were inclined to give only secondary importance to the introduction of costly modern inputs as a means of increas-

[1] India, Ministry of Community Development, *Jawaharlal Nehru on Community Development* (Delhi, 1957), 13.

3

ing agricultural productivity. Instead, they devised agricultural development programs based on "intensive cultivation of land by hand—and improving conditions of living in rural areas through community projects, land reforms, consolidation of holdings, etc."[2] Indeed, the planners' strategy for agricultural development rested on the capacity of the Community Development Program to mobilize more than 60 million peasant cultivators for participation in labor-intensive agricultural production programs and community works, including the construction of capital projects. The crux of the approach—the major inducement to greater effort on the part of the small farmers—was the promise of social reform held out by large-scale initiatives for institutional change. The highest priority was assigned to rapid implementation of land reforms, including security of tenure, lower rents, transfer of ownership rights to tenants, and redistribution of land. Meanwhile, state-partnered village cooperatives were created to fortify small farmers with cheap credit facilities and economies of bulk purchase and sale of agricultural commodities.

In retrospect, it was probably inevitable that a development strategy requiring extensive land reforms and institutional change as preconditions for success should meet with powerful opposition from landed groups; and that in a political democracy, where land-owning interests are heavily represented in the legislatures, this resistance should manifest itself in a go-slow approach toward agrarian reform. By the early 1960's, most legislation on tenancy reform and ceilings on land ownership had not been effectively implemented. Yet, in the absence of agrarian reform it proved impossible to provide attractive incentives to the majority of small farmers for participation in labor-intensive agricultural production programs.

Actually, as early as 1958, lagging growth rates in the

[2] P. C. Mahalanobis, *Talks on Planning* (Bombay: Asia Publishing House, 1961), 69.

4

agricultural sector became a serious limiting factor on the overall rate of economic advance. By the middle of the Third Plan, four years of relatively static production levels (1960-61 through 1963-64) convinced the Planning Commission that continuation of shortfalls in agriculture would jeopardize the entire program of industrial development. Of necessity, some retreat from the social goals of planning had to be contemplated. In 1964, therefore, the planners announced "a fresh consideration of the assumptions, methods, and techniques as well as the machinery of planning and plan implementation in the field of agriculture." Two major departures from previous policy were initiated as a result of this reappraisal: (1) development efforts would subsequently be concentrated in the 20 percent to 25 percent of the cultivated area where supplies of assured water created "fair prospects of achieving rapid increases in production"; and (2) within these areas, there would be a "systematic effort to extend the application of science and technology," including the "adoption of better implements and more scientific methods" to raise yields.[3] In October 1965, the new policy was put into practice when 114 districts (out of 325) were selected for an Intensive Agricultural Areas Program (I.A.A.P.). A model for the new approach already existed in the 15 districts taken up under the pilot Intensive Agricultural Development Program (I.A.D.P.), beginning in 1961. Initially pioneered by the Ford Foundation, the I.A.D.P. emphasized the necessity of providing the cultivator with a complete "package of practices" in order to increase yields, including credit, modern inputs, price incentives, marketing facilities, and technical advice.

The economic rationale of an intensive agricultural areas program was considerably strengthened by the technical breakthrough reported from Taiwan and Mexico in 1965 of the development of new varieties of paddy and wheat

[3] India, Planning Commission, *Memorandum on the Fourth Five-Year Plan* (Delhi, October 1964), 26, 29.

seeds, with yield capacities of 5,000 to 6,000 pounds per acre, almost double the maximum potential output of indigenous Indian varieties; and also by the development at Indian research stations in the late 1950's of higher yielding hybrid varieties of maize, bajra, and jowar. In all cases, the availability of controlled irrigation water and the application of the package of modern inputs, especially very high doses of chemical fertilizer and pesticides, were essential preconditions for realizing maximum yield potentials. By November 1965, the Food Ministry was ready with a full-blown version of the "New Strategy": in essence it called for the implementation of a High Yielding Varieties Program in districts that had already been selected for intensive development under the I.A.D.P. and I.A.A.P. schemes, following the same extension concepts embodied in the Package Program.

In the last few years, the High Yielding Varieties Program has assumed "crucial importance" in the Planning Commission's agricultural development strategy. During the period of the Fourth Plan, 1969-74, it is proposed to bring approximately 60,000,000 acres under high-yielding varieties of wheat, rice, maize, jowar, and bajra. Yet, while this area represents less than 30 percent of the total acreage under these crops, over two-thirds of the additional production of food grains targeted for the Fourth Plan is expected to come from it.[4] The 1969 report of the Food Ministry's Expert Committee on Assessment and Evaluation of the Intensive Agricultural District Program enthusiastically endorsed this strategy and recommended "not merely the continued use of the I.A.D.P. approach, but its extension as a spearhead of the total agricultural modernization program for the country as a whole."[5]

[4] India, Planning Commission, *Fourth Five-Year Plan 1969-74* (Delhi, 1970), 138.
[5] India, Ministry of Food, Agriculture, Community Development, and Cooperation (Department of Agriculture), Expert Committee

The New Strategy already has spectacular economic gains to its credit. For example, with the rapid introduction of high-yielding wheat varieties, production reached a record high of 16.6 million tons in 1967-68, one-third more than the previous peak output of 12.3 million tons achieved in the last good weather year of 1964-65. Moreover, despite a recurrence of drought and other unfavorable seasonal conditions, wheat production in 1968-69 exceeded this new level, giving substance to the slogan of a "green revolution" in the wheat areas. Indeed, in 1969-70, national wheat output rose to another record high of approximately 20 million tons.

The new paddy varieties have shown less striking results. Important technical problems remain to be fully solved. Imported varieties show higher vulnerability to plant diseases than do local strains; crop duration of the nonphotoperiod sensitive exotic varieties is commonly too long for the main *kharif* season in many parts of the rice growing south where the plants come to maturity with the onset of the northeast monsoon; and the coarse grain quality of the imported varieties compares unfavorably with the finer grained local plants. Nevertheless, with the All-India Coordinated Rice Improvement Project conducting large-scale experiments in hybridization—to evolve new shorter duration nonphotosensitive strains having the high yield potential of imported varieties and the disease resistance and finer grain quality of local plants—many or all of these problems may be solved. In fact, while the total rice output in 1967-68 remained disappointingly lower than the previous peak level of 1964-65 (37.9 million tons compared to 39 million tons) production recovered in 1968-69 to the previous record. Moreover, in 1969-70, rice output resumed its upward climb and reached an estimated total of 40.4 million tons.

on Assessment and Evaluation, *Report on the Intensive Agricultural Program* (*1960-68*), Vol. I (New Delhi, 1969), 4.

Most significant, despite the poor weather conditions of 1968-69, total food grains output of 94 million tons approached the record production of 95.6 million tons achieved in 1967-68 (as against the previous peak of 89 million tons in 1964-65) suggesting the power of the new technology to liberate the fortunes of Indian agriculture from the vagaries of the monsoon. Prospects for such a breakthrough seemed even brighter in 1969-70, when estimates of total food grains output indicated a landmark achievement of nearly 100 million tons. On the strength of this stability in the improved performance of the agricultural economy, the Food Ministry has substantially reduced its annual imports of food grains and confidently predicts that India will be completely self-sufficient in 1972.

Ordinarily, the success of the New Strategy should elicit only expressions of deep satisfaction. Certainly, the potential economic benefits are great. The production gains of the last few years, while still modest, offer the most hopeful sign since the beginning of planning that modern science and technology can break through India's long closed circle of poverty to spearhead an agricultural "take-off" that will provide the missing momentum in rural resources and demand for rapid industrialization. Paradoxically, however, the improved prospect for higher rates of agricultural growth has created considerable uneasiness among policymakers whose concerns also include orderly social and political development through a democratic framework of government. Over the last few years, long-standing assumptions about the positive relationship between more rapid economic growth and the promotion of democratic stability have been badly shaken by growing instances of rural violence. It now appears that in the agroeconomic environment of the Indian countryside, high rates of economic development may actually exacerbate social tensions, and ulti-

8

mately undermine the foundations of rural political stability.

It was always clear, of course, that the intensive areas approach would accentuate regional disparities in development. Specifically, the dry areas of the country, the one-third of the sown area receiving less than 30 inches of rainfall annually, will inevitably fall farther behind. But more recently, it has been recognized that despite efforts at prevention, a capital intensive agricultural strategy tends to increase disparities *within* selected districts also, with tenants and small farmers "shar[ing] less than larger farmers in the gains from the application of the new technology,"[6] largely for lack of capital to invest in costly land improvement schemes. Moreover, in the rice growing districts, where there is a relatively high ratio of agricultural labor to the number of farms, the introduction of modern methods may add to employment opportunities from intensive cropping, but still "increases problems of income inequality."[7] The destabilizing impact of rapid modernization within an agro-economic context that favors the large farmers was highlighted by the Home Ministry's 1969 report on "The Causes and Nature of the Current Agrarian Tension."[8] Citing an increase from 19 to 43 reported cases of agrarian conflict in one year (from 1967 to 1968), the Home Ministry found that over 80 percent of the agitations were led by the landless against landowners, and concerned demands for increased agricultural wages, security of tenure, larger crop shares, and most important, redistribution of land. Indeed, the report found that it is "agitations for distribution of land to the landless which have elicited the maximum re-

[6] *Report on the Intensive Agricultural District Program (1960-68)*, Vol. I, 12.
[7] *Ibid.*, 31.
[8] For a summary of the contents of the Home Ministry's report, see P. C. Joshi, "A Review Article" in *Seminar*, May 1970, New Delhi.

9

sponse and have also had a wide geographical spread." The causes of agrarian tension are complex. "Predisposing" factors were identified as the failure of land reforms to provide tenants with security of tenure or fair rents, or to correct inequalities in landownership through redistribution of surplus land (i.e., land held by individual cultivators in excess of legally established ceilings). However, the "proximate" causes which actually converted latent discontent into open conflict were located in the new agricultural strategy and green revolution. Poor peasants who had appeared resigned to their handicaps under the existing agrarian structure as long as the prospect for material improvement was relatively limited, had become increasingly resentful of institutional arrangements which deprived them of "their legitimate share" in the greatly increased production now possible with modern technology. "One bad agricultural season," the report warned "could lead to an explosive situation in the rural areas."

In a sense, the problem of Indian agricultural planning has come full circle. Once more there is increasing concern about ensuring all classes of agriculturists—landlords and tenants, landowners and laborers, large and small farmers —an equal share in the benefits of the new technology. Certainly, part of this renewed interest springs from growing evidence that as economic disparities increase so does the likelihood that social discontent will be transformed into political violence by radical parties interested in launching a class struggle movement in the countryside.

This study is an enquiry into the socioeconomic and political aspects of the new strategy of agricultural development. It represents a preliminary assessment of the impact of modern technology, including the High Yielding Varieties Program, on patterns of income distribution among various classes of agriculturists; the stability of traditional patron-client relationships between landowners and the landless; and types of political participation among the peasantry. Inasmuch as broad social changes associated with agricultural modernization should be more highly advanced in districts experiencing the longest period of intensive development, five of the original I.A.D.P. districts were chosen for study: Ludhiana, Punjab; West Godavary, Andhra Pradesh; Thanjavur, Tamil Nadu, Palghat, Kerala; and Burdwan, West Bengal.

Most of the data presented in this study was collected in India between February and August in 1969. At the State level, interviews were conducted with officials having responsibility for the subjects of agriculture, rural development, irrigation, cooperation, and land reforms. In the districts, interviews were held with the Project Officer and the I.A.D.P. staff, the Chairmen and officers of the Central Cooperative Bank and the Land Mortgage Bank, and, in Ludhiana, with economists at the Punjab Agricultural University. Written materials have been utilized when available. In the main, however, the study relies on information collected during interviews with agriculturists. In each district, in order to assure as broad-based a sample as possible, two or three Blocks representing the major natural or agroclimatic divisions were selected. Within each Block, three villages rated as good, average, and below average with respect to the adoption of modern techniques of agriculture were chosen. One officer of the I.A.D.P. staff, as well as the Block Development Officer accompanied me on field trips to the selected villages. The regional officer of the Planning Commission's Program Evaluation Organization also travelled with me and acted as interpreter in interviews with informants from the major agricultural classes: small, medium, and large farmers; tenants; and agricultural laborers.

2. Ludhiana, Punjab

No STATE is more closely identified with the gains of the green revolution than Punjab, and within Punjab, no district is more enthusiastically advanced as a model for emulation—by other parts of the region and the country—than Ludhiana. There are a number of sound achievements behind this enthusiasm. On virtually all indices of agricultural modernization Ludhiana has scored spectacular progress. Even to cite the statistical record, a dull but obligatory exercise in empirical studies, is, in the case of Ludhiana to make an eloquent statement of the agricultural transformation occurring in the district. Among the most striking changes are the following. Between the pre-package year of 1960-61 and 1968-69, the area under irrigation increased from 45 percent to 70 percent, mainly as the result of the rapid installation of tubewells. Again, between 1960-61 and 1967-68, consumption of fertilizer increased more than 13 times, from 17.6 pounds to 242 pounds per cultivated acre. More dramatic still, in the short period between 1965-66 and 1968-69, the acreage under the new Mexican dwarf varieties expanded from a minuscule 170 acres to an overwhelming 420,000 acres, or an area accounting for 90 percent of the total acreage under wheat. Finally, and the surest measure of success, yields per acre in Ludhiana increased from an average of 1,385 pounds in 1960-61 to over 3,280 pounds in 1968-69 (i.e., by over 120 percent). Moreover, during the last few years, Ludhiana has seen a trend toward mechanization which promises even greater efficiency in the exploitation of the new technology for inten-

12

sive cropping. Exact estimates of the number of tractors now in use in the district are difficult to come by, but in April 1969 they were not less than 2,500 and possibly as many as 5,000, most representing purchases over the past two years. The major suppliers of tractors in Ludhiana, Massey-Ferguson and International Tractor, estimated that orders currently on file with all dealers totaled at least another 2,500. Even larger increases in the demand for smaller machines, especially seed and fertilizer drills and threshers are reported.

The sum total of all these changes—i.e., the installation of thousands of tubewells to bring extensive new areas under irrigation; the rapid rise in the consumption of chemical fertilizers; the widespread coverage of the wheat acreage by the high-yielding varieties; and the trend toward mechanization—does indeed add up to an agricultural revolution. The increases in yields achieved in Ludhiana must be considered a change in kind rather than degree; so must the growing trend away from labor to capital-intensive methods of production. Together, they signal the beginning of a transformation of agriculture from an impoverished "way of life" to a profitable business occupation. Indeed, those who have been most closely associated with the agricultural breakthrough in Ludhiana see in it even wider implications. They are inclined to view Ludhiana as a model and guidepost not only for the Punjab and other parts of the wheat growing region, but for the future development of the Indian agricultural economy as a whole. For many, Ludhiana has become a symbol of the power of the new technology to break through the seemingly eternal circle of India's poverty by spearheading an agricultural "take-off" that will finally provide the momentum in rural resources and demand to boost India into a period of self-generating industrial growth.

These hopes are nowhere more in evidence than at the

13

Punjab Agricultural University (P.A.U.) in Ludhiana among the economists who have worked so hard to ensure the success of the green revolution in the Punjab. Their projections of the future development of the Indian agricultural economy—based mainly on their experience of recent changes in districts like Ludhiana—is a familiar model in the West. It is rooted in the principle of economic rationalization, and assumes that as in the United States and Canada, so in India, the average size of operational holding will gradually expand to coincide with the increase in the minimum power unit now available. They predict that with the progressive displacement of bullock power by tractors and other machines, Indian farmers will for the first time be able to enjoy the economies of scale that have made agriculture a profitable business enterprise in advanced countries. As for the inefficient cultivators, the small farmers who cannot afford the new technology, ultimately, this class will find the gap in returns to investment on large and small farms so great that they will sell their holdings and leave agriculture. Similarly, the tenant class will begin to disappear: specifically, the owner-cum-tenant cultivator who used to rely on leased-in land to create an economic unit of operation will sell his small and scattered holdings as he finds large farmers unwilling to rent land that can be cultivated directly at a higher profit.

It is striking that the agricultural economists at P.A.U. do not view the displacement of small farmers and owner-cum-tenant cultivators with alarm. On the contrary, they assume that economic rationalization will proceed in response to changing opportunity costs; i.e., that the class of inefficient cultivators—small farmers and tenants—will leave agriculture because as economic men they become aware of better opportunities in the urban sector. Partly on the same assumption, the P.A.U. economists also tend to reject the thesis that mechanization will lead to greater unemployment among landless laborers. First, they suggest that while machinery may displace labor from some agricultural operations, on balance, farm modernization will probably increase employment by (1) stimulating greater intensity of cropping, and (2) enhancing the intensity of farm practices per crop; e.g., by resulting in a higher number of irrigations, ploughings, and weedings. But even if the demand for labor is somewhat decreased, they argue, agricultural laborers—like the small farmers and tenants—will willingly move off the land because they discover better opportunities in the urban sector. In fact, these opportunities are linked, indeed they will be created, by the very agricultural revolution that drives them from the land. According to S. S. Johl, an enthusiastic advocate of this model, mechanization

would create new types of jobs such as those of drivers, mechanics and semi-skilled laborers attending to the machinery and machine operations. This will put more demand on training institutions and there will crop up workshops and spare shops, etc. Further, the mechanization of farm operations will push up the demand and production of machines, implements and allied farm inputs which can be expected to create more jobs in the industrial sector. All this will lead to a chain reaction creating more and better jobs outside of agriculture. Thus, the overall impact of mechanization would be creation of more and better jobs in the economy. We have the example of Punjab State before us. . . . This experience is replicable in other parts of the country, it may vary only in degree and speed.[1]

Such projections, are, of course, questions for empirical investigation. How realistic is the assumption that the ex-

[1] S. S. Johl, *Problems and Prospects of Indian Agriculture*, 6-7. Mimeo.

15

perience of Ludhiana is replicable—in other parts of the Punjab? in the wheat growing region as a whole? in the rest of the country?

· I ·

Even a casual review of the background of the green revolution in Ludhiana reveals that the district presented an unusually favorable environment for the rapid modernization of the agricultural economy once modern techniques became available. Located in central Punjab, Ludhiana forms part of the fertile Indo-Gangetic plain, and is especially fortunate in having large quantities of good subsoil water that can easily be tapped through minor irrigation works. The fertile land and high water table actually facilitated the development of irrigation works in an indirect way: since most areas were equally capable of irrigation, popular support could be mobilized for large-scale programs of land consolidation. In Ludhiana, like other parts of the Punjab (but unlike most other areas in the wheat belt), consolidation of holdings was carried out on a large scale, leaving cultivators with compact and economic units for land development. By 1961, almost 50 percent of the net cropped area was irrigated, mainly from privately owned wells and tubewells.

Ludhiana was fortunate in addition to these natural features. Like other areas with fertile land and extensive possibilities for irrigation, the district is densely populated. In 1961, a population of more than one million persons was concentrated in a small area of 1,324 square miles, resulting in a population density of 773 persons per square mile.[2] Yet, the district also had the greatest concentration of small-scale industries of any area in the Punjab. Indeed, Ludhiana city, with a population of some 240,000 was styled the

[2] Census of India, 1961, Punjab, *District Census Handbook*, No. 11, *Ludhiana District*, 1965, 27.

16

"Small-Scale Industrial Capitol of India." It boasted hundreds of manufacturing enterprises in the fields of hosiery, cycles, machine tools, motor parts, agricultural machinery, oil engines, and a variety of other consumer goods.[3] Of the total population in the district, 31 percent were classified as urban.[4] Of the total work force, more than 65 percent were employed outside of agriculture.[5]

The rapidly growing rates of urbanization and industrialization were reflected in an unusually favorable land-man ratio for a high population density area. In 1961, there were 130,000 cultivators and agricultural laborers on a net cropped area of 662,500 acres, giving an availability of land per adult worker of approximately 5 acres.[6] Moreover, taking into account only the households engaged in cultivation (some 46,000 farm families), there were fewer small-sized operational holdings in Ludhiana than in the state as a whole. Surveys conducted between 1961 and 1964 revealed that fully 80 percent of cultivating households operated holdings of 10 acres or above, an astronomical figure by all-India standards, but high even for the Punjab, where the mean size of some 58 percent of all holdings is less than 10 acres.[7] Actually, in Ludhiana, 37 percent of all cultivators operated holdings of 20 acres or more, accounting for about 55 percent of the total cultivated area of the district. Another 43 percent had holdings between 10 acres and 20 acres, taking up another 35 percent of the area. Only 20 percent of cultivating families operated holdings of less

[3] Ibid., 21.
[4] Expert Committee on Assessment and Evaluation, Ministry of Food and Agriculture (Department of Agriculture) Intensive Agricultural District Program, Report (1961-63), 169.
[5] District Census Handbook, No. 11 Ludhiana District, 35.
[6] Intensive Agricultural District Program, Report (1961-63), 170-77.
[7] K. S. Mann, An Analysis of the Expected Shifts in Cropping Pattern of the Punjab (India) Resulting from the Introduction of High-Yielding Varieties of Crops, OSU-USAID Contract Program (Ludhiana, Punjab Agricultural University, 1967), 16.

than 10 acres and they accounted for only 10 percent of the cultivated land. Table 1 shows the distribution of cultivators and cultivated areas in Ludhiana by size of holdings.

TABLE 1

Distribution of Cultivators and Cultivated Areas
in Ludhiana District by Size of Holdings

	Holding size			
Item	Less than 5 acres	5 acres to 9.9 acres	10 acres to 19.9 acres	20 acres and above
Percentage of cultivators in the group to the total sampled	4	16	43	37
Percentage of the cultivated area for the group to the total	1	9	35	55

SOURCE: Intensive Agricultural District Program, *Second Report* (*1960-65*), 273.

Moreover, although the incidence of tenancy was high—even the official estimate being that 46 percent of all cultivators took some land on lease—the proportion of "pure" tenants was believed to be only 4 percent of the total.

The district had other advantages. Compared to a literacy rate of 24.2 percent for Punjab State as a whole, the literacy percentage in Ludhiana was 36.3 percent. Even in rural areas, almost 42 percent of adult males were literate; among males working as cultivators, this proportion was 31 percent.[8]

Yet another, intangible, factor has often been mentioned as an important element in the rapid progress of Ludhiana and the state as a whole. In Ludhiana, the majority population, about 63 percent, are members of the Sikh commu-

[8] *District Census Handbook*, No. 11 *Ludhiana District*, 32, 37, 168.

18

nity,[9] a religious group which separated from Hinduism in the 15th century as part of an effort to overturn Muslim domination. Initially organized for purposes of battle, the Sikhs have retained their reputation as an aggressive and innovative community. Many Sikhs still carry on the military tradition by serving in India's armed forces and many work for brief periods in Commonwealth countries to accumulate capital for investment. As a result, Sikhs are usually exposed to modern values and foreign ways in larger numbers than their Hindu neighbors, and are a major source for promoting change when they return to their villages. In Ludhiana, the dominant landowning caste, the Jats, is drawn mainly from the Sikh community.

Of course, there are depressed groups in the district. Indeed, in 1961, over 22 percent of the population were former untouchables, Harijans, or members of the Scheduled Castes,[10] drawn both from the Sikh and Hindu religions. The overwhelming majority, 87 percent, lived in rural areas, and constituted the major supply of village menials and agricultural laborers.[11] Literacy among this group was lower than 14 percent, almost the same as for agricultural labor, which was mainly recruited from the Harijan castes.[12] However, even this group could nurture some

[9] *Ibid.*, 33.
[10] *Ibid.*, 252. The practice of untouchability was prohibited by Article 17 of the Indian Constitution. The designation Scheduled Castes refers to the lists of these communities drawn up by the central government and appended to the Constitution under provisions for special reservation of seats in the parliament and in the legislative assemblies of the states for members of untouchable castes in proportion to their population, and also for their appointment to reserved posts in the civil service of the states and the union. Although these reservations were supposed to lapse after ten years, they have been extended for additional ten year periods twice since independence (in 1959, and 1969). Untouchable castes are also referred to as Harijans in ordinary conversation, a term coined by Mahatma Gandhi meaning "children of God." Altogether, the Scheduled Castes account for about one-seventh of the total population.
[11] *Ibid.*, 252.   [12] *Ibid.*, 252.

19

hopes of social mobility. The few who managed to pass their matriculation or get a B.A. were eligible for appointment to a reserved place in government service, either as a peon or junior grade officer. Others could follow the traditional avenue of social mobility and join the army. Most important, the existence of good roads and transportation made it possible for some agricultural laborers to find alternative employment in local factories in Ludhiana city or other towns while still maintaining their homes in the village. Indeed, according to the *District Census Handbook*, by 1961, there was "a dearth of agricultural laborers in the District because the growing industries afford the labor better opportunities and remuneration."[13]

· II ·

When the I.A.D.P. was started in Ludhiana district in 1961, crop demonstrations showing increased yields of 40 to 65 percent per acre with the application of the improved "package of practices" quickly convinced all categories of farmers of the superiority of modern methods. For example, during the first four years of the package program, between 1961-62 and 1964-65, the consumption of nitrogenous fertilizer increased by about 8 times, and of phosphatic fertilizer by over 20 times.[14] This achievement was facilitated by a very liberal policy of government loans to cultivators. Village level extension workers were authorized to issue spot loans of Rs. 150 for fertilizer; and Block Development Officers and District Agricultural Officers could authorize loans up to Rs. 1,000. Cooperative societies, which covered the great majority of cultivating families by the early 1960's, were another source of cash loans that could be used to purchase fertilizers and pesticides. Data col-

13 *Ibid.*, 36.
14 Intensive Agricultural District Program, *Second Report (1960-65)*, 267.

lected during this period reveals that small farmers did not lag very much behind larger cultivators in their willingness to adopt modern methods. In 1963-64, 60 percent of farmers with holdings of more than 10 acres, 60 percent of farmers with holdings between 5 and 10 acres, and 50 percent of farmers with holdings as small as 5 acres were applying fertilizer. Indeed, while small cultivators could not afford to cover as large a proportion of their holdings, those with the smallest farms actually applied higher doses of nitrogen on the area treated than cultivators with larger holdings.[15] The major constraint on the small cultivator was not conservative resistance to change but limited resources. This is indirectly illustrated by the wide disparities in the size of average loans borrowed by small and large farmers from both governmental and cooperative agencies during 1963-64. Cultivators having 5 acres or less received an average advance of Rs. 39.17. By contrast, farmers with holdings of 20 acres or more borrowed Rs. 517.63.[16]

Nevertheless, it seems clear that during the first years of the I.A.D.P. at least some farmers in all size categories were able to take advantage of the intensive development program to increase yields per acre through the application of modern methods, especially chemical fertilizers. At the same time, a serious disparity rapidly emerged between the large farmers with holdings of 20 acres or more, and the majority of other cultivators.

The prospects of achieving optimum increases in yield levels with the new package of inputs, improved seeds, chemical fertilizers, and pesticides depended on the availability of an assured water supply. In Ludhiana district, where canal irrigation covered only some 17 percent of the area under crops (water from which was itself dependent on the monsoons), the introduction of modern practices required the installation of minor irrigation works, especially

[15] *Ibid.*, 274, 278.   [16] *Ibid.*, 282.

21

percolation wells, pumpsets, and tubewells to provide an assured source of water all year round. Large capital investments in land improvement were actually a prerequisite to the efficient utilization of modern methods. The cost of installation of the smallest tubewell, one commanding an area of about 20 to 25 acres, was about Rs. 4,000 to Rs. 6,000. Cultivators belonging to the groups with the largest holdings already tended to have private tubewells. Generally, only cultivators with 20 acres or more were in a position either to finance new minor irrigation works from their own savings or to finance agricultural investment through loans. In fact, while the volume of government loans for percolation wells, pumping sets, and tubewells increased by over ten times between 1960-61 and 1964-65, the Department of Agriculture itself insisted that only cultivators having 20 acres or more of owned land could be eligible for minor irrigation loans.

As a result, during the first phase of agricultural modernization in Ludhiana, i.e., prior to the introduction of the high-yielding varieties, the large farmers with holdings of 20 acres or more made the greatest gains. With assured water, and the ready availability of modern inputs, especially chemical fertilizers, it became possible for them to replace less profitable crops like wheat plus gram mixture, and gram, with wheat. Actually, a substantial increase in wheat production in Ludhiana between 1960-61 and 1965-66 came from a striking shift in the cropping pattern. During this period, the acreage under wheat increased by more than 20 percent—from 280,000 acres to 339,000 acres—while the area under wheat plus gram mixture declined from 157,000 acres to 86,000 acres; and the area under gram from 44,000 acres to 25,000 acres.[17] At the same time, yields

[17] Intensive Agricultural District Program, Ludhiana (Punjab) *Report on the Analysis of Crop Cutting Experiments, Rabi,* 1967-68, 11-13.

per acre for wheat also showed an impressive improvement with the application of fertilizer, from an average of 1,020 pounds in the base period 1958-61 to an average 1,698 pounds between 1961-65.[18] Altogether, from both these sources, total production of wheat increased from an average of 135,300 tons in 1958-61 to 241,500 tons in 1961-65, a rise of over 78 percent.[19] The largest cultivators therefore benefited in two ways: by bringing a substantial portion of their holdings under the better paying wheat crop; and by increasing their yields per acre through the application of chemical fertilizer. By contrast, the gains of small farmers were limited mainly to some improvement in yields during good weather years arising from an increase in the application of fertilizers.

· III ·

The advent of the new dwarf varieties of Mexican wheat in 1966-67 marked the beginning of a second stage of agricultural development in Ludhiana district that opened unprecedented opportunities for increasing net returns to farm management. The advantages of the Mexican varieties are by now well known. Essentially their superiority over conventional strains derives from their capacity to withstand much higher doses of chemical fertilizer without lodging. While the Mexican varieties show an average response ratio of 17 to 18 pounds per acre to additional applications of nitrogen up to doses of 100 to 120 pounds, the fertilizer response ratio of conventional varieties is roughly 1:10, with yield decline occurring at applications above 40 or 50 pounds per acre. In short, with the advent of the dwarf varieties, it became possible to double output per acre from one season to the next—over and above the yield

[18] Intensive Agricultural District Program, *Second Report* (*1960-65*), 287.
[19] *Ibid.*, 289.

23

increases that had already been achieved with local varieties after five years of intensive development.

The implications of this productivity breakthrough for the profitability of wheat cultivation in Ludhiana is roughly illustrated by the following figures. In 1966-67, the average yield of local wheat varieties was 2,108 pounds per acre, a little less than 10 quintals. During the same year, those farmers who adopted the Mexican varieties (mainly Lerma Rojo) achieved an average yield of 4,235 pounds per acre, about 20 quintals or exactly twice the first amount.[20] Given the procurement price of Rs. 76 per quintal for Mexican varieties, the innovative farmer grossed about Rs. 1,520 per acre. Allowing for cost of cash inputs of some Rs. 260 per acre, the net return to management was about Rs. 1,260. By contrast, the farmer growing local varieties, who probably sold his output at a somewhat higher price, of about Rs. 80 per quintal, grossed only Rs. 800 per acre. Allowing for a lower cash expenditure on purchased inputs of about Rs. 40-Rs. 100, the net income per acre was about Rs. 700 to Rs. 760.[21] *On the average*, therefore, Ludhiana farmers who adopted the high-yielding varieties in 1966-67 doubled their output, and in one swoop, increased their net income by over 70 percent.

Given the powerful demonstration effect of the success of the new technology, it is not surprising that the spread of the dwarf wheats was rapid. Between 1966-67 and 1967-68, the area growing Mexican varieties jumped from 18,000 acres to 245,000 acres. A second spectacular increase occurred in 1968-69: almost the entire wheat area was covered, approximately 420,000 acres out of 450,000 acres.[22] It

[20] AID/W, *Outline for Country-Crop Papers: Country, India, Crop, Wheat.* First Draft, March 1969, 7. Mimeo.

[21] *Ibid.*, 44.

[22] Intensive Agricultural District Program, Ludhiana (Punjab), *Report on the Analysis of Crop Cutting Experiments, Rabi,* 1967-68. Final estimates are available only through 1967-68. The estimate of

24

is this comprehensive coverage that suggests all classes of cultivators in Ludhiana district are participating equally in the green revolution.

Nevertheless, discussions with the Project staff, the agricultural economists at Punjab Agricultural University, and most important, the testimony of the cultivators themselves, indicates that while most classes of cultivators have made some gains, proportionately a much greater share has continued to go to farmers with holdings of 20 to 30 acres or more. Indeed, over the last four years, economic disparities between large and small farmers have significantly increased as a result of the introduction of the high-yielding varieties.

It is not surprising that the large farmers, those with 20 acres or more, were the first to adopt the high-yielding varieties. The successful cultivation of the dwarf wheats depends even more heavily on assured supplies of water. In fact, irrigation at fixed times in the growth cycle of the plant is essential to the realization of its high-yield potential. Only cultivators with assured water, i.e., large farmers having private tubewells, could initially take up the cultivation of the Mexican varieties. In addition, the new wheats also require more sophisticated farm equipment to produce optimum yields: improved ploughs, discs, and harrows for proper land leveling; seed and fertilizer drills for shallow planting and exact spacing of seedlings; and plant protection equipment to ward off rusts and other diseases. Only the large farmers, most of whom had already made capital investments in tubewells and improved equipment were initially in a position to adopt the new high-yielding seed varieties. Many were able to double (or even treble) their output and net income with very little extra capital outlay.

420,000 acres under the high-yielding wheat varieties for 1968-69 is an unofficial figure provided by the Pilot Project officer, I.A.D.P., Ludhiana.

Some large farmers made even more spectacular gains. With the release of more disease resistant Mexican varieties (PV 18, S 227, and S 308) in 1967-68, there was such a high demand for scarce supplies that many cultivators took up production of seed rather than grain, and sold their stocks at "fantastic" prices of about Rs. 150 per quintal. Most important, the large farmers used a substantial part of their additional income from the dwarf wheats for reinvestment in the land, and for the purchase of agricultural machinery —tractors, threshers, and seed drills. The replacement of bullock power with tractors and threshers made agriculture more efficient, permitting cultivators to double and even triple crop, and in addition to diversify their cropping pattern in order to include more profitable commercial crops like sugar cane, cotton, and orchards. Some also used their capital to establish ancillary enterprises like poultry farming, or even to start small-scale industries, e.g., dealerships in spare parts for the new machinery that came flooding into the villages. Indeed, as a result of all these innovations, each of which was related to the introduction of the high-yielding varieties, farmers with very substantial holdings of 50 acres or more experienced a qualitative change in their standard of life which represents a new departure for rural India. They attained a level of prosperity in terms of consumption and the acquisition of amenities, including refrigerators, telephones, and even cars, that compares favorably with upper-middle class life in urban areas, and which has never before been seen in a village setting. Indeed, with land values increasing from about Rs. 1,000-Rs. 5,000 per acre of irrigated land five years ago to Rs. 5,000 to Rs. 10,000 and even Rs. 15,000 an acre, a Ludhiana landowner with 50 irrigated acres now owns (untaxable) landed assets worth some Rs. 2.5 lakhs to Rs. 7.5 lakhs, and must be considered a wealthy man.

26

INDIA'S GREEN REVOLUTION
· IV ·

All this is not to say that smaller farmers, those with holdings of 10 to 20 acres have not adopted the high-yielding
varieties. They have, and in overwhelming numbers. But
the circumstances under which the small farmers have done
so—especially those with 10 to 15 acres—sharply limit their
gains.

Probably the greatest aid to the smaller farmer in adopting the high-yielding varieties has been the relaxation of
criteria for eligibility for tubewell loans both by government agencies and land mortgage banks. In 1967, the Agriculture Department lowered its requirement for land ownership to make farmers with 15 acres of owned land eligible
for minor irrigation loans. By 1969, cultivators with holdings as small as 5 acres became eligible for government
loans for tubewells. The Land Mortgage Bank followed
suit: they advanced loans for tubewells to cultivators with
5-acre holdings. Given the appreciation of land values over
the last five years, small farmers experience little difficulty
in providing the necessary security for such loans. For example, the Land Mortgage Bank places the value of unirrigated land at Rs. 5,000 an acre, and advances loans at the
rate of one-half the value of land offered as security. A
farmer need therefore only mortgage 2 acres of unirrigated
land to qualify for a loan of Rs. 5,000, repayable in seven
equal installments. Under an even more liberal scheme being operated by the Land Mortgage Bank (but financed by
the Agricultural Refinance Corporation), small farmers are
able to get larger amounts on even easier terms: Rs. 6,500
for a tubewell, repayable over nine years, with only repayment of interest during the first year. The easy credit terms
have seen the business of the Land Mortgage Bank double.
In 1967-68, the Bank advanced a total of 31 lakhs in loans,
of which about 20 lakhs was for tubewells. During 1968-69,

27

total advances jumped to Rs. 60 lakhs of which Rs. 42 lakhs was for tubewells.[23] According to the Chairman of the Land Mortgage Bank, the majority of these loans for minor irrigation has gone to small farmers with 10 acres or less.

There is also a large amount of production credit available from the cooperatives. In Ludhiana, virtually all cultivating families are members of primary agricultural credit societies. Assuming that members are not defaulters, they can get personal surety loans at the standard scale of Rs. 300 per acre of wheat, distributed mostly in kind. In fact, in 1967-68, the Punjab Government took special steps to see that adequate credit facilities were available with the cooperatives by financing a large new subscription to the share capital of the Central Cooperative Banks. Compared to the 7.33 lakhs of government share capital invested in the Ludhiana Central Cooperative Bank in 1966-67, there was Rs. 59.33 lakhs in 1967-68. Together with modest increases in share capital from member societies, reserves, and other funds, the Bank's total owned funds increased from Rs. 56.56 lakhs in 1966-67 to Rs. 128.48 lakhs in 1967-68. As an A class Bank with a borrowing capacity of four times owned funds from the Reserve Bank, the State Government's additional contribution to share capital actually created an extra borrowing capacity of Rs. 200 crores. In fact, the Bank's working capital did increase from Rs. 392.10 lakhs in 1966-67 to Rs. 520.05 lakhs in 1967-68. The most striking evidence of increased business activity, however, came from the sharp spurt in advances for short-term loans between 1967-68 and 1968-69—from Rs. 250 lakhs (Rs. 86 lakhs in cash and Rs. 164 lakhs in kind) to Rs. 451 lakhs (Rs. 103 lakhs in cash and Rs. 348 lakhs in kind).[24] Discus-

[23] Figures provided by the Secretary of the Land Mortgage Bank, Ludhiana.
[24] The figures are compiled from materials supplied by the Punjab State Cooperative Bank, Chandigarh, especially, *A Short Note on the Working of the Punjab State Cooperative Bank, Ltd.*, showing the

sions with officials of the Central Cooperative Bank again confirm that advances to the small farmer, particularly cultivators with 10 to 15 acres, were mainly responsible for this striking increase. It is this class of cultivator that is relying most heavily on the cooperatives for financing the costlier inputs required by the high-yielding varieties.

One obvious implication is that a substantial part of the profits that can be expected from the introduction of the high-yielding varieties on small farms will be siphoned off by debt repayment at least for the next few years. More serious, once having incurred this indebtedness, the small farmer is at a disadvantage in maximizing returns to his investment. Foremost among his limitations, is the small size of the farm itself. At present, the command area of the smallest tubewell is about 20 to 25 acres. Extension workers and the economists at P.A.U. agree that the optimum size of holding for the efficient cultivation of the high-yielding varieties, assuming a tubewell and bullock power, is about 20 to 25 acres; this floor can be reduced with efficient management to 15 acres, but not below. Necessarily, therefore, the small farmer is denied the economies to scale enjoyed by larger landowners. The returns to his investment in a tubewell will be lower than on 20 to 25 acre farms.

The limitation of size is also a crucial constraint with respect to mechanization. In Ludhiana district, replacement of bullock power by tractors and other machines is considered economic only on holdings of 25 to 30 acres and above. Not only does a tractor represent a major capital investment —ranging from the black market price of the smallest Rus-

---

breakup of advances made by Central Cooperative Banks to societies during *Rabi* 1967-68 and 1968-69; and a separate mimeographed statement showing the comparative position of shares, owned funds, and deposits of the Central Cooperative Banks from 1965-66 through 1967-68. The Ludhiana Central Cooperative Bank, Ltd., Ludhiana, also made available comparative figures from 1960-61 to 1967-68 in a mimeographed statement, "Goals and Achievements of Cooperatives in I.A.D.P., Ludhiana."

sian built tractor at about Rs. 15,000, to Rs. 24,000 or more for a large Massey-Ferguson, but annual maintenance, calculated on the basis of a 30-acre holding, amounts to some Rs. 300 a year for servicing; Rs. 600 for spare parts; and Rs. 400 for diesel or gasoline. Other machines are less costly, but still expensive for the small farmer, e.g., small threshers cost about Rs. 720; a small combination thresher-winnower, Rs. 1,600, and a seed and fertilizer drill, another Rs. 275-Rs. 300.[25]

Nevertheless, the startling fact is that the majority of loan applications received for tractors by the Pilot Project Officer comes from farmers with 15 acres or less. The Land Mortgage Bank has recently had a similar experience. Since 1963, when it first began giving loans for tractors, and until 1967, only the larger farmers with holdings of 30 acres or more applied for such loans. Within the last two years, however, the Land Mortgage Bank reports more loan applications from 15 to 25 acre farmers than from cultivators with 30 acres or more. Since criteria for credit-worthiness are established on the same principles as for tubewells, except that loans are advanced at one-half the value of irrigated land—placed at Rs. 8,000 an acre—a cultivator with about 6 acres of irrigated land to mortgage would be eligible for a tractor loan of about Rs. 24,000.

Despite the confidence of the small farmer, the Land Mortgage Bank has viewed the recent trend with mounting alarm. In fact, so concerned did the Bank become at the large number of small farmers taking loans for tractors that as of March 1969, it was decided to limit the percentage of loans allocated for tractors to 15 percent of the total advanced. The view that mechanization is not an economic proposition for the small farmer, in this context meaning cultivators with less than 25 or 30 acres, is also shared by

[25] Estimates and prices as given by the sales managers for Massey-Ferguson and International Tractor in Ludhiana.

the principal suppliers of agricultural machinery in Ludhiana district. They suggest that easy credit is tempting small farmers to purchase machines without much thought for how they will repay their loans, in some cases, simply for prestige reasons. In any event, there is virtually unanimous agreement that the present demand for tractors and other machinery among this class of cultivator is completely unjustified on economic grounds, and that it will collapse within a few years as the farmers themselves discover it to be an uneconomic proposition. Once again, the small farmer is unlikely to find the same opportunities for maximizing farm income through double and multiple cropping that have come to large cultivators with the spread of mechanization.

There are other reasons why returns to the small farmer from the introduction of the high-yielding varieties are apt to be less than on larger farms. First, considering the high costs involved, they are less likely to use optimum doses of chemical fertilizer, and to achieve the maximum yield potential of the new varieties. This is indirectly confirmed by the decrease in average yields per acre of Mexican wheats reported in 1968-69 compared to 1966-67, from 20 quintals an acre to 14 quintals.[26] In the earlier year, mainly large farmers were involved; two years later, almost all cultivators had adopted the new varieties. Second, the cost of the inputs have themselves increased over the last few years, so that returns to investment are now less.

In sum, once all these limitations are taken into account, the 10 to 15 acre farmer can only make marginal gains from the introduction of the high-yielding varieties for some years to come. This is confirmed by interviews with cultiva-

[26] According to page 3 of the *Report on the Analysis of Crop Cutting Experiments*, I.A.D.P. (Ludhiana), average yields of Mexican wheat were only 3,628 pounds per acre or approximately 16 quintals in 1967-68. During 1968-69, it is estimated that this declined further to an average of 3,280 pounds per acre or about 14 quintals.

31

tors in this size class who report only modest increases in net income after the introduction of the high-yielding varieties—certainly not enough to make any qualitative change in their standard of life, but sufficient to improve the general level of consumption. As one 10 acre farmer put it, "we are feeling just a little better after passing through very bad days."

Actually, the 10 to 15 acre farmers who have adopted the high-yielding varieties at great cost in indebtedness are in a much more vulnerable position than they realize. The prospect that they can liquidate their debts and continue to make a modest gain from their investment rests heavily on maintaining the current procurement price of Mexican wheat at the artificially high level of Rs. 76 per quintal. Yet, with the large spurt in wheat production over the last few years, open market prices for Mexican wheat—without price support—are estimated at Rs. 60 to Rs. 65 per quintal.[27] In 1968-69, the Punjab Government did succeed in persuading the Center not to reduce the procurement price to Rs. 70 a quintal; equally determined efforts succeeded in 1969-70. But it is unlikely that the central government can continue indefinitely to purchase virtually the entire Mexican wheat crop at these rates, especially when the new varieties do not find a ready market—their brown color marking them as inferior to the amber colored local varieties in the minds of most consumers. In fact, the central government has been able to sustain the high procurement prices for Mexican wheat until now, only because they could compensate for the high costs of domestic stocks by pooling them with low priced imported food grains, and issuing all grains through the fair-price shops at a price that struck an average between the two. Specifically, the economic issue price of P.L. 480 wheat being some Rs. 65-66 per quintal,

[27] *AID/W Outline for Country-Crop Papers: Country, India, Crop, Wheat,* 29.

and the economic issue price of Mexican wheat (given procurement rates of Rs. 76 per quintal) being Rs. 87-88 per quintal, the government was able to avoid large losses on its distribution system by setting the price of all coarse grains at Rs. 78 per quintal.[28] But once concessional imports of food grains are phased out after 1971, the central government will find it impossible to maintain the present procurement price without heavy losses. Indeed, the Food Minister has already given warning that procurement prices of Mexican wheats will have to be lowered and issue prices stepped up.

· V ·

In Ludhiana, however, it is the bottom 20 percent of cultivators, with holdings of less than 10 acres, who have fared worst as a result of the green revolution. These farmers may have been able to make some marginal gains in good weather years by applying small additional doses of chemical fertilizer to Mexican wheats, but, in general, they have not been able to sustain the indivisible inputs—tubewells and agricultural machinery—required for the efficient cultivation of the new varieties. Actually, there is some reason to believe that their position may have suffered an absolute deterioration as a result of the green revolution.

It has already been mentioned that the incidence of tenancy in Ludhiana is quite high. Official estimates are that 46 percent of all cultivators take some land on lease. The Pilot Project Officer and the economists at P.A.U. estimate that about one-fourth of the cropped area in Ludhiana is currently cultivated by tenants. While exact figures are not available to indicate the rented in component of operational

[28] Estimates of economic issue prices compared to actual issue prices of Mexican wheat and of the rough adjustments permitted by the availability of low-priced imports of P.L. 480 wheat are taken from an interview with the Managing Director of the Food Corporation of India, in New Delhi, August 1969.

33

holdings by different size classes in Ludhiana district, an investigation of selected sample villages in Punjab State as a whole, conducted by the P.A.U. in 1966-67, indicated that this proportion is as high as 27 percent on holdings of less than 10 acres. Significantly, it declines to 15 percent on medium-size holdings of about 20 acres; and to little over 2 percent on large holdings of 50 acres.[29]

There is little doubt that the position of tenants has become more difficult as a result of the green revolution. With profits from direct cultivation rising, there are now more farmers who want to lease in land than lease out. Moreover, farmers now find a positive advantage in larger units of management, given new possibilities for more efficient agriculture with mechanization. Those large farmers who still give out some land on lease usually demand a premium in higher rents. Compared to six years ago, cash rents on leased land have increased from about Rs. 300-Rs. 350 to Rs. 500 per acre. More commonly, sharecropping arrangements are made. In some cases, the traditional rate of a 50-50 division of gross output between the owner and the tenant is maintained; the owner may also pay half the cost of fertilizers and diesel for irrigation. In many instances, tenants are not so fortunate. Landowners may ask for a 70 percent share of the crop, arguing that with new methods, the tenant still receives a larger absolute portion from 30 percent of a higher output than 50 percent of a lower one. But since most small owner-cum-tenant cultivators cannot afford to invest in optimum production practices, they find the new rentals uneconomic, and gradually are forced to give up as cultivators. One solution has been to "rent" out small holdings of 2 to 4 acres to large farmers, who then supply the actual owners with modern inputs for cultiva-

[29] K. S. Mann, *An Analysis of the Expected Shifts in Cropping Pattern of the Punjab (India) Resulting from the Introduction of High-Yielding Varieties of Crops*, 16-17.

tion and take 50 percent of the crop as their share. Some small owners have decided to take advantage of rising land values and sell their holdings, either to liquidate debts, or to start a new enterprise, such as poultry farming. Pure tenants, those with no land or bullocks to sell or "rent" are in the worst position. They may be taken on as a sharecropper by a large farmer who supplies all the inputs, and pays the tenant 20 percent of the crop as his share.

· VI ·

The situation of landless laborers in Ludhiana district appears much more favorable at first glance. Accounting for only 18 percent of all agricultural families, they have never been so numerous as to suffer from the worst extremes of rural underemployment. Even before the introduction of the high-yielding varieties, agricultural laborers could generally find some work eight months a year. Moreover, during the peak harvest period, there was always a relative shortage of labor. Indeed, many farmers have traditionally relied on migratory workers from Uttar Pradesh to supplement the local labor force.

During the first stage of agricultural modernization in Ludhiana, it appears that the position of agricultural laborers improved. The growing prosperity of the larger farmers generated an increased level of economic activity that added to employment opportunities during the off-season, especially in the construction of houses and roads, and in land improvement schemes like the installation of tubewells, drains, and culverts.

With the large-scale introduction of the high-yielding varieties in 1967-68, the economic situation of landless laborers seemed to improve further. Compared to a few years earlier, when a laborer remained idle for three or four months a year, he now found employment all year round. This was due mainly to more intensive cropping with the

35

large increase in irrigation facilities; more labor intensive farm practices per crop; and diversification of the cropping pattern which creates additional demand for workers during traditionally slack seasons, e.g., during December to mid-March for crushing sugar cane, and during July and August for hoeing and weeding maize. Moreover, the new level of affluence of many cultivators accelerated the pace of new investment, creating additional employment in the off-season for installation of tubewells, land leveling, repair of irrigation channels, and also for construction of roads and houses.

At the same time, cash wages for casual labor increased. Rates generally doubled over the last few years from about Rs. 2.5 to Rs. 5 plus tea. In areas where local labor was particularly scarce, rates went as high as Rs. 6, and in some cases also included food. Work on construction projects during the off-season also brought about Rs. 5 per day. During the peak harvest season, when labor was most scarce, reports of wages as high as Rs. 8 or Rs. 10, even Rs. 12 per day plus food were common.

Notwithstanding all this, laborers generally do not feel they have made any substantial net gains over the last few years. They tend to argue that the rise in prices of essential commodities has neutralized any improvement arising from higher levels of cash income. The fact is that the laborers of Ludhiana still judge the real level of their well-being not in terms of cash earnings, which are devalued by inflation, but by the market price of the crop share they have traditionally received at harvest. It is largely on the basis of this yardstick that laborers assert they have experienced little improvement in real income over the last few years.

The reality of the laborers' situation is more complex. Initially, the introduction of the high-yielding varieties enhanced the economic position of agricultural laborers by increasing their bargaining position at harvest time. Large farmers engaged in multiple cropping were greatly concerned with speedy harvesting of standing crops. In addition, with larger crops to handle, more laborers were required to complete the job within the allotted time. Finally, whereas the local varieties could be harvested over a period of 20 days or so, the dwarf wheats tend to shatter unless they are harvested within 10 or 15 days. With such a high premium placed on timely labor, agricultural workers attempted to exploit their new advantage by bargaining with landowners for increased wages, often threatening to work elsewhere if their terms were not met. But with migratory labor also available, these techniques were only partially successful.

Far from believing that the laborers deserve any increase in wages, landowners are convinced that with the output of the new varieties roughly doubled, they would be justified in reducing the laborers customary crop share from 1/20 to 1/40 of the harvest. The laborers, for their part, assert that they should share in the increased output in the same proportion as the landowners, i.e., that the traditional rate of 1/20 should be maintained. Over the last couple of years, a compromise has been struck which has seen the customary rate reduced from 1/20 to 1/30. Agricultural laborers now receive every thirtieth bundle they tie before putting the grain on the threshing floor. Their gains under this formula are limited but real. To illustrate, using local varieties, there are normally 80 bundles to one acre. Under the old system of division, 4 bundles, i.e., 1/20, averaging about 16 kilos each was paid for harvesting. Using the high-yielding varieties, there are now some 120 bundles in an acre: at the new rate of 1/30, 4 bundles are still paid as wages, but each now weighs 20 kilos to 25 kilos depending on the condition of the crop.[30] The net gain to the laborer, therefore, is about 25 percent in real income, compared to increases

[30] Estimates supplied by S. S. Johl, Professor of Economics, Punjab Agricultural University, Ludhiana.

of 50 percent or 75 percent or even 100 percent realized by the landowner. The increase is sufficient to permit some significant improvement in the general standard of living: e.g., to provide better food, a change of clothing, a cleaner home, cups and saucers (instead of metal glasses), in some cases, the margin necessary to send a son to school or to keep cows or goats for milk, and even to buy a luxury item like a transistor.

Unfortunately, these gains are likely to cost the laborers dearly in the future. Already, landowners are resentful at what they consider the laborers' blackmailing tactics. They have agreed to pay the higher wages, but have retaliated by applying other economic pressures; e.g., by denying laborers traditional rights of taking fodder from the fields for their animals, or additional payments in kind of fuel and vegetables. A greater hardship for many laborers is the landowners' refusal to advance interest-free loans, which used to be done, they explain for "goodwill," but which they accuse the laborers of breaching by adopting bargaining tactics. More serious, is the landowners' determination, reinforced by rising prices for food grains, to convert all kind payments into cash. They have already succeeded in substituting cash for the traditional payment in kind given for winnowing operations, and they clearly intend to press this pattern for harvesting operations as well.

Actually, the large farmers believe that the laborers' new bargaining power is bound to be transitory. They are aware that it is only at harvest time "that the laborers are our masters, and during the rest of the year we are their masters." The large farmers are determined to mechanize harvesting operations as quickly as possible, in order to be rid entirely of their dependence on agricultural laborers. Indeed, they are convinced that with the advent of labor-saving machines, e.g., thresher-winnowers, which not only represent large capital outlays by the cultivator but also substantially

38

reduce the manual labor exerted during farm operations, the traditional system of payment in kind now operates to exploit the innovative landowner. Assuming that the pace of mechanization does increase, especially if combines or other mechanical harvesting devices are introduced on a large scale in Ludhiana, the laborers will have lost their major advantage, and their best prospect of realizing significant gains from the green revolution.

· VII ·

If one reviews the experience of Ludhiana as a whole, it appears that most classes of cultivators have made some gains as a result of the green revolution. Nevertheless, the benefits have been heavily weighted in favor of the large farmer (the cultivator with 25 to 30 acres or more) who has been able to exploit the full potential of the new technology for multiple cropping and diversification of the cropping pattern by large capital investments in land improvement and mechanization. Although 15 to 25 acre farmers have also experienced absolute increases in output and income, the gap between the large and medium farmers has undoubtedly widened. Small farmers, those with 10 to 15 acres have so far made only marginal gains, and ultimately they may even find their farm operations overcapitalized and uneconomic. Some farmers with less than 10 acres have experienced an absolute deterioration in their economic position with the increasing difficulty of finding leased land on reasonable terms. The condition of landless laborers has improved, but at a proportionately smaller rate than that of large landowners, and these gains are threatened by the rapid drive toward more complete mechanization.

Ludhiana being the best case, it is extremely doubtful that the present trend toward mechanization will have the sanguine outcome that the P.A.U. economists project; i.e., an increase in the average size of holding to coincide with the

39

new minimum power (tractor) unit, while displacing only small numbers of agricultural workers who can be absorbed by the creation of new job opportunities in industry. This, no doubt, is the Western model, and it appears to be the model for Ludhiana. But Ludhiana is atypical even for the Punjab. The mean size of holdings is larger, extending opportunities for modern farming to more cultivators. There is also a relatively well-developed industrial sector, as well as a tradition of army recruitment in order to help absorb displaced tenants, small farmers, and agricultural workers. Where these advantages do not exist, and they do not in some districts of the Punjab, rapid mechanization has already produced "large numbers of unemployed or under-employed young men in the villages . . . who may present serious socio-economic and law and order problems in the years to come."[31] Perhaps more immediately serious, is the rapid deterioration in "good relations" between landowners and agricultural laborers in the context of an accelerated erosion of traditional ties based on payments in kind. Even in Ludhiana, where agricultural workers are the most prosperous in the state, the sense of injustice nurtured by this change has led to the first confrontations between "landlord" and "laborer" factions in the villages. With a rapid increase in political awareness among the Scheduled Castes, even conservative political leaders predict that if nothing is done to check growing inequalities at the village level, economic and class issues will increasingly replace communal problems as the foremost political concern in the state.

Indeed, the Punjab is entering a new period in its postindependence political development. Until 1966 when the boundaries of the state largely coincided with India's share of the pre-independence province after partition, the basic

[31] *The Statesman*, May 23, 1969.

social issues were communal.[32] Roughly two-thirds of the population were Hindus; one-third were Sikhs. An aggravating factor was the geographical concentration of both communities in compact areas: the Sikhs in the Punjabi-speaking region of the state where they enjoyed a 55-42 percent edge over the Hindu population; and the Hindus in the Hindi-speaking Haryana region where they accounted for 90 percent of the population. Although both major religious groups were also internally stratified between high-caste proprietor classes, and Harijans and other low-caste agricultural labor and tenant classes, the overriding communal issue prevented economic questions from being raised.

The demand for a separate Punjabi-speaking state, Punjabi Subah, taken up by the Sikh based Akali Dal shortly after independence, dominated Punjab politics for almost two decades. After being rejected by the 1956 States Reorganization Commission as a communal and religious rather than linguistic demand, the call for Punjabi Subah triggered numerous agitations, demonstrations, and riots. Apart from the Communist party which supported the demand on linguistic grounds in an attempt to exploit popular religious sentiments for political gains, the other major parties in the Punjab offered staunch opposition. Among these, the Jan Sangh, a communally oriented Hindu party, was concerned about protecting the substantial Hindu minority in Punjabi-speaking areas, and forestalling any attack on Hindi. The Congress party, officially committed to a secular state, refused to make any overt communal appeal.

Indeed, until 1962, the Congress party was able to use its secular stance to good advantage, establishing its dominant position in the state by appealing to the fears of both the Hindu minorities in the Punjabi-speaking region and to

[32] For an excellent account of Punjab politics see Baldev Raj Nayar, "Punjab" in Myron Weiner, ed., State Politics in India (Princeton University Press, 1968).

41

Sikh minorities in the Hindu area who were apprehensive of the growing demand, supported by the Jan Sangh, for a separate Haryana state. Moreover, the lavish use of patronage by Congress governments to woo the support of the Sikh community actually resulted in a brief merger of the Akali Dal and the Congress party between 1956 and 1960. Even when the Akali Dal reconstituted itself as an independent party in 1960, a majority of Akalis remained inside the Congress party.

By the mid-1960's, however, the precarious balancing act performed by the Congress party was in danger of being upset. Intense factional conflict between and within the ministerial and organizational wings of the Punjab Congress party virtually paralyzed the state government. At the same time, a split in the Akali Dal produced a new militant faction which was determined to revive and win the demand for a Punjabi Subah. By 1966, in the wake of continuous mass demonstrations that created alarm in New Delhi for national security on the tense Indo-Pakistani border, the central government finally announced the creation of the two states of Punjab and Haryana.

Since 1966, the major political parties have found it more difficult to use religious issues as a diversionary tactic in maintaining communal solidarity that cuts across class lines. The credibility of such appeals has been seriously undermined since the 1967 elections when the Congress party failed to win a majority of seats in the Legislative Assembly, and both the Akali Dal and Jan Sangh agreed to participate in a United Front government with other opposition parties to prevent the Congress from forming a ministry. In the event, the United Front government collapsed after only eight months in office following the defection of the Education minister and 15 dissident legislators who formed a new United Punjab Janta party, and ruled as a minority government with Congress support until the declaration of President's Rule in November 1968. Nevertheless, the brief experience of a United Front regime was sufficient to alert the landowning classes to the future dangers of a direct challenge to their political hegemony from Harijans and other landless groups.

Indeed, the large landowners who provided the leadership of the Janta party justified their defection at least partly by patriotic concern over what they considered subversive activities of Communist constituents in the United Front government. Their major worry was not the Communist party of India (C.P.I.) which, like the Akali Dal, had built a political base among the Sikh proprietor castes by exploiting the communal demand for Punjabi Subah. Rather, it was the newly formed C.P.I. (Marxists) which had split off from the national C.P.I. in 1964 over policy differences on questions of party ideology and program. Rejecting a parliamentary strategy limited to electoral exploitation of local issues, the Marxists were oriented toward creating a mass movement in the countryside through direct organizational work among the most impoverished sections of the population, especially the Harijans and other landless castes. Although the Marxists won no more than 3 percent of the popular vote in the 1967 elections, and had only 3 seats in the Legislative Assembly they were accommodated in the United Front government. Almost immediately, Janta Party leaders became disturbed by what they believed were efforts by Marxists to use their official position for subversive activities, including the penetration of government security networks and encouragement of strikes by urban factory workers to provoke a law and order crisis. However, they were most alarmed by Marxist efforts to carry Communist propaganda to the countryside and to develop an extensive network of political cells reaching into the villages; they were further angered by Marxist

43

proposals for new legislation to establish an 8-hour day for agricultural laborers.

Whatever the motives behind the Janta party's defection, it seems clear that their alarm was genuine, and that it was shared by the political leadership of other parties. During the mid-term elections of February 1969, the Akali Dal limited its electoral adjustments to the Jan Sangh and the C.P.I.; and both the Akali Dal and the Congress party demonstrated a "rightward swing" in its attitude. Specifically, both parties omitted standard promises of land reforms from their political platforms, and concentrated instead on issues having the greatest appeal to landowners, e.g., higher procurement prices for food grains, and all-weather roads linking villages to market towns.[33]

As a political strategy to damp down new economic demands by Harijans and other landless castes, the maneuver was successful. The landowning castes, whether in the Akali Dal, the Jan Sangh, or the Congress party maintained their leadership over local politics with little difficulty. In Ludhiana, as in most other districts of the Punjab, no Marxist was elected.

The strategy was less successful as a blueprint for political stability. The Akali Dal did improve its position vis-à-vis the Congress party, but it remained dependent on Jan Sangh support in forming a ministry. Within a year, however, internal dissensions within the Akali Dal again led to mass defections from the government, this time including the majority Akali Dal faction and the Jan Sangh. A new government formed by the Akali-Jan Sangh defectors in March 1970 was in turn almost defeated in July when the Jan Sangh withdrew from the ruling coalition after accusing the Akalis of communal bias in reorganizing the universities of the state. The decision in November of the warring factions of the Akali Dal to compromise their differences and

[33] *Economic and Political Weekly*, Annual Number, January, 1969.

reunite as one party appeared to return state politics to its essentially communal character. Meanwhile, all major parties continue to respond to the economic grievances of the landless by the same expedient of ignoring their existence.

It is a moot question how long this tactic will succeed, especially if future political instability puts a premium on alliances of convenience. In a state like the Punjab, where inequalities are much less pronounced than in other parts of India and where all sections of the agricultural population are among the most prosperous in the country, it might well serve for some time to come. Yet, there are already signs that the general prosperity of the state is not a sure safeguard against rural upheaval. In the summer of 1970, the sudden murders of several prominent landowners stunned the Akali Ministry, and created a law and order crisis in some villages as local landowners also resorted to violence against Harijans.

If a policy of studied avoidance of economic issues is likely to prove inadequate in the Punjab, it is certain to be less effective in other parts of the wheat belt.

In states like Uttar Pradesh and Bihar where over 80 percent of cultivating households operate holdings of less than 10 acres, where 15 percent to 30 percent of workers in agriculture are laborers, and where the level of industrial development is still very low, it is difficult to see how more than a small section of the agricultural population will be able to realize significant benefits from the wheat revolution. By comparison with the Punjab, gains in these areas are likely to be even more heavily weighted, increases in disparities larger, and the rate of displacement greater than can reasonably be expected to be absorbed through the creation of alternative job opportunities outside agriculture. Occurring as these changes are in a social context characterized by an erosion in traditional ties, and an incipient polarization on the basis of class, it would not be surprising

45

if efforts by political parties to mobilize social discontent for power purposes would lead to increasing instances of class confrontation in rural areas.

In the rice belt, where each of these problems is magnified several fold, and all tend to occur together, the dilemma of ensuring a reasonable degree of equity in the distribution of gains from the new technology is even more formidable—as is likely to be the law and order problem arising from a failure to do so. This emerges clearly from a consideration of agricultural modernization and social change in the predominantly paddy growing districts of West Godavary, Thanjavur, Palghat, and Burdwan.

3. West Godavary, Andhra Pradesh

SITUATED to the west of the Godavary River which runs the length of the district, the delta areas of West Godavary contain some of the most fertile lands in Andhra Pradesh. Except for the small sandy coastal belt along the Bay of Bengal to the south, rich alluvial and black soils occur throughout the district. Government canals branching off from the Godavary Anicut have brought irrigation water to more than half the cultivated area since the middle of the nineteenth century.

The richness of the deltaic tract accounted for the selection of West Godavary as one of the first intensive development districts in 1961. Yet, its very advantages were the source of a major limitation. By 1961, West Godavary was one of the most overpopulated areas in the rice belt. With almost two million persons living in an area of 3,009 square miles, population density was only moderately high at 657 persons per square mile.[1] However, 85 percent of the total population lived in rural areas, and more than 68 percent of the work force were employed in agriculture.[2] Altogether, there were 630,000 cultivators and laborers on a net sown area of 1 million acres, resulting in an availability of land per adult worker of 1.4 acres.[3] Aggravating the problem, alternative opportunities for employment were very

[1] Census 1961, Andhra Pradesh, *District Census Handbook, West Godavari District*, 1967, i, xxi.

[2] *Ibid.*, i, xxv.

[3] Intensive Agricultural District Program, *Report (1961-63)*, 94, 96.

limited. In 1961, West Godavary had only 10 large and medium-size factories.[4] The majority of industrial establishments were small-scale agricultural processing units which provided steady employment to few workers and offered low rates of pay. The most attractive jobs were in the government services, but these were available only to the educated. In 1961, this was a very limited group. Although the literacy rates were considerably higher in the district than in the state as a whole, reaching almost 31 percent in West Godavary compared to 23.4 percent in Andhra Pradesh, less than 4 percent of the total population had completed primary school.[5] Moreover, literacy declined precipitously at lower levels of the economic and social ladder. In 1961, one-half of all male cultivators were classified as illiterate.[6] This rate jumped to 79 percent in the case of agricultural laborers.[7] Among the Scheduled Castes who alone accounted for about 17 percent of the rural population, the rate of illiteracy was as high as 82 percent.[8]

When the I.A.D.P. was introduced in West Godavary in 1961, another constraint on rapid agricultural advance became apparent. Compared to yield increases in Ludhiana of 40 percent to 65 percent with the application of the improved package of practices to wheat, yields obtained on local demonstration plots for paddy were only some 17 percent to 19 percent higher than on the control plots.[9] Although the offtake of nitrogenous fertilizer did increase by 2 1/2 times and of potassic fertilizer by almost 6 times between 1960-61 and 1964-65,[10] average yield per acre, after an initial upward spurt, quickly reached a plateau; this pat-

---

[4] *District Census Handbook, West Godavari District,* lxxi.
[5] *Ibid.,* 30.   [6] *Ibid.,* 30.
[7] *Ibid.,* 30.   [8] *Ibid.,* 113.
[9] Intensive Agricultural District Program, *Second Report* (1960-65), 153.
[10] *Ibid.,* 155.

tern was repeated for total production of rice crops. Table 2 shows the progress in yields per acre and total production of rice for both major crops in West Godavary district from 1961 to 1965.

TABLE 2
Average Yield and Production of Rice in West
Godavary District
1961-62 to 1964-65

Crop	Year	Yields (pounds per acre)	Total Production (tonnes)
Rice (First crop)	Average for 3 years (1958-61)	1196	371,300
	1961-62	1487	458,200
	1962-63	1214	398,000
	1963-64	1425	462,800
	1964-65	1425	443,100
Rice (Second crop)	Average for 3 years (1958-61)	1188	123,700
	1961-62	1377	137,100
	1962-63	1601	161,100
	1963-64	1478	159,900
	1964-65	1408	171,400

SOURCE: Intensive Agricultural District Program, *Second Report* (*1960-65*), 176-77.

Also in striking contrast to Ludhiana, coverage under high-yielding paddy varieties expanded very slowly. In West Godavary district, about 900,000 acres are normally under paddy, 700,000 acres during the first *kharif* crop, and 200,000 acres during the second *rabi* crop. The first introduction of I.R. 8 occurred during *rabi* 1966-67 when it was planted on an area of 687 acres. Subsequently, during

1967-68, I.R. 8, and Taichung Native 1 were planted on 7,540 acres and 36,276 acres during the *kharif* and *rabi* seasons, respectively. In 1968-69, the targets were raised to 20,000 acres for the first crop and 50,000 acres for the second.[11] A more ambitious program was projected for 1969-70, with 30,000 to 40,000 acres in *kharif* and 100,000 during *rabi*. Even so, these targets accounted for only 15 percent of the total paddy acreage.

This slow pace of adoption can be partly explained by the relatively modest increase in profit margins from the cultivation of I.R. 8 and other high-yielding varieties over returns from improved local varieties. As reported in interviews with cultivators, cash input costs for I.R. 8 commonly range between Rs. 350 and Rs. 400. Average yields per acre tend to fluctuate between 22 to 26 quintals (4,840 to 5,720 pounds). At the 1968-69 procurement price of Rs. 49 per quintal, gross returns varied between Rs. 1,078 and Rs. 1,235, and net profits ranged between Rs. 728 and Rs. 885. By contrast, estimated production costs for local varieties are lower (about Rs. 150 to Rs. 200). Yields vary widely and may be as low as 7 quintals (1,650 pounds) in bad weather years. However, in normal seasons, most cultivators using the recommended practices report average yield levels of 12 to 15 quintals (2,805 to 3,300 pounds). Moreover, the local varieties produce finer grain than I.R. 8 and commanded a premium price in the market of Rs. 55 per quintal. Gross returns therefore ranged from approximately Rs. 660 to Rs. 825 and net profits from Rs. 460 to Rs. 625. The net gain to the cultivator of growing I.R. 8 in preference to local varieties is relatively unstable. In the best case, it may be as high as Rs. 425 (Rs. 885 minus Rs. 460) and represent an increase over previous levels of cash income of about 50 percent; on the other hand, it may be no more

[11] I.A.D.P., Eluru, *District Agricultural Plan and Plan of Action, 1968-69*, West Godavari District, 33, 35.

than Rs. 103 (Rs. 728 minus Rs. 625), only 16 percent higher than previous levels. Average returns to additional investment for I.R. 8, as estimated by the Project Officer, are
somewhere between these extremes, at about Rs. 200 in
cash per acre, or an increase of one-third to one-quarter
above previous levels.

Even so, an average gain of 25 percent to 30 percent per
acre from the cultivation of high-yielding paddy varieties
would usually be considered sufficient incentive for adoption—assuming the rate of return to additional investment
was assured. In the West Godavary environment, however,
the opposite is the case. Risks of cultivating the new varieties are still so high that while farmers may win an extra
Rs. 200 or so, they are liable to lose double that amount in
production costs if the crop fails. Actually, an investigation
into the conditions surrounding the successful adoption of
the high-yielding paddy varieties in West Godavary reveals
that only large farmers in irrigated areas, cultivators with
10 acres or more, are in a position to overcome these obstacles by making the large capital investments in minor
irrigation works needed to realize the full yield potential of
the dwarf paddy varieties.

· I ·

The dwarf varieties of paddy, like the dwarf wheats, de-
rive their basic superiority over conventional strains from
better resistance to high doses of fertilizer. Compared to
recommended applications for local varieties of 15 to 30
pounds of nitrogen per acre, 20 to 30 pounds of phosphates
and 30 pounds of potash, dosages for the high-yielding varieties are set at 80 to 100 pounds of nitrogen per acre, 40 to
50 pounds of phosphate and 40 pounds of potash.[12] The difference this makes to productivity is best summed up by the
average yield rates reported in 1966-67 in West Godavary

[12] I.A.D.P., West Godavari District, Resumé of Work, 1967-68, 14.

51

for local varieties, and I.R. 8 respectively, of 1,500 pounds per acre and 4,620 pounds.[13]

However, I.R. 8 and other dwarf paddy varieties have a number of limitations that considerably raise the risk of adoption. The short height and heavy tillering of the dwarf varieties—the very characteristics associated with high fertilizer responsiveness and increased yields—also provide a more favorable environment than tall, thinly tillering indigenous plants for planthoppers and gall midge. During the high humidity of the monsoon season, one variety, Taichung Native 1, proved so susceptible to bacterial leaf blight that it was all but completely rejected for future planting by the farmers. Even I.R. 8 requires very elaborate —and expensive—plant protection measures, involving at least four prophylactic sprayings and two dustings during the crop cycle and constant inspection of the plants in the fields to detect the first signs of disease and apply immediate curative treatment.

The second major limitation of the high-yielding paddy varieties in West Godavary district is a growth cycle basically unsuited to the monsoon patterns of the main *kharif* season. Under the conventional cropping pattern, sowing, transplanting, and harvesting are adapted to the onset and departure of the southwest and northeast monsoons. Cultivators plant their seedlings sometime in June—with the arrival of the southwest monsoon—transplant in mid-July and harvest in December—after the retreat of the northeast monsoon that brings particularly heavy rains during September and October. Local varieties are specially adapted to the monsoon patterns in two basic ways: they are long duration strains and photoperiod sensitive. This means that indigenous rice varieties "flowered and went into their re-

13 I.A.D.P., Andhra Pradesh, Agricultural Information Unit, Eluru, *Souvenir*, 1969. P. P. V. Krishna Murthy, "Yield Trends in West Godavary District during 1961-62 to 1967-68," 37, 40.

52

productive phase of growth when day length reached a certain critical number of minutes. After flowering there was a fixed time to maturity, an interval sufficient for the monsoon to retreat and the rice to ripen ready for harvest under sunny skies."[14]

By contrast, the high-yielding dwarf varieties of paddy are short duration and nonphotoperiod sensitive. When planted during the main *kharif* season, e.g., in mid-June, varieties like I.R. 8 will flower and come to maturity within a fixed period of about 107 to 115 days; i.e., by mid-October or during the worst period of the northeast monsoon. Harvesting must then take place under conditions of heavy rain, and unless mechanical drying equipment is immediately available, much of the crop is lost. There are still other disadvantages: very heavy rains during the southeast monsoon may submerge the seedlings and cause serious damage to the plants; also, the heavy cloud cover of the monsoon season deprives the paddy plants of the strong sunlight they need for photosynthesis at the end of the growth cycle to achieve optimum yields.

The result is that the dry and sunny *rabi* season, which traditionally extends from the end of January to late April or May provides the best conditions for the cultivation of high-yielding paddy varieties. Yet, I.R. 8, like the dwarf wheats, can be cultivated successfully only on land having assured supplies of water. In West Godavary, as in Ludhiana, maximum yields are realized under conditions of controlled water management. In effect, an essential prerequisite of the efficient cultivation of the high-yielding paddy varieties during the *rabi* season is an assured supply of supplementary irrigation water from a privately owned minor irrigation facility, either a filter point or tubewell.[15] This re-

[14] AID/W *Outline for Country-Crop Papers, Country, India, Crop, Rice,* first draft copy, March 1969, 112.

[15] A tubewell essentially consists of a deep bore drilled into the ground for the purpose of tapping groundwater through one or a

quirement can be better appreciated after a review of the irrigation facilities currently available in West Godavary.

· II ·

Of the 1 million acres constituting the net sown area in West Godavary, only about 50 percent is classified as delta, receiving water supplies from the canal system of the Godavary River. With the onset of the southwest monsoon (usually by June 15th), the first waters are released. However, supplies are sufficient only until mid-March or the latter part of the second crop season; then water shortages become acute. Moreover, there is not sufficient water in the canals to ensure even all delta farmers of adequate water for a second crop every year. Instead, a rotational system is followed under which canal irrigated areas are divided into three zones. In the first or "permanent" zone, farmers receive water for *rabi* cultivation every year. Altogether, this area accounts for about 100,000 acres, including 69,000 acres situated near Kolleru Lake, which regularly overflows during the southwest monsoon, submerging the *kharif* crops and causing serious loss of *kharif* plantings to the farmers. The remainder of the permanent zone represents mainly "tail-end" areas, i.e., areas at the outer limits of the irrigation canals which are supposed to receive adequate water supplies during the *kharif* season, but often do not due to

---

series of permeable layers of water bearing strata. The bore is installed with an assembly of blind pipes and perforated pipes so that the latter come opposite the water bearing strata. Water is pumped from the pipes either by horizontal centrifugal pumps or by deep bore hole turbine pumps. The major variables in the installation of a tubewell are the hardness of soil and the depth of subsoil water: it may be necessary to drill anywhere from 120 to 400 feet; and to use mechanical rigs rather than hand boring sets for drilling. By contrast, in coastal and deltaic areas where the substrata soil is soft and groundwater is plentiful, water may be efficiently withdrawn by a small filter point tubewell having a bore of only some 35 or 40 feet. Filter points can be driven with hand boring sets and they are operated by electric or diesel pump sets installed at ground level.

54

pilferage. The remainder of the delta area is divided between biennial and triennial zones, receiving water for a *rabi* crop every second and third season, respectively. Even during rotational years, however, the farmers still face water shortages by mid-March.

The situation is much worse in the uplands area of the district which accounts for little less than one-half the net sown area, or just under 500,000 acres. Approximately 100,000 acres is served by tanks, but water supplies are directly dependent on rainfall. As a result, most uplands farmers lose at least some part of the first *kharif* planting because of water shortages during the latter part of the season; and usually, they take only ground-nut or gingelly as a second crop.

Given the limitations of water supply, the second paddy crop has not only been limited in area (to about 200,000 acres annually) but also in yields due to water shortages beginning in mid-March. One innovation early sponsored by the I.A.D.P. was a plan to advance the planting of the second crop by one month in order to make more efficient utilization of available water supplies. Under the traditional cropping pattern, water in the canals was not utilized (except for perennial crops like sugarcane and banana) between the first week of December when the *kharif* crop was normally harvested, and the middle of February when the *rabi* crop was planted. If seedlings could be planted during the second week of December (instead of mid-January) and transplanted during the second week of January (instead of mid-February), the shorter duration varieties raised in the *rabi* season would come to harvest by the last week of March or early April, thus avoiding the worst effects of prolonged water shortages in the latter part of the season. Initially, this scheme was unsuccessful. The low temperatures during December affected the growth of seedlings in the nursery; and the seedlings also suffered

55

from severe attacks of stemborer in the nursery and in the field which resulted in total or partial failure of the crop. By 1964-65, however, the Department of Agriculture and Agricultural Research Stations succeeded in perfecting a package of fertilizer and plant protection practices that was effective against both these problems. By *rabi* 1967-68, an area of about 100,000 acres was planted with an early second crop; and in 1968-69, the target was 150,000 acres.[16]

Nevertheless, this innovation did not significantly help in extending the area under the high-yielding paddy varieties during the *rabi* season. I.R. 8, while a "short-duration" *kharif* variety when compared to local strains, was actually 20 to 25 days longer than the local varieties used during the *rabi* season. Even when planted as an early second crop, it could not be harvested until late April, i.e., well after the period of water scarcity set in. Possibly, the release of Padma in 1968 (a hybrid produced by crossing an indigenous variety with Taichung Native 1) will make this limitation less serious. Compared to I.R. 8 which requires 107 to 115 days to flower, Padma needs only some 81 days. But as a fine-grained variety, the average yields of Padma are less than I.R. 8, usually not more than 3,700 pounds.[17] In any case, the need for controlled water management and timely operations will still place a premium on the availability of supplementary water from minor irrigation works.

· III ·

Actually, a number of benefits would flow to cultivators from the rapid expansion of minor irrigation in the delta. First, while the southwest monsoon rarely fails completely,

[16] The difficulties and achievements of raising an early second crop are outlined in *District and Agricultural Plan and Plan of Action, 1968-69*, West Godavari District, 56-57.

[17] The comparative advantages of Padma and I.R. 8 are analyzed in S.V.S. Shastry, "New High-Yielding Varieties of Rice: Jaya and Padma," *Indian Farming*, February 1969.

it is often delayed. Cultivators are supposed to receive the first water from the canals by June 1; they are fortunate if it comes by June 15. Those with holdings at the bottom of the supply channel may have to wait an additional month for their first water. Such delays may prolong the period of the first crop well into December, and reduce the cultivator's opportunity of taking an early second crop to avoid the serious water shortages beginning in March. By contrast, with a filter point or tubewell, the farmer does not have to wait for the release of the canal waters to begin cultivation of the *kharif* crop. He can plant his seedlings in early May; transplant by mid-June, and harvest by mid-November, gaining ample time for an early *rabi* crop of high-yielding paddy varieties. Second, while the average rainfall in West Godavary is high—about 40 to 45 inches annually—it is also erratic. In some years, water shortages develop earlier and are more acute. Again, with a filter point or tubewell, the farmer can be certain of supplementing canal irrigation at the end of the crop season to avoid any loss in yields from water shortages. Finally, there is the advantage of being able to double crop paddy land every year, even if the holding is located in a biennial or triennial rotation zone. Actually, the I.A.D.P. staff is convinced that triple cropping would also be feasible with short duration varieties "under assured irrigation facilities, if provided from early in the month of May until the end of April."[18]

There are other ways in which the expansion of minor irrigation works could transform the agricultural economy of the district. At present the uplands area hardly has any assured supplies of water. Cultivators mainly grow millets (gram, bajra, and jowar) and put a small part of their holding under paddy only to lose at least part of the crop because of water shortages late in the season. Occasionally,

[18] *District Agricultural Plan and Plan of Action 1968-69*, West Godavari District, 66.

57

there are drought conditions year after year. In one uplands village, Pangidigudem, drought for three consecutive
years had dried up virtually all minor irrigation tanks and
wells. Out of a net sown area of 1,544 acres, 1,027 acres had
to be left fallow; and of the 455 acres normally planted
under paddy, perhaps 15 or 20 acres had been cultivated.
Losses to the cultivators were staggering. Farmers subsisted
on some small returns from groundnut plantings, occasional work as agricultural laborers, loans from the local
money lenders, and by misutilization of loans for land development taken from the local Land Mortgage Bank. By
contrast, if these same cultivators had borewells, they
would be assured of one paddy crop a year, and an additional lightly irrigated cash crop during the *rabi* season.
Not only would they be guaranteed a relatively stable
standard of living from year to year, but according to estimates of the local extension staff, they could double or even
treble their average annual net income.

If the rapid installation of minor irrigation works would
be desirable, estimates of underground water resources in
West Godavary suggest that a large expansion program
would also be feasible. Indeed, some preliminary ground
water surveys have indicated that "all uplands areas of
[West Godavary] district are particularly well endowed
with vast underground water resources."[19] The situation in
the delta areas is less certain. But apart from some stretches
where the subsoil water is known to be saline, it appears
that there is also substantial scope for the development of
supplementary irrigation works.

Yet, whatever the future benefits, the installation of a
filter point or tubewell by a cultivator requires an immediate capital investment of very substantial proportions. In

[19] Agricultural Information Unit, Eluru, *Souvenir*, T. V. Ratnakar
Rao, "Prospects of Underground Water Exploitation in West Godavary District," 6.

the delta area where the water table is relatively high, the cost of installation for a filter point may vary between Rs. 500 to Rs. 2,000; adding another Rs. 2,500 for an electric motor or Rs. 3,500 to Rs. 4,000 for an oil engine, the total cost of a filter point can range anywhere between Rs. 3,000 to Rs. 6,000. In the uplands area, where underground water is often much deeper, and power drills are required to sink borewells and tubewells, the total cost of installation may range as high as Rs. 2,500 to Rs. 7,500. Adding the expense of an electric motor or oil engine, the total cost may come to Rs. 5,000, reaching as high as Rs. 10,000 or Rs. 11,000.

There are two major sources of finance for such investments: personal savings or loans. In the prosperous delta area where conditions are suitable, i.e., where the subsoil water is not saline, farmers with 10 acres or more are often able to finance filter points and pumpsets from their own resources. In the relatively backward uplands area, greater reliance is placed on loans from the Land Mortgage Bank.

The Ellore Cooperative Land Mortgage Bank serving the uplands area has recently taken a liberal view in establishing criteria for land development loans. It has introduced a scheme under which landowners may receive loans for borewells at 50 percent of the *potential* value of the mortgaged land; i.e., the value it would acquire after being irrigated. Arriving at a valuation of Rs. 3,000 per acre of irrigated land (by analyzing the sales statistics in the Registrars office over the last seven years, and averaging the prices for land transactions), a cultivator may receive Rs. 1,500 per acre of mortgaged land toward the price of a borewell. Under this policy, there has been a steady increase in the number of loans sanctioned for borewells from 124 in 1965-66, to 159 in 1966-67, to 287 in 1967-68, and 362 during the first nine months of 1968-69. During 1965-66 and 1967-68, the number of loans sanctioned for oil engines and electric motors also increased from 16 to 40 to 80, respectively.[20] Yet, with the total cost of borewells and pumpsets in the uplands area at a minimum of Rs. 5,000, and often closer to Rs. 10,000, a cultivator must still be in a position to mortgage about 4 to 7 acres of land in order to be eligible for a loan. In fact, the officials of the Land Mortgage Bank estimate that about 60 percent of loans for borewells have gone to agriculturists with 10 to 15 acres or more; and the bulk of the remainder to farmers with 5 to 10 acres. Altogether, the area irrigated through bores and tubewells is estimated at about 65,800 acres.[21]

In both the delta and uplands areas, however, the large majority of cultivators (farmers with less than 5 acres) have not been able to afford the large capital investment for minor irrigation works. As a result, they have been excluded from the green revolution not only as narrowly defined, i.e., as the adoption of high-yielding varieties, but from the gains in output and income that become possible only with assured irrigation water: more efficient utilization of modern inputs; the introduction of intensive cropping; and the diversification of the cropping pattern to include more profitable commercial crops.

· IV ·

This state of affairs is not surprising once attention is focused on the agroeconomic pattern of West Godavary district. While potentialities of underground water exploitation may not be much less favorable than in Ludhiana, the small size of the average holding and high rentals for leased land prevent the majority of farmers from accumulating any surplus capital for investment in land development.

According to an agroeconomic survey conducted in West Godavary district between 1961 and 1964, fully 50 percent

[20] Data supplied by Secretary of the Ellore Cooperative Land Mortgage Bank, Ltd.
[21] T. V. Ratnakar Rao, "Prospects of Underground Water Exploitation in West Godavary District," 6.

INDIA'S GREEN REVOLUTION

of all cultivators operated holdings of less than 2.5 acres. Another 21 percent had holdings between 2.5 acres and 5 acres. Of the remaining 29 percent, 14 percent operated farms between 5 and 10 acres, and 15 percent had holdings of 10 acres or more. Table 3 shows the distribution of cultivators and cultivated areas in West Godavary by size of

TABLE 3

Distribution of Cultivators and Cultivated Areas
in West Godavary District by Size of Holdings

Item	Holding size			
	Less than 2.5 acres	2.5 acres to 4.9 acres	5 acres to 9.9 acres	10 acres and above
Percentage of cultivators in the group to the total sampled	50	21	14	15
Percentage of the cultivated area for the group to the total	12	16	22	50

SOURCE: Intensive Agricultural District Program, *Second Report (1960-65)*, 162.

holdings. Using the rough rule of thumb applied by the Ellore Cooperative Land Mortgage Bank, that 3 acres is an economic unit in the irrigated delta area, and 10 to 15 acres in the dry uplands area, it appears that the majority of cultivators were operating uneconomic holdings at the time the I.A.D.P. was introduced in West Godavary district in 1961.

Actually, the situation was worse than the data on the size of holding suggests. Although the official survey estimated that 14 percent of all farmers cultivated some land on lease (accounting for only 10 percent of the total), this figure was certainly too low. A field investigation by Wolf Ladejinsky in 1965 concluded that one-half of all cultivators took some land on (oral) lease, and actually operated about

61

50 percent of the total area.[22] In the villages visited during April 1969, upwards of 30 percent of all cultivators were reported to be leasing some land, and estimates of the area that was operated by tenants ranged to 50 percent (two villages), 30 percent (two villages) and 20 percent (one village). Moreover, the rates of rental, while variable, were always so high as to prevent the cultivator from accumulating a surplus for investment in land improvement.

The most common tenancy arrangement in the delta area is the fixed share system. Under this scheme, rentals are set at a fixed number of bags of paddy per acre,[23] regardless of actual output. Over the last five years this rate has been increasing by about one bag annually to about 11 bags per acre in 1968-69. Since the landowner receives the same payment regardless of output, he has no incentive to advance production loans to tenants. Some landlords, it is true, do advance interest-free loans as a matter of "goodwill," but many, especially "absentees," who may live in another village, do not. Since the overwhelming majority of tenants cultivate on oral lease and are not generally members of the cooperatives (or, if members, eligible only for very small personal surety loans), they must rely mainly on private moneylenders for production credit. In most cases, therefore, they apply little or no fertilizer and no pesticides on leased lands, and yield levels during the *kharif* season have tended to remain relatively constant. Assuming average yields of 15 bags to 18 bags per acre, rentals account for about 60 percent to 70 percent of the total *kharif* crop in delta areas.

It is clear that the fixed share system leaves tenants such a bare margin over costs that they cannot possibly sustain increased expenditure on improvement of leased land. In

[22] Wolf Ladejinsky, *A Study on Tenurial Conditions in Package Districts* (New Delhi: The Planning Commission, 1965).
[23] One bag of paddy is the equivalent of 165 pounds.

a representative case, a cultivator pays 11 bags of paddy in rent for every acre of paddy land leased. His yields with local varieties are 17 bags. After paying rent, the tenant is left with 6 bags. Cash input costs account for another 4 bags. He is therefore left with a net income of 2 bags. In cash terms, each bag of paddy is valued at about Rs. 41 so that net income from one acre of leased land is Rs. 82.

Nevertheless, tenants who cultivate under the fixed share system in the delta during the *kharif* season are in a better economic position than those who lease land on a proportional crop share basis in the less productive uplands areas and in parts of the delta liable to submersion because of proximity to Kolleru Lake. Tenancy arrangements in Ganapavaram Block which has both uplands area and land subject to submersion either resulted in no profit at all or involved cultivators in net losses during *kharif* 1968. The standard crop division in one village visited, Thokalapalli, was 60:40 in favor of the landlord, with the cost of fertilizer shared between the landlord and tenant in the same proportion. In Bylepalli and Chinatalindrakolamu villages, rentals were higher involving a 70:30 division of the crop between landlords and tenants, with the cost of fertilizer shared between them in the same proportion. Of the four tenants interviewed taking land on a proportionate crop share basis, one managed to break about even on his investment and three reported net losses. While this is by no means an adequate sample, it is at least suggestive. To cite the most favorable case: the tenant paid 70 percent of the output as rent on every acre of paddy land leased. His yields were 15 bags per acre during the *kharif* season. With each bag valued at Rs. 41, the gross value of his output was Rs. 615. Seventy percent, i.e., 10.5 bags or Rs. 470 was paid to the landlord as rent, leaving the tenant with 4.5 bags or Rs. 184. After taking account of his cash production costs at Rs. 174, he was left with a net profit of Rs. 10 per acre. In the other instances, the farmers were less fortunate. For example, one tenant who also paid 70 percent of the output as rent on every acre of paddy land leased realized an average yield during the *kharif* season of only 10 bags per acre. After paying 7 bags, or Rs. 287, to the landlord, the tenant was left with three bags valued at Rs. 123. By contrast, his cash input costs were Rs. 145, leaving him with a net deficit of Rs. 22 per acre.

If there is a second *rabi* crop of paddy, the more typical sharecropping arrangement is an equal division of 50:50 between the landlord and the tenant with landlords sharing the costs of fertilizers and pesticides. However, if I.R. 8 is adopted, landlords usually demand a crop division of 70:30, or even 75:25, although in the latter case, they pay the full cost of fertilizers and pesticides. Normally, tenants will not risk cultivating I.R. 8 during rotation years for fear of losing extra investment funds in the event of crop damage from inadequate water or pest attack. Instead, they grow a second paddy crop of local varieties every two or three years, sharing the output with the owner on a 50:50 basis, and increasing their return over *kharif* levels by 2 or 3 bags per acre. This is probably a prudent choice judging by the experience of one tenant-cultivator who did try I.R. 8 on leased land during the *rabi* season. Cultivating on the basis of a 70:30 crop share division, with the landowner sharing costs for fertilizers and pesticides in the same proportion, the tenant experienced a net loss at the end of the season. Estimating his own cash input costs at about Rs. 233 per acre, and yields from I.R. 8 (in the absence of assured water supply) at about 15 bags per acre, his gross returns at Rs. 37 per bag were Rs. 555. Of this, 10.5 bags or Rs. 388 went to the landowner as rent. The tenant remained with 4.5 bags or Rs. 167. Compared to production costs of Rs. 233 he suffered a net loss per acre of Rs. 66.

Fortunately, most cultivators taking land on lease also

64

have small ownership holdings of 1, 2, or 3 acres. Generally, they tend to apply higher doses of fertilizers on owned land, although still less than recommended doses, and over the last ten years this has given them some gain in yields. But the only improvements mentioned by this class of owner-cum-tenant cultivator were extremely modest, amounting to no more than increased consumption of vegetables, or a change of clothing, and in rare cases, the ability to send a son through trade school or secondary school.

Actually, under these circumstances, the small farmer with less than 5 acres who does not try to extend his holding size with leased land may come out in a better economic position than the 2 or 3 acre owner who takes an additional 3 or 4 acres on lease and then finds he has to make up losses on leased land by profits on owned land. Yet, it is clear that the small owner-cultivator is also unable to accumulate any capital surplus for investment on land improvement, especially minor irrigation.

Owner cultivators with small farms in the uplands areas have fared worst. In a good weather year, they may get as much as 20 bags of paddy using improved practices: allowing for an expenditure of about Rs. 200 or 5 bags (each valued at about Rs. 40), they may net as much as 15 bags or Rs. 400 per acre. But in drought years, they lose practically the entire crop. As a result, any improvement in their condition over the last few years has been extremely limited: perhaps substitution of rice for gruel as the main diet in good weather years; and finer varieties of cotton shirts and *dhotis*. Farmers in the delta areas have done better. They have managed small, but reliable increases in the yields of *kharif* paddy crops from the application of fertilizer, totaling about 1 to 3 bags per acre over the past six or seven years. Yet, rising costs of cultivation, especially for labor, have absorbed much of the increase. Generally, they report no substantial improvement in real income. During

65

rotation years, small farmers avoid using the high-yielding varieties. They are afraid of the high expenditure, and of damage to the crops from inadequate water or pest attack that would leave them with losses they could not withstand.

· V ·

The fear of crop failures, and the consequences of defaulting on loans from the local cooperatives plays a large part in the reluctance of small farmers to take large production loans for the cultivation of the high-yielding varieties. About 75 percent of all agricultural families are now members of primary agricultural credit societies served by the three Central Cooperative Banks in West Godavary district. Nevertheless, many small farmers prefer to deal with local moneylenders who charge 24 percent to 36 percent interest per annum, but are flexible about security for loans and schedules of repayment.

In theory, tenant-cultivators and small farmers can now borrow up to Rs. 1,500 on personal surety loans; i.e., on the personal guarantee of two landowners, subject only to the requirement of maintaining a 10:1 ratio between loans received and share capital owned. In practice, however, tenants and small farmers are considered poor loan risks, and personal surety loans, when they are sanctioned tend to be much lower than the maximum permitted. In most cases, the amount of the loan advanced is determined according to the value of the security, i.e., land, offered by the member. For this reason, the crop loan system introduced in *kharif* 1966 has never worked properly. Although loans are supposed to be advanced according to scales of finance based on the production costs per acre of paddy—set at Rs. 350 per acre in *kharif* 1968—small cultivators often have to mortgage part of their land to get the full amount.

Moreover, the attempt to divide production loans into three cash and kind components—(A) Rs. 200 cash; (B)

66

Rs. 100 in fertilizer; and (C) an optional supplementary advance of Rs. 50 to cover the labor costs of fertilizer application—was never successful. Members refused to lift the fertilizer component of the loan, partly because of the red tape involved, partly because they were obliged to take only the variety available at the cooperative, but also because private dealers were willing to advance fertilizers on delayed repayment terms, compared to the cooperatives' insistence on a fixed schedule of repayment. The response of the cultivators was so poor, that starting with *kharif* 1969-70, the entire loan amount has become available to cultivators in cash.

Even so, the Eluru Central Cooperative Bank anticipates that it will be difficult to meet its lending targets. Compared to a target of Rs. 2 crores in short-term loans for *kharif* 1967-68, the Bank advanced about Rs. 1.3 crores; in 1968-69, the target was raised to Rs. 3.5 crores with achievement estimated at Rs. 3 crores. Bank officials expect that advances will stabilize at about this level, with perhaps some small increase to 3.5 crores.[24]

This is not due to want of funds. In fact, compared to the present borrowing power of the Bank (at twelve times share capital and reserves) of Rs. 7-8 crores annually, it currently borrows about Rs. 3 crores, including deposits and advances from the Reserve Bank. The main reason adduced by Bank officials is "lack of demand" for loans. Actually the situation basically reflects two factors: an Individual Maximum Credit Limit for short-term loans of Rs. 10,000 in the delta, and Rs. 6,000 in the uplands, prohibiting larger advances to big farmers; and more important, the inability of small farmers to absorb larger loans as long as they do not have assured sources of water. If, having incurred large debts for the application of improved prac-

[24] Data provided by the Secretary of the Cooperative Central Bank, Ltd., Eluru.

tices, especially for the cultivation of I.R. 8 during the *rabi* season, inadequate water and/or pest attack damages the crop, small farmers will be left without means of repayment—and fear that they will ultimately lose their land.

By contrast, there is striking evidence of the willingness and ability of small farmers to make full use of cooperative credit for adopting the high-yielding varieties once they are assured of adequate irrigation facilities. In one delta village, Achanta, groups of neighboring farmers, each with 5 acres of land or less, managed to pool their resources in proportion to the land each owned, and meet the capital expenditure and operation costs of a filter point and electric motor. The advantages of an assured water supply as explained by one 5-acre partner were dramatic. Prior to joining this group in 1964, his net income from 5 acres of paddy was about Rs. 2,000 during the *kharif* season. Two years out of three, he netted another Rs. 500 during the *rabi* season from the cultivation of gingelly and groundnut, bringing his total income to Rs. 2,500. During the third rotation year, he gained roughly another Rs. 2,000 from a second paddy crop of local varieties, raising his annual income to Rs. 4,000. After acquiring the additional facility of a filter point, this cultivator put 3 of his 5 acres under high-yielding varieties during the *kharif* season. Partly as a result of rising yields and partly because of higher prices for food grains, in *kharif* 1968 he realized gross returns of Rs. 4,200. In addition, he was able to take a second crop of I.R. 8, grossing another Rs. 5,400 for a total cash income of Rs. 9,600. Under the new circumstances created by access to assured water, the high level of indebtedness readily incurred by this cultivator to finance production costs turned out to be sound economics. Taking into account his loans, both repayment to the cooperative of Rs. 1,080 (including 8 percent interest) and to a private lender of Rs. 944 (including 18 per-

68

cent interest), his total debt repayment for the year amounted to Rs. 2,024. Adding an additional expenditure of Rs. 1,600 from his own resources to meet the full cost of cash inputs, his total investment was Rs. 3,624. Against a gross income of Rs. 9,600, he was left with net earnings of Rs. 5,976. Altogether, therefore, this 5-acre farmer managed to increase his net income over previous levels in nonrotational years by almost 100 percent, and in rotational years by close to 50 percent. Improvements were apparent in all aspects of his life. He had made further investments in land, buying an additional acre in a neighboring village (which he gave on lease) and on leveling his own holding. He also reported a change for the better in virtually all items of consumption—food, clothing, housing, and furniture.

Unfortunately, such cases represent the exception rather than the rule in West Godavary. It is more common to hear reports of 2, 3, and 4-acre farmers selling their holdings to take advantage of the sharp rise in land values: some to clear off old debts, others to buy larger farms in areas where land prices are lower, especially on sites that may eventually be irrigated under the Tungabadra or Nagarjunasagar Projects. Although there is no readily available data to document these transactions, it is generally believed that outsiders, including businessmen, and richer farmers resident in the village, usually those with contiguous holdings, are buying the land for direct cultivation. This points to yet another difficulty that is slowly emerging to handicap small farmers. In areas where I.R. 8 has proved successful, large cultivators are becoming more reluctant to give land on lease. The innovation mentioned earlier, of leasing *rabi* land on a 75:25 crop share basis, with the landowner meeting the full costs of modern inputs, is really a step in the direction of reducing tenant-cultivators to permanent laborers. In fact, it is clearly perceived by the landowners as a

69

method of ensuring the day-to-day field supervision necessary for the successful cultivation of the high-yielding
varieties.

· VI ·

The first visible signs of increasing prosperity in West
Godavary occur only among medium holders with farms of
5 to 10 acres, who have managed to increase yields by 25
percent to 30 percent with improved practices, and have
also benefited from the rise in prices for food grains. Even
among this group, however, gains have usually been sufficient only to provide for higher levels of consumption, leaving little surplus for investment in land improvement.

Actually, it is still unusual in the delta areas for cultivators with holdings below 10 acres to have a filter point—
possibly because the smallest command area of a filter point
is about this size. Although there is no way to estimate the
total number of filter points installed by large farmers over
the last few years, it is not uncommon to hear that in villages with good subsoil water, 100 or more filter points have
been sunk in the last two or three years alone; and there is
general agreement that every year the number installed is
increasing.

Access to assured irrigation has brought the large farmer
a new level of prosperity. Water not only assures a second
crop every year, but also higher yields from *rabi* plantings,
especially with the adoption of I.R. 8 on suitable land.
Moreover, with filter points and perennial irrigation, many
large farmers are diversifying their cropping patterns to include profitable commercial crops like sugarcane. Over the
last few years alone, large farmers estimate that they have
doubled their net income from all these sources. A great
deal of the gain has gone into consumption: large houses,
consumer durables like electric fans, radios, cycles; even
refrigerators, air-conditioning, and cars; and the purchase

70

of gold ornaments. Some is also going for the education of sons. But undoubtedly, a good deal is also being invested in buying additional land and improving land already under cultivation. As the technical problems associated with the high-yielding paddy varieties are progressively solved, this tiny class of large farmers will be in the most favorable position to maximize gains from the new technology. The social implications of this point are more forcibly made when it is remembered that in West Godavary only 15 percent of cultivators have holdings of 10 acres or more, but this small minority operates 50 percent of the total cultivated area. Indeed, those with 20 acres or more are in a position to emulate their counterparts in Ludhiana by increasing their advantages even farther through mechanization of farm operations. Already, many large farmers have shown an interest in acquiring tractors for more efficient utilization of the land, e.g., for more rapid puddling and threshing operations to facilitate double cropping—and also to save on labor costs. Between 1961 and 1966, the number of tractors in West Godavary district increased only from 278 to 416.[25] But three years ago, loan applications with the Land Mortgage Banks more than doubled, from about 23 per annum to 75; this trend has steadily increased until in 1968-69, a total of 200 applications were received—all from farmers with 20 acres or more.[26] In fact, the demand is now so high that many loans cannot be sanctioned for want of available tractors.

· VII ·

With so much attention focused on the cultivator as the primary agent of agricultural modernization, it can be forgotten that in West Godavary about 60 percent of agricul-

[25] West Godavari Zilla Parishad, Eluru, *Handbook of Statistics, West Godavari District*, 1966-67, 88.
[26] Data supplied by the Secretary of the Ellore Cooperative Land Mortgage Bank, Ltd.

71

tural workers are actually farm laborers.[27] It is estimated that the majority of them, over 60 percent, work as casual laborers; and the rest are permanent workers.

Compared to very small farmers and tenant cultivators, it appears that agricultural laborers have experienced some greater, albeit modest, improvements over the last few years. Permanent laborers have benefited least. Generally, payments have not increased over the last ten years, or only by marginal amounts of 1/2 bag or 1 bag of paddy per year. Payments to permanent laborers are variously 20 to 22 bags of paddy with no other facility; or 15 or 16 bags of paddy, and some food, clothing, and shoes during the year. The cash value of these annual payments is usually little more than Rs. 700 per year.

On the other hand, casual laborers reported some improvement. Opportunities for employment have increased with more intensive cultivation and the introduction of new crops. Cultivators estimate that the new rice varieties require an extra 15 to 20 man days of employment per acre during the *rabi* season. More important, intensive cropping and new crops have increased the work available throughout the year. In the delta areas, laborers find no difficulty in getting work for 10 1/2 to 11 months a year; even in the uplands laborers find assured employment for at least 8 months a year as more farmers sink borewells and grow a second crop. During the off-season, laborers find employment in a variety of activities: cutting sugarcane, transporting manure, loading lorries, leveling land, deepening and desilting canals, collecting firewood, making bristles from palm fibre, and constructing houses and roads.

Rates for casual labor have also increased, generally by two times over the last six years. In the uplands, laborers can make about Rs. 3 per day during the season (for transplanting and harvesting crops), compared to Rs. 1.8 six

[27] *Handbook of Statistics, West Godavari District, 1966-67*, 15.

years ago; and Rs. 2 during the off-season. In the delta areas, laborers do a little better, earning Rs. 3.5 or Rs. 4 for transplanting and harvesting, compared to Rs. 2 or Rs. 3 five years ago, and Rs. 2 or Rs. 2.5 off-season. In cash terms, many casual laborers still earn no more than permanent workers. Yet, some actually do better, earning as much as Rs. 900 or more a year. Moreover, despite rising costs, virtually all casual laborers cite modest improvements in their standard of living, especially better quality of food, e.g., two meals of rice per day instead of millets, along with some coffee or tea; the purchase of some brass vessels or stainless steel plates, or a charpoy and chairs. Some also report that they are now less in debt.

Perhaps the greatest and most striking gain, however, has been in social and psychological freedom. With greater opportunities for work, casual laborers can now earn as much or more than permanent laborers. The landless no longer need to seek the protection of a permanent patron-client relationship in order to ensure their livelihood. On the contrary, they are in a position to choose their employer and even bargain over terms. This increase in bargaining power is reflected in new forms of social interaction which concede the independence and dignity of Harijans and low-caste agricultural laborers. Although economic gains are still limited, yet landowners and laborers agree that the relationship between the two sides has been transformed. Casual laborers in West Godavary have long been accustomed to negotiate with landowners on wages through a *maistry* or team leader (heading about 10 men), but they have traditionally done so in the attitude of suppliants, knowing that their livelihood depended on striking a working relationship with the landowner. Even when laborers were employed as casual workers, moreover, they maintained the deferential behavior of clients toward patron, e.g., declining to sit in the presence of the landowner, and often performing personal services in addition to agricultural duties. The increase in work opportunities, reducing the overwhelming bargaining advantage of the employer, has made the value of the goods and services exchanged between laborer and landowner more nearly equal. Indeed, during the peak period landowners now speak of the laborers as "our masters"; and the laborers confirm that they insist on shorter working hours, and breaks for lunch, as part of their "contract" with employers. Landowners complain that laborers take the same wages but work "less sincerely" and that it now takes 5 men to do the work of 3. But laborers clearly feel these concessions justified as a measure of their worth, and also, as assertions of personal dignity. Many now say that they would no longer work as permanent laborers even at higher wages, because they do not want to be servants at the beck and call of the landowner at all hours of the night and day. Harijans and low-caste casual laborers may still be reluctant to sit in the presence of the landowner, but not to declare in his hearing that they are their own men. Landowners grumble at these trends, yet seem reconciled to the erosion of old status relationships and their replacement by new contractual arrangements based on mutual satisfaction of both sides. Perhaps for this reason, efforts by Communist parties to organize agricultural laborers for strikes against landowners at harvest time have not had any marked success so far.

· VIII ·

Agricultural laborers have nevertheless expressed their sympathy for the Communist party at the polls. Actually, in Andhra, the Communists have always followed a rural strategy, concentrating their organizational and electoral efforts in the delta districts which have the highest percentage of agricultural laborers. While the votes of Harijans and other low-caste laborers do not guarantee Communist

74

victories, they have been responsible for a much greater Communist vote in the delta than in Andhra Pradesh as a whole.

Indeed, the total Communist vote in Andhra has been declining—from 22 percent in 1957, to 19 percent in 1962, to 15.5 percent in 1967. On a statewide basis, the Congress party has consistently outpolled the Communists by about two to one, winning 41.7 percent of the popular vote in 1957, 46 percent in 1962, and 45 percent in 1967.[28] Yet, in West Godavary, Communist party candidates often come within a few percentage points of defeating their Congress party rivals; in many cases, they emerge victorious. An example is the record of both parties in elections to the Lok Sabha or national parliament. In 1957, the Congress party was successful in the Eluru parliamentary constituency with 51.2 percent of the popular vote compared to 48.8 percent for the Communists; in 1962, the Communists were victorious with 47.4 percent of the popular vote compared to 46.9 percent for the Congress party; and in 1967, the Congress party managed to regain the seat by little more than one-half of one percent, winning 41.8 percent of the popular vote compared to 41.3 percent for the Communists.[29] A similar pattern occurs in Narsapur parliamentary constituency. In 1957, the Communists were successful with 51.6 percent of the popular vote as opposed to 37.9 percent for the Congress party. In 1962, the Congress party made a strong comeback winning 50.4 percent of the vote compared to 46 percent for the Communists. In 1967, the Congress party was again victorious with 44.5 percent of the vote, although the Communist defeat was clearly due to the split within the national party. Together, the regular C.P.I. and the C.P.I.(M) polled a clear majority of the popular vote, 51.5 percent.[30] Fluctuations in the fortunes of Com-

[28] *India Votes: A Source Book on Indian Elections* (New York: Humanities Press, 1968), 718.
[29] *Ibid.*, 366, 535.   [30] *Ibid.*, 364, 365, 525.

munist candidates with respect to assembly seats in West Godavary have been much more extreme. In 1957, the Congress party made almost a clean sweep, winning 13 out of 14 seats, and losing only one to the Communists. In 1962, the Congress party was cut back to 8 seats while the Communists captured 5. In 1967, the Congress party reestablished its commanding position, winning 10 seats, while the Communists (C.P.I.(M)), won only 2.[31]

One feature distinguishing West Godavary from other parts of the rice belt where Communist parties have established reliable strongholds among landless laborers is that political polarization on class lines has not led to open conflict between landowning and landless groups. Some possible explanations emerge from an examination of the origins of the Communist party in Andhra.

As Selig Harrison pointed out,[32] the Andhra Communist party was formed in the 1930's when the slump of agricultural prices impoverished many delta farmers and made them receptive to Communist slogans of equality. One result was that the Andhra Communist leadership is recruited from the dominant agricultural caste in the delta, and Communist leaders at the local level are "predominately of rich and middle peasant stock." Another factor peculiar to Andhra is the historic rivalry between the two dominant agricultural castes in the state, the Kammas and the Reddis. The Kammas, who are geographically concentrated in the delta districts, were originally drawn to the Communist party partly as an expression of opposition to dominant Brahman elites who controlled the Congress party leadership. Later, when the more numerous Reddis, centering in the western districts of Andhra, gradually succeeded the Brahmans as the dominant group in the Congress party,

[31] *Ibid.*, 364, 366, 535.
[32] Selig S. Harrison, *India: The Most Dangerous Decades* (Princeton University Press, 1960), 204-45.

many ambitious Kamma politicians decided to remain in the Communist party, converting it into a vehicle for political competition with their traditional Reddi rivals. While hard core electoral support for the Communists came from the landless laborers, the margin of victory was generally supplied by the ability of the leadership to attract a share of the Kamma vote. In the delta districts, therefore, the Communists have tried to conciliate the middle peasantry. Even when the Communists experimented with guerrilla warfare between 1948 and 1951, and carried out land redistribution in "liberated" villages, they usually spared all but the largest farmers.

Nevertheless, the Andhra Communist leadership could not succeed in this strategy without the cooperation of the agricultural workers and poorer peasants who constitute their political base in the countryside. Weiner's study of the Congress party in another delta district (Guntur)[33] suggests what may be the most important factors in the acquiescence of Harijan and low-caste laborers. At the village level, the primary political unit is not caste or class, but faction. The leaders of each faction are prominent families of the same landowning caste or rival agricultural castes who compete with each other for social and political ascendency in the village. The families may have been rivals for several generations; in any case, they are traditional landowning patrons who owe their influence to support from kin groups and families of other castes economically dependent on them, especially tenants and agricultural laborers. Normally, each faction allies itself with a political party or a faction of a political party in the district. During general elections, the faction leader will act as a broker between the village group and the political party, delivering peasant votes in return for promises of preferential treatment (for

[33] Myron Weiner, *Party Building in a New Nation: The Indian National Congress* (University of Chicago Press, 1968), 133-209.

his faction and/or village) if the candidate is successful. Conversely, sitting M.L.A.s or M.P.s may help the faction to win village elections by supplying money or other less tangible assets, such as prestige, to the faction leader. While competition between the Congress party and the Communists for control of village *panchayats* (councils) is keen, the Congress party has so far been victorious in most local contests. An important factor, as suggested by Weiner, has probably been the practice of voting by a show of hands rather than secret ballot in many village elections, and the reluctance of client groups to alienate the patron family.

Yet, there appears to be another reason as well. The primary target of political competition at the local level is control of the village council. With the advent of adult suffrage, each faction leader is forced to extend his following by attracting the allegiance of those villagers who have usually not participated in traditional power struggles. The most obvious source of new popular support are the large numbers of unattached laborers, many of whom are slowly increasing their bargaining power as a result of growing economic opportunities. Since village leaders cannot command the support of uncommitted individuals, they must cajole it. At the very least, this involves being civil to Harijans, even solicitous of their needs. High-caste leaders who have traditionally considered Harijans outside the pale of Hindu society and were accustomed to ignoring even the existence of Harijan households in estimating the effective strength of the village, now routinely visit the Harijan section to ask for votes at election time. High-caste leaders also bestow more tangible benefits. Often, one of the first priorities for a successful candidate is redeeming his campaign pledge to arrange a new drinking water well or school building or radio for the Harijan quarter. Such considerations by the dominant castes tend to blunt the hostilities of Harijans and convince them that social conditions are improving.

78

Yet, it is problematical that Harijans and low-caste laborers will indefinitely be satisfied with their role of "follower" in local politics. First, the very accommodations forced on upper-caste leaders by adult suffrage as a means of protecting their hegemony has further eroded traditional status relationships. High ritual position and economic standing no longer automatically confer authority. A candidate must ask for support, indeed he has to bargain for it. In many cases, he literally pays for it, not only by feasting large groups of his supporters, but also by giving cash bribes to individuals. If some landless laborers are already advancing independent economic demands, it should not be long before they begin to assert a separate political role as well. Indeed, there are strong incentives to do so. Under the prevailing pattern of factional politics, there is a very low ceiling on the benefits that come to Harijans and low-caste groups. In fact, as long as economic values, especially rights in land, are so unequally divided between leader and follower groups, there can be little substantial improvement in the income or standard of living of most Harijan families even when their faction is victorious. On the contrary, as modernization gains momentum, disparities can be expected to widen, and the gains that trickle down due to the enlightened self-interest of village leaders will appear less and less significant in relative terms. At some point, therefore, the low castes may well decide that only a direct challenge to the power of the dominant landowning castes can bring about a fundamental improvement in their condition. Yet, once the interests of the traditional agricultural castes and the landless are perceived as antagonistic, the multi-caste (class) faction will no longer be a viable political unit. Already, there are cases in the delta of village elections being fought between the Harijans on one side and the dominant agricultural caste on the other, that can best be described as "class struggles."

West Godavary is only in the first stages of the green revolution. Nevertheless, the overwhelming majority of cultivators have already been defined out of the modernization process by various barriers: the small size of landholding, the high rates of rental for leased land, and the lack of capital for investment in land improvement. In West Godavary, any rapid acceleration of agricultural modernization will inevitably produce far wider disparities than in Ludhiana between the large landowners and small cultivators-cum-tenants, with the additional crucial difference that in West Godavary the first group represents a small minority of agriculturists and the second, the majority. Moreover, it is doubtful that agricultural laborers will long remain satisfied with predominately social and psychological gains. At the moment, West Godavary presents a very peaceful picture. Developments in other districts that are similarly situated suggest this may not be a lasting peace.

4. Thanjavur, Tamil Nadu

A PREDOMINANTLY delta area lying along the coast of the Bay of Bengal, Thanjavur is the proverbial "rice bowl" in Tamil Nadu State. One of fourteen districts, it alone accounts for nearly one-fourth of the total acreage under paddy and more than a quarter of the total output of paddy.

Historically, the area has been benefited by the availability of natural flow irrigation from a number of rivers which pass through the region. The largest of these, the Cauvery, has a length of 500 miles from its source in neighboring Mysore State to its outlet in eastern Thanjavur. Altogether the Cauvery and its tributaries irrigate about 1,700,000 acres in Tamil Nadu. More than two-thirds of the delta area is concentrated in Thanjavur.

There seem to have been efforts dating from very early times to control the flow of water from the Cauvery for more efficient irrigation. But by the turn of the nineteenth century, little remained of the ancient canal network. The first attempt in modern times to rebuild the irrigation system came with the construction of the Cauvery and Vennar regulators in 1886. Apart from distributing the waters of the two rivers more efficiently, the regulators also protected the farmers' fields from flooding. The area commanded by the Cauvery and Vennar regulators, accounting for about 900,000 acres, became known as the Old Delta of Thanjavur after new construction in the 1920's and 1930's extended the area under canal irrigation. Between 1925 and 1934, there were two major improvements. The Mettur Reservoir was constructed near the Tamil Nadu-Mysore border over a

81

catchment area of 16,300 miles. At the same time, a new canal, called the Grand Anicut Canal, was built to provide irrigation facilities for an additional 300,000 acres in Thanjavur. Known as the Cauvery Mettur Project, or C.M.P., the area under the Grand Anicut Canal is still referred to as the "new delta" in the district.

In 1961, the total area commanded by the Cauvery and Vennar regulators, and the C.M.P., about 1,200,000 acres, accounted for 80 percent of the net sown area in Thanjavur. With about 80 percent of the cultivated area also under paddy, almost all of the paddy crop was grown under irrigated conditions. It was this extensive irrigation system, together with the fine alluvial soil in large parts of the Cauvery delta that marked Thanjavur as one of the districts with the highest potential for development when the I.A.D.P. was first introduced in 1960-61.

Yet, it was precisely the unusually favorable agronomic conditions that accounted for some of Thanjavur's most severe problems. In 1961, Thanjavur supported a population of 3,240,000 persons on 3,648 square miles, resulting in a population density of about 900 persons per square mile. Moreover, about 80 percent of the total population lived in rural areas.[1] Altogether, there were 941,000 cultivators and farm laborers dependent on a total cropped area of 1,458,000 acres for their livelihood.[2] The availability of land per adult worker was only 1.5 acres, one of the lowest landman ratios in any region of India.

There were other problems. Field experience revealed that the irrigation position was less favorable than first appeared. As in West Godavary, the canal system is dependent on rainfall for its water supplies. While the agricultural economy of the rest of Tamil Nadu revolves around the

[1] Expert Committee on Assessment and Evaluation, Ministry of Food and Agriculture (Department of Agriculture), Intensive Agricultural District Program, Report (1961-63), 77.

[2] Ibid., 77, 78.

northeast monsoon from October to December, Thanjavur is dependent on the weaker southwest monsoon from June to September that feeds the catchment area of the Cauvery-Mettur system in Mysore. The southwest monsoon rarely fails; nevertheless, it is frequently delayed, and once begun, often does not continue in full force. Consequently, the first waters from the Mettur Reservoir may not be released until early July, reaching the higher elevations only in August. Then, depending on the strength of the northeast monsoon, and local rains in January, crops may suffer from acute water shortages beginning in February. By contrast, in some years, the northeast monsoon is so heavy that fields are flooded. Even in a normal season, the low lying coastal areas in the eastern part of the district (accounting for about 100,000 acres under paddy), are plagued by inadequate drainage; in years of particularly heavy rainfall, the entire crop is menaced by submersion. Moreover, seasonal imbalances in water supply, whether the problem is one of too little or too much, are aggravated by the old construction of the irrigation system. Channels are very wide, inadequately lined, and irregular. It is therefore necessary to maintain maximum flow in order to bring sufficient water to farmers' fields. In normal or below average rainfall years, a great deal of water is unnecessarily wasted; in years of very high rainfall, the problems of drainage and flooding are intensified.

The uncertain water situation depresses overall production in another way. It places a low ceiling on the extent of the area that is double-cropped. In 1961, the area covered by both a *kurvai* or *kharif* crop (from June to September-October) and a *thaladi* or *rabi* crop (from October-November to February) accounted for less than one-third of the net acreage under paddy, i.e., a little under 300,000 acres. This area was mainly concentrated on low-lying lands situated nearest to the canal outlets. On other lands, double-

83

cropping was considered too hazardous on a routine basis unless the cultivator had access to supplementary water facilities. Delays in the southwest monsoon meant late seedlings and late harvests extending into October and November when heavy rains caused serious damage to crops from lodging of plants. Further, delayed harvesting of the *kurvai* crop automatically postponed seedlings for the *thaladi,* and exposed the cultivator to the double jeopardy of crop losses at the end of the *rabi* season from extended water shortages beginning in February. Not surprisingly, uncertainty about the time of the onset of the southwest monsoon, combined with lack of availability of strains that could withstand the heavy rains of the northeast monsoon in the event of delayed planting, convinced many farmers of the wisdom of taking only one long duration *samba* crop from August-September to January-February. This solution did not eliminate the danger of yield losses from water shortages during the tail end of the *samba* season in February, but it did save the cultivator from the double risk of losing both the *kurvai* and *thaladi* crops if the rains failed.

Nevertheless, in 1961 when the I.A.D.P. was first introduced in Thanjavur, the development staff was hopeful. The results of crop demonstrations using the full package of modern practices were more favorable than in West Godavary. Yields of paddy on treated plots increased by about one-fourth, and in some cases, the gains were well over 40 percent. Moreover, the economics of modern practices also appeared attractive. It was estimated that for each additional rupee spent on the package of practices, the return to the cultivator was Rs. 2.62.[3]

Yet, Thanjavur's farmers responded even more slowly than the cultivators of West Godavary to these incentives. During the period 1960-61 to 1964-65, the offtake of nitrog-

[3] Intensive Agricultural District Program, *Second Report* (*1960-65*), 121.

84

enous fertilizer increased by only 140 percent and that of phosphatic fertilizers by 230 percent.[4] The slow rate of progress in the adoption of modern inputs was reflected in the average yield rates: with the exception of upward spurts in the good weather years of 1961-62 and 1964-65, average yields per acre of rice remained virtually stationary during the period 1960-61 and 1965-66. Average yield rates for each crop season in Thanjavur district are presented in Table 4.

TABLE 4

Average Yield of Rice in Pounds Per Acre for Each Season
in Thanjavur District, 1960-61 to 1965-66

Year	Kurvai	Samba	Thaladi	Total crop
1960-61	1445	1347	1285	1347
1961-62	1490	1570	1517	1517
1962-63	1552	1366	1249	1356
1963-64	1445	1338	1267	1320
1964-65	1562	1591	1455	1565
1965-66	1509	1332	1129	1340

SOURCE: *Progress of I.A.D.P., Thanjavur, 1960-67,* 67.

Certainly, the vagaries of annual water supply played a large role in damping down the average yield levels over a period of years. Without minimizing the limitations of the irrigation system as an explanation of the slow progress in Thanjavur, it is necessary to recognize that another substantial constraint on the progress of agricultural modernization also existed. Indeed, it was the inability of most cultivators to absorb any losses in bad weather years that contributed to a widespread lack of willingness to make costly innovations. As in West Godavary, the unfavorable agroeconomic setting was at least as important as the shortcomings of the irrigation system in accounting for the poor progress of the agricultural economy during the first five years of the I.A.D.P.

[4] *Ibid.,* 122.

85

· I ·

Agroeconomic surveys conducted in the district in 1961-62 revealed that 73 percent of all holdings were less than 5 acres. Another 15 percent were between 5 and 10 acres in size. Only 12 percent were above 10 acres. Even in respect of area, holdings of less than 5 acres accounted for 36 percent of the total cultivated land. Another 22 percent of the area was operated in holdings of 5 to 10 acres. Little more than 40 percent of the land was cultivated in holdings of over 10 acres. By contrast, the minimum size for an economic holding in Thanjavur district, according to estimates by the development staff, is 3 or 4 acres of double-cropped paddy land, or 6 acres of single-cropped land. Thus, the majority of cultivators in Thanjavur, like their counterparts in West Godavary, were operating uneconomic holdings at the time the I.A.D.P. was introduced. Table 5 shows the 1961 distribution of cultivators and cultivated area according to size of holdings.

TABLE 5

Distribution of Cultivators and Cultivated Areas
in Thanjavur District by Size of Holdings

	Holding size			
Item	Less than 2.5 acres	2.5 acres to 4.9 acres	5 acres to 9.9 acres	10 acres and above
Percentage of cultivators in the group to the total sampled	46	27	15	12
Average size in acres	0.49	1.43	2.62	6.69
Percentage of cultivated area for the group to the total	13	23	22	42

SOURCE: Intensive Agricultural District Program, *Report* (1961-63), 82.

Comparable land tenure problems also existed. Even official estimates indicated a very high rate of tenancy. Nearly 20 percent of all cultivators were described as pure tenants, and another 20 percent were said to be leasing some part of their holding. Altogether, the area operated under tenancy arrangements was placed at about 20 percent of the total cultivated land in the district.[5] Nevertheless, official estimates were certainly too low. Ladejinsky's field investigation in 1965 concluded that about one-half of all cultivators were taking some land on lease, and that as much as 50 percent of the total area was operated under tenancy arrangements.[6] Visits to selected villages in 1969 produced data in support of the higher estimates for the densely populated Old Delta area. In three villages of Tiruvaiyaru Block, Kargudi, Royampettai, and Peramur, the percentage of cultivators who were either pure tenants or taking some part of their holding on lease was roughly 48 percent, 45 percent, and 77 percent, respectively. More striking was the estimate of the percentage of the total cultivated area operated under tenancy arrangements: 75 percent in Kargudi, 30 to 40 percent in Royampettai, and 60 percent in Peramur. Conditions were more or less similar in Kaivalur Block in the coastal area of eastern Thanjavur. Sixty-four percent of the cultivators of Valivalam village, 45 percent of Thaevur village, and 75 percent of Therkkupanaiyur village were classified as pure tenants or owner-cum-tenant cultivators operating about 33 percent, and 40 percent of the total area under paddy in their respective villages. Only in the "new delta" area, where most farmers are small owner-cultivators, was the incidence of tenancy negligible.[7]

[5] *Ibid.*, 132.
[6] Wolf Ladejinsky, A *Study of Tenurial Conditions in Package Districts*, 3.
[7] The three villages of Thambikottai, Maharajasamudrapuram, and Aladikumulai in Pattukottai Block of the "new delta" area were visited. In the first two villages 10 to 13 percent of all cultivators

The most favorable terms for leased land are offered by temples, which own about 200,000 acres of land in the district, most of it concentrated in the Old Delta. Customary rates ranging from 4 1/2 to 7 1/2 bags of paddy per acre,[8] depending on soil quality and suitability for double-cropping, were reported. Assuming average yield levels of about 10 bags per acre at the time the I.A.D.P. was introduced, rentals on temple owned lands were absorbing about 35 percent of the gross output on double-cropped land and about 45 percent on single-cropped land. By contrast, the rates charged by individual *mirasdars*, many of whom were absentee landlords, ranged from 9 to 15 bags of paddy per acre for single-cropped and double-cropped land, respectively. They were so high that except in extremely good weather years, leasing arrangements were likely to prove uneconomic for the cultivator.

From the outset, therefore, the I.A.D.P. faced two crippling agroeconomic limitations with respect to its program for rapid diffusion of modern practices: (1) the small size of most cultivators' holdings which prevented the accumulation of any surplus capital for investment; and (2) the high rate of tenancy among small farmers on terms which siphoned off anywhere between 35 percent to 80 percent of the gross produce in rent. Far from having any surpluses to invest on agricultural innovations, a sizable segment of agriculturists lived on the margin of subsistence, and actually required rehabilitation before they could make any contribution to development.

This basic fact of agrarian life in Thanjavur was indirectly reflected in the figures for the adoption of the new

leased some land, and this land accounted for 12 percent and 20 percent of the total cultivated area, respectively. In Aladikumulai, less than 1 percent of all cultivators operated leased land, accounting for less than 1 percent of the cultivated area.
[8] 1 bag = 125 pounds.

techniques. As early as 1961, survey results indicated that all classes of farmers were psychologically receptive to economic innovations: "almost all the farmers in the district applied organic manures or chemical fertilizers to their crops."[9] Yet, while Thanjavur was considered "one of the most advanced districts in the country in respect of the use of manures and fertilizers," the small farmers were clearly hampered in their efforts to adopt modern inputs by the absence of resources for investment. During *kharif* 1963-64, 74 percent of cultivators with holdings of 10 acres or more were reported to have applied some chemical fertilizer. More remarkable, as many as 57 percent of farmers with holdings of 2.5 acres or less also did so.[10] But as in Ludhiana, the percentage of area treated was much lower on small than on large holdings, and small farmers actually applied higher doses of nitrogenous and phosphatic fertilizer to treated areas in an apparent effort to maximize output and income from investment.[11] The financial constraints on small farmers were further illustrated by available information for cooperative credit. An initial drive to increase membership in the cooperatives was very successful. Between 1959-60 and 1964-65 membership almost doubled, from 274,000 to 434,000.[12] But the inability of small farmers to absorb larger amounts of credit was quickly reflected in the deterioration of the economic position of the cooperatives. Between 1959-60 and 1963-64, the total amount of loans advanced increased from Rs. 214 lakhs to Rs. 426 lakhs. But by 1964-65, this amount had declined to Rs. 325 lakhs. During the same period, moreover, the percentage of overdues increased from 5 percent to 37 percent.[13]

[9] Intensive Agricultural District Program, *Second Report* (*1960-65*), 135.

[10] *Ibid.*, 136.   [11] *Ibid.*, 138.

[12] *Ibid.*, 127.   [13] *Ibid.*, 128.

· II ·

The availability of I.R. 8 and other exotic paddy varieties could do little to change the dim prospect for the agricultural economy of Thanjavur. The short-duration imported strains were higher yielding than the short-term local variety, ADT 20, but significantly inferior in their ability to withstand flooding and heavy rains during the northeast monsoon. Nevertheless, in 1964, a breakthrough by local researchers in evolving the Japonica-indica hybrid ADT 27, unexpectedly transformed the public image of Thanjavur from one of stagnation and failure to dynamism and success as the vanguard district of the green revolution in the rice areas.

ADT 27 is not as high-yielding as the exotic varieties. Under the most favorable field conditions, output reaches some 4,600 pounds, an increment of about 45 percent over the maximum yield potential of the local variety, ADT 20.[14] Yet, it has other striking advantages: it gives reliable yield increases; requires minimum changes in cultivation practices; is relatively disease resistant; and produces fine grain that fetches the highest procurement price. As early as the *kharif* season, 1965, when ADT 27 was cultivated on 5,000 acres, these qualities prompted the press to dub the new variety with such extravagant names as "the seed of destiny" and "heavenly gift."[15] But the greatest attraction of ADT 27 for the average cultivator was fortuitously revealed in *kharif* 1966 when the Agriculture Department's plan to cover about 200,000 acres in Thanjavur was jeopardized by the late arrival of the southwest monsoon, and a delay in the opening of the Mettur Reservoir until July 21. With the rest of the State facing serious food shortages under pervasive drought conditions, the extension staff persuaded the farmers to take late seedlings of ADT 27 "in spite of the risk of

[14] *Progress of I.A.D.P., Thanjavur, 1960-67*, 27.
[15] *Ibid.*, 55.

the crop being damaged by rains with the noble objective of saving Tamil Nadu State from famine conditions."[16] Subsequently, the prospects of the crop were further dimmed by a failure of the monsoon during the growing period, and the heaviest rainfall ever recorded in October and November (28 inches as against an average of 8 inches). Despite all these adversities, and the fact that the crop was harvested during the "dreaded" rains of November, the average yields obtained with ADT 27 were about 3,000 pounds.[17] The lesson was not lost on the farmers of Thanjavur. Not only was ADT 27 as short-duration (about 105 days) and fine grained as ADT 20, and higher-yielding in good weather years, but it was also more resistant to lodging in heavy rains. Even if caught in the northeast monsoon as a result of delayed planting, yields would still exceed output of ADT 20 by a comfortable margin.

The dramatic achievement of the 1966 *kharif* season provided the foundation for a projection of the "green revolution" into Thanjavur. Enthusiastic I.A.D.P. officers argued that the advent of ADT 27 presented the opportunity to convert most of the single-cropped area into double-cropped land, and to reverse the traditional ratio of double and single-cropped land from the proportion of 1:3 to 3:1, i.e., from 300,000 acres out of 1,200,000 acres to 900,000 acres out of 1,200,000 acres.[18] This program of "mass conversion" which was started in 1967 not only caught the public imagination, but also attracted the ingenuity and resources of the Ford Foundation and the Food Corporation of India, and within a short period 30 mechanical dryers were installed in different centers of the district to guarantee drying facilities for the wet paddy harvested. All of this had its effect. In addition to widespread adoption of ADT 27 on traditionally double-cropped land, in 1967-68 and again in 1968-69, an additional 200,000 acres of *samba*

[16] *Ibid.*, 44.   [17] *Ibid.*, 44.   [18] *Ibid.*, 44-46.

land was planted with ADT 27 and a second medium-duration crop. Altogether, the double-cropped area was increased from 300,000 acres to 500,000 acres. Equally striking, average yield per acre during the *kurvai* season in 1967-68 was estimated at 1,752 pounds compared to 1,235 pounds in the previous year.[19]

Yet, careful analysis of the dimensions of the green revolution in Thanjavur produce a number of caveats which suggest serious limitations on its capacity to transform the agricultural economy of the region. It now appears that limitations on the *samba* conversion program are greater than was originally anticipated. Compared to the target of converting 600,000 acres of traditional single-cropped land into double-cropped land (which was supposed to be achieved in one year, by 1967), actual accomplishment in 1967-68 and 1968-69 was about 200,000 acres. In 1969-70, an additional 100,000 acres is expected to be converted. I.A.D.P. officers now believe that 300,000 to 400,000 acres represents the maximum new area that can be brought under double-cropping. Problems of poor drainage, inadequate water, and alkaline and saline soils are all more intractable than anticipated in carrying out any further expansion of the *samba* conversion program. Moreover, there are also agroeconomic limitations: these cannot be quantified, but are nevertheless serious constraints. A number of small farmers simply have no money to grow a second crop; if they are tenant-cultivators they often have no incentive as well. Farmers with very small holdings also face physical limitations; e.g., they do not have raised platforms for threshing, although they cannot use the roadside when the harvest occurs in heavy rains. Once all these constraints are taken into account, it is probable that in most years about half the acreage in Thanjavur will remain single-cropped land.[20]

[19] *Ibid.*, 67.
[20] A major agronomic limitation of ADT 27 is that the variety is photosensitive and cannot be planted during the *thaladi* or *samba*

While rather significant limitations on the ability of small farmers to participate in the new technology have been cited above, it is true that ADT 27 has been adopted by both large and small farmers. Indeed, this fact has encouraged the notion, also prevalent in Ludhiana, that all classes of cultivators can participate equally in the green revolution. Yet, as in Ludhiana, an inquiry into the distribution of benefits from the new technology between small and large farmers leads to the conclusion that economic disparities have been substantially increased as a result of the introduction of ADT 27. Even when small farmers adopt the new practices, the multiple handicaps under which they do so, operate to bring about a relative deterioriation in their economic position.

· III ·

It is true that compared to I.R. 8, ADT 27 can be cultivated successfully on land that does not have an assured supply of supplementary water from a filter point or tubewell. This was dramatically demonstrated during the 1966 *kharif* season when despite late planting of seedlings, drought conditions during the growing season, and the worst November rains on record, the average yield of ADT 27 was about 3,000 pounds. Undoubtedly, this was a striking improvement over the performance of ADT 20, which even under optimum weather conditions could give little

seasons. No other high-yielding varieties have yet been evolved which are suitable for either the second crop or the *samba* crop, although at present, they account for two-thirds of the total area under paddy. This limitation on further agricultural development is illustrated by available figures on yields per acre for Thanjavur district as a whole in 1966-67 and 1967-68. While the *kurvai* season saw average yields per acre of rice increase from 1,235 pounds to 1,752 pounds, yields for both the *thaladi* and *samba* crops were pushed down to a new low by adverse weather conditions, from 1,121 pounds per acre to 837 pounds per acre and from 1,370 pounds per acre to 1,223 pounds per acre, respectively. As a result, average yields per acre for the total crop registered a slight decline from 1,292 pounds per acre to 1,262 pounds per acre. The same marginal decline was reported for total output from 866,746 tonnes in 1966-67 to 807,442 tonnes in 1967-68. *Ibid.*, 67-68.

more than 2,500 pounds, and in bad weather years, 1,500 to 1,900 pounds. Nevertheless, the average yield level of ADT 27 under adverse weather conditions was still about 35 percent less than *its own* maximum yield potential of 4,600 pounds. The fact is that only farmers with a filter point or tubewell can achieve optimum yield levels with the adoption of the new variety.

Actually, there are multiple advantages of having supplementary minor irrigation. First, cultivators do not have to wait until water is released from the Mettur Reservoir to plant. Even if the monsoon is delayed (or their fields are at tail end areas of the canal network), they can begin cultivation of the *kuruai* crop in June. The ability to plant early permits farmers to harvest the crop before the onset of the northeast monsoon in November and to prevent yield losses caused by germination after exposure to heavy rains. Moreover, yields are further protected against the effects of water shortages during key stages of the growth cycle if the monsoon does not continue in full force after planting.

There are other important advantages of supplementary water facilities in maximizing returns to investment on improved practices. Seedlings for the second *thaladi* crop can be planted early in October; and the unfavorable effects of water shortages during the end of the *rabi* season can be eliminated. Also, a filter point or tubewell can be used for a third summer crop, between February and May, to increase income from lands that are generally given over to dry fodder crops. Alternatively, agricultural operations can be diversified to bring some land under more profitable commercial crops such as sugarcane and banana.

The Cauvery Basin is a rich belt for tapping underground water through filter points. Indeed, between 1965 and 1967 official estimates are that over 4,200 filter points were sunk.[21] But as in West Godavary, the large majority

[21] *Ibid.*, 40.

94

of farmers, i.e., those with less than 3 or 4 acres of owned land, have not been able to raise the large capital outlays required to exploit these resources.

Installation costs for a filter point in parts of the delta where the subsoil water is near the surface may range from Rs. 500 to Rs. 1,500. Additional outlays for an electric motor or oil engine may bring the total cost to Rs. 4,000. In areas where underground water is deep and power drills are required to sink borewells and tubewells, the minimum cost of a minor irrigation facility will rise to Rs. 6,000 and is usually closer to Rs. 8,000 or Rs. 10,000. Farmers with 10 acres or more can generally manage to meet these outlays from their own resources. Cultivators with smaller holdings are likely to rely on the Department of Agriculture or the Land Mortgage Banks for loans. Yet, to tap these sources, a cultivator must be in a position to mortgage at least 3 or 4 acres of land. Far from having such assets, most farmers are so impoverished that I.A.D.P. officers believe even the operational costs of using large State-financed community tubewells may prove beyond their means. State schemes that now envisage large tubewells serving 60 to 70 cultivators also project a rise in the water rate (to meet the operational costs of a turbopump and permanent staff) from Rs. 20 per acre for double-cropped canal irrigated land to a total of Rs. 100 per acre. Although this is roughly the same expense that large farmers now absorb on privately owned filter points, it is considered too high for many small cultivators who tend to consume a large portion of additions to output.

Those small farmers who have adopted ADT 27 therefore have done so without access to assured water from supplementary minor irrigation works. As a result, their gains from the introduction of the new seeds are sharply limited from the outset. Lack of timely irrigation may delay planting for the *kurvai*, advancing the harvest date to November when heavy rains cause yield losses from lodging. Moreover, postponing planting for the second *thaladi* crop also reduces output through prolonged exposure to water shortages at the end of the *rabi* season. Equally damaging, while severe water shortages may not actually occur more than one or two years in five, chronic uncertainty about the availability of adequate water in any given year creates an unwillingness to invest in recommended doses of modern inputs. As a result, even in good weather years yield levels fall below the maximum obtainable.

The reluctance of the small farmer to risk high expenditures on fertilizer, as long as the availability of water is uncertain, is illustrated by the inability of the agricultural credit societies to close the large gap between loans sanctioned—on the basis of the requirements of members as determined by standardized rates of finance per acre in both cash and kind—and amounts actually disbursed or lifted by farmers. The two Cooperative Central Banks in Thanjavur district, Kumbakonam and Thanjavur, include 555 primary agricultural credit societies which have a membership estimated at 390,000 or about 85 percent of all agricultural families.[22] Yet, in 1968-69 the Joint Registrar of Cooperative Societies for Thanjavur had to remind the district officers that only one-third of the existing membership was actually borrowing from the credit societies, and "the other 2/3rds ununderstandably have kept aloof from facilities that cry to be used."[23] Compared to Rs. 12 crores of agricultural credit sanctioned for the district as a whole in 1967-68, only Rs. 4 crores was actually disbursed. Even so, overdues

[22] Estimate supplied by the Secretary, Central Cooperative Bank, Thanjavur.

[23] *Circular of the Joint Registrar of Cooperative Societies Thanjavur Region, Thanjavur*, dated 10-4-68, 2.

amounted to 24 percent of the total advanced.[24] The inability of the cooperative societies to utilize existing resources is also strikingly demonstrated by the gap between the present borrowing power of the Central Banks (at twelve times share capital and reserves) and the amount currently borrowed (including deposits and advances from the Reserve Bank). In 1968-69, the Cooperative Central Bank at Kumbakonam was eligible to borrow Rs. 5.8 crores; actual borrowings outstanding were Rs. 1.4 crores, leaving the bank with a borrowing reserve of Rs. 4.3 crores. The situation was similar at the Thanjavur Cooperative Central Bank. Compared to a borrowing power of Rs. 8.7 crores, borrowings outstanding were Rs. 5.9 crores, with a reserve borrowing power of Rs. 2.8 crores. Altogether, for the district as a whole, resources amounting to over Rs. 7 crores remained idle for lack of applications for credit.[25]

This lack of demand can be traced to the same two factors which were already noted in West Godavary: (1) an Individual Maximum Credit Limit of Rs. 15,000 (rising to Rs. 20,000 for sugarcane) that prevents expansion of loan business through larger advances to big farmers; and (2) the inability of small farmers to utilize their maximum borrowing power even at the modest rates of finance per acre now provided. In Thanjavur, there are two main reasons for the second problem: the relatively high kind component in the loans advanced, coupled with the reluctance of small farmers to draw the fertilizer component in full without an assured supply of water; and the unwillingness of the primary agricultural credit societies to recommend tenants as good credit risks, despite official policy providing cultivation loans for tenants "with or without lease deeds" up to an amount necessary to cultivate 5 acres of land.

[24] Figures supplied by the Secretary, Central Cooperative Bank, Thanjavur.
[25] *Ibid.*

97

Compared to estimated cultivation costs of ADT 27 of about Rs. 450 per acre,[26] the rate of finance for paddy was Rs. 250 in 1968-69. Only Rs. 90 was disbursed in cash, and the remainder in seeds, fertilizers, and pesticides, with the major part, valued at Rs. 120, representing fertilizers. Landowners were eligible for an additional cash component at the rate of Rs. 25 per acre before the harvest of the paddy crops, collectable immediately by procurement of produce.[27] Bank officials acknowledge that most borrowing members take only the first cash portion in full, and much smaller proportions of the kind component. The decision to raise the scale of finance starting in 1969-70 to Rs. 300 per acre provides that the cash component will remain the same, and presumably so will the farmers' response.

Many cultivators, however, do not even get the opportunity to exercise such an option. These are tenants who are considered bad credit risks by the cooperatives. According to official regulations, tenants with or without lease deeds are eligible for personal surety loans up to Rs. 1,000 (compared to Rs. 5,000 for landowners). In practice, however, primary agricultural credit societies will sanction loans only to permanent or hereditary tenants; i.e., only to cultivators who enjoy a customary, if not legal, right to till the same holding from year to year. Yet, the bulk of sharecroppers in Thanjavur are shifted from one plot to another in order to avoid the provisions for security of tenure under state tenancy legislation; consequently, they are generally denied loans by the cooperatives. Ironically, at the same time that the tenants are excluded from access to low-cost credit that might help them benefit from the new production potential

[26] India, Planning Commission, Programme Evaluation Organization, *Evaluation Study of the High Yielding Varieties Program, Kharif*-1967, August 1968, 30.

[27] *Norms for Financing Agricultural Operations by the Cooperative Central Banks in Thanjavur District during 1968-69.* Mimeo. Supplied by the Secretary, Central Cooperative Bank, Thanjavur.

of ADT 27, *mirasdars* have been raising rentals on paddy land by about one bag annually over the last three or four years, citing higher productivity rates with the introduction of the new technology.

Once all the handicaps under which small farmers operate are taken into account, it is not surprising that the majority of cultivators in Thanjavur have experienced only minimum benefits from the introduction of ADT 27. Indeed, farmers with holdings of less than 5 acres are almost automatically excluded from exploiting the greatest potential economic advantage opened up by ADT 27, the possibility of converting some portion of single-cropped to double-cropped land. Considering the high cost of conversion—Rs. 450 per acre for ADT 27 when optimum cultivation practices are used—small farmers, especially predominantly tenant cultivators, find it too risky to invest (borrowed) funds on a second crop given the high probability of yield losses from delayed or inadequate irrigation water. For this group of single-crop farmers, the I.A.D.P. has offered little more than the chance of maintaining constant levels of consumption in the face of rising costs. Over the last six or seven years, some small farmers have managed to increase their yields anywhere from 10 percent to 40 percent, mainly from the adoption of the superior seed variety CO 25 for CO 19 or ADT 10 during the *samba* growing season. In a few cases, cultivators have also substituted medium-duration strains such as ADT 8 or GEB 24 for CO 19 on part of their holding, and succeeded in making modest additions to net income from double-cropping with groundnut or maize. Yet, compared with steadily rising living costs, the extra cash income generated by such innovations has proved sufficient only to provide for growing families, and/or increase the quantity and quality of food consumed, e.g., from one to two meals a day, or from ragi to rice, and to repay outstanding debts.

99

Actually, even small farmers who have always double-cropped a portion of their holding (mainly those with land closest to canal outlets) report little more by way of improvement in real income or standard of living as a result of adopting ADT 27. It is striking, for example, that no respondent in this size class achieved maximum potential yields with ADT 27. The damaging effects of late irrigation, delayed planting, inadequate water, small doses of chemical fertilizer, and late harvest in heavy rains are reflected in yield levels that may be as low as 1,900 pounds per acre, and rarely more than 3,400 pounds. Not surprisingly, predominantly owner-cultivators are much more likely to achieve yield levels at the higher end of the continuum; pure tenants rarely realize even 3,000 pounds per acre—the average output estimated for ADT 27 in a bad weather year. The point here is not that small farmers, especially tenants, fail to obtain any benefit in yields or net income from the adoption of the new seeds, but that these gains fall much below the maximum potential now possible with modern methods. A few owner-cultivators did report average yield gains of up to 50 percent an acre along with increases in cash income of 35 to 40 percent; even predominantly tenant-cultivators estimate their gains in output and income at about 25 percent. Yet, given the low ceiling on overall gains imposed by tiny holdings, both categories of small farmers agree that these rates of return are sufficient only to maintain current standards of living in the face of rising costs, allowing perhaps for modest improvement in some items of consumption. Indeed, even among the small group of "medium" size farmers, i.e., the 16 percent of cultivators with holdings between 5 and 10 acres, this picture is not significantly altered, except in the case of predominantly owner-cultivators. For example, one 8-acre farmer managed to convert 3 acres of his traditionally single-cropped holding into double-cropped land with the

INDIA'S GREEN REVOLUTION

introduction of ADT 27. As a result, he increased his net income per annum by over 30 percent from the additional *kurvai* crop; and by using CO 25 instead of local varieties for the *samba* and *thaladi* crops, and applying optimum doses of chemical fertilizers and pesticides in place of organic manures, managed to increase his yields per acre by about 80 percent and his net income some 35 percent during good weather years. This cultivator's new prosperity was reflected not only in a subjective feeling of definite improvement, but in newly acquired assets, including a terraced house and jewelry, as well as a Bose plough[28] and Burmese Satoon.[29] By contrast, predominantly tenant-cultivators in this size group reported only modest gains in average yields and net income per acre, mainly from the application of small doses of chemical fertilizer to local varieties. Such increases were unfortunately neutralized by rising costs. The main exception to this rule was the experience of farmers who were able to substitute ADT 27 for a local variety on a small area of owned land that had always been double-cropped. Cultivators who could afford to apply the recommended package of practices increased yields by some two-thirds and net income by about 50 percent per acre in good weather years. However, even allowing for such cases, it is clear that the majority of cultivators in

[28] The Bose plough is locally manufactured in Thanjavur and is especially suitable for efficient preparation of paddy fields. It consists of a wooden beam and body with one handle, a steel socket share and cast steel moldboard, and is drawn by a pair of bullocks. The plough partially inverts the soil and has a cutting action. In black soil, the width of the cut is 4 to 5 inches and the depth is 3 inches.

[29] Adapted from an implement used in Burma, the Burmese Satoon is an improved device for puddling wet land. It can prepare an area of 3½ to 4 acres a day for the transplantation of paddy seedlings. It has a 6 to 7 foot long shaft to which 6 to 8 blades or discs are fixed with cast iron hubs. It tramples or softens the soil in standing water to provide the proper consistency for the protection of the fine and weak roots of the paddy seedlings. It also turns under green leaves which are used as manure for paddy. It is light and can be drawn by a pair of bullocks.

101

Thanjavur, as in West Godavary, experienced a relative deterioration in their economic position as a result of the introduction of ADT 27 once the gains of the small minority of large landowners—the 9 percent of all cultivators having holdings of above 10 acres—are taken into account.

· IV ·

Farmers with holdings of 10 acres or more enjoy decisive advantages in exploiting the full potentiality of modern methods. Most are owner-cultivators, or lease only a small portion of their holding. They alone reap the returns to additional investment on improved practices. Second, the large size of the farm unit is itself a major advantage. Most of the additional output generated by application of modern inputs represents a net surplus over consumption and is disposed of on the market. With the price of food grains rising over the last few years, even modest increases in yield levels are capable of creating significant improvement in cash income per acre; on large farms aggregate increases are quite substantial. In fact, even before the introduction of ADT 27, many of the largest farmers, those with holdings of 30 acres or more, responded to market incentives for increasing production by applying the package of improved practices recommended under the I.A.D.P., and more important, undertaking large capital investment on land improvement, especially for minor irrigation works. In addition, they acquired a whole array of improved agricultural implements to enhance the efficiency of farm operations, including sprayers, dusters, and puddlers.[30] Ten or 20-acre farmers who often

[30] These are wet land puddlers designed to churn the soil in standing water. The puddlers break up clods and lumps in the soil and bring the finest particles to the surface in order to provide the most favorable growing environment for the fragile paddy seedlings. The ordinary puddler is somewhat more rudimentary in construction and less efficient than the Burmese Satoon. It consists of 3 angular bladed cast iron hubs rigidly fixed to a hollow horizontal pipe which rotates when drawn by a pair of bullocks.

could not afford the capital outlays on minor irrigation, were still in a position to withstand production losses in bad weather years, and this permitted them to adopt a wide variety of modern inputs. For example, they substituted CO 25 for lower yielding *samba* varieties; applied the recommended fertilizer and pesticide doses; and bought Bose ploughs, Burmese Satoons, and sprayers. Depending on the monsoon, they saw their yields increase anywhere from 20 percent to 60 percent per acre, and these gains were magnified by rising prices for food grains into higher cash income per acre, averaging from 50 to 60 percent. Certainly, a significant portion of this gain was neutralized by rising costs, but it seems clear that even before the introduction of ADT 27 large farmers as a group did experience a definite improvement in real income. Evidence for this assumption comes from reports by farmers of purchases during the 1960's of new furniture, cycles, transistors, jewelry, and electric fans, and also of investment in additional land and improved agricultural implements. By the time ADT 27 was introduced in 1965, this class of cultivators had accumulated sufficient savings to sustain much of the additional expenditure needed to realize optimum returns from the adoption of the new seeds.

The largest landowners, those with 30 acres and above, many of whom had already invested in filter points or borewells, or had ready access to capital for land improvement schemes, made the greatest absolute—and relative—gains. Having access to an assured supply of water, they were able to achieve reliable yield increases ranging from 50 to 200 percent over previous levels, realizing per acre output of 3,750 pounds to 4,500 pounds, or the maximum potential yield of ADT 27. Corresponding increases in cash income per acre tended to be at least three times higher than previous levels; some farmers reported gains of as much as eight times. In the case of one large estate of 600 acres, the

103

substitution of ADT 27 for local varieties on 300 acres of traditionally double-cropped land resulted in yield increases for the *kurvai* crop of about 50 percent per acre and a rise of cash income by almost five times. In absolute terms, total net income from the *kurvai* crop jumped from about Rs. 30,000 to almost Rs. 117,000. Such increases in cash income from the *kurvai*, along with more modest gains from the introduction of improved practices during the *thaladi* and *samba* seasons, permitted large farmers to accumulate substantial surpluses. These were used to pyramid their earlier gains by financing the purchase of additional land, the improvement of owned land, the conversion of larger proportions of owned holdings into double-cropped land, the planting of some acreage with more profitable commercial crops such as banana and coconut, and even the investment of some capital in small industries. Perhaps the most striking evidence of the large gains among this group—and of their growing orientation toward commercial agriculture —is the acute shortage of bulldozers and tractors that recently developed in Thanjavur district. Compared to less than 200 tractors available for distribution in the whole of Tamil Nadu State, during 1968, the Thanjavur Land Mortgage Bank alone received 200 loan applications for tractors —all from farmers with 30 to 40 acre holdings.[31] Given the demonstration effect exercised by these large farmers and the concrete gains that have already come to cultivators with 10 acres and above from the application of improved practices in good weather years, it is likely that more and more farmers in this size group will be able to sustain capital outlays on minor irrigation, and will begin to approach their larger neighbors in the ability to exploit the full range of new production opportunities opened by the advent of modern technology in Thanjavur.

[31] Estimate supplied by the Secretary of the Thanjavur Land Mortgage Bank.

· V ·

Standing in striking contrast to the bright prospects of the minority of large landowners is the unchanging poverty of the largest section of the agricultural population, the landless laborers. Accounting for almost one-half of all agricultural families and most of the Scheduled Castes, they have been excluded almost entirely from participating in the benefits of the green revolution. Indeed, in parts of Thanjavur, the several years since the introduction of the I.A.D.P. has seen the condition of agricultural workers deteriorate.

Farm workers in Thanjavur are about evenly divided between those who are permanent laborers, i.e., attached to the family of one *mirasdar* or landlord and those who work as hired labor on a daily basis. Of the two groups, it appears that attached laborers who still receive the greater amount of their annual earnings in kind, have fared better.

Permanent laborers generally receive food, housing, and some clothing from *mirasdars*. In addition, depending on individual arrangements, they receive monthly payments, both in cash and kind, or in cash only. Those permanent laborers who receive the largest portion of their monthly wage in kind enjoy the most favored position. In such cases, a laborer typically receives one and one-half bags of paddy per month, plus Rs. 2 in cash; during harvest there are additional kind payments of about two Madras Measures[32] of paddy per day. While these rates have remained substantially unchanged over the last ten years, their cash equivalent has risen along with the price of food grains from less than Rs. 400 to about Rs. 560 during this period. Other laborers who have customarily received their monthly payments in cash are less fortunate. A laborer who ten years ago, received Rs. 100 annually (in addition to food, cloth-

[32] One Madras Measure equals 1.22 kilograms or 2.7 pounds.

ing, and housing) may now be paid Rs. 300 per year, an increase of three times, but still lag behind the purchasing power of workers getting constant payments in kind.

The economic position of casual laborers tends to vary from one part of the district to another, depending on the extent of new employment opportunities opened up by the conversion of single-cropped to double-cropped land, diversification of the cropping pattern, and the level of associated off-season activities. Nevertheless, even in areas of intensive farming, the general oversupply of agricultural labor has tended to keep wage rates frozen at the same level for the past several years. This is particularly true of that portion of the farm workers income still paid in kind, i.e., wages for harvest. In the most prosperous western portion of the delta, agricultural laborers usually receive about six Madras Measures per day for harvesting work, valued at about Rs. 4. In most cases, this is the same rate of payment as received over the past five or six years. Even if an agricultural worker is fortunate enough to find harvest work during two crop seasons, i.e., for about two months a year, he can earn the equivalent of only some Rs. 240 during the peak seasons. It is true that daily cash wages for other agricultural work (ploughing, transplanting, land leveling or farm operations for sugarcane and betal vine) have increased over the last five or six years from rates that were as low as 75 n.p. per day for men, to Rs. 2-3; and from 50 n.p. for women to Rs. 1.8. Still, if an agricultural worker were fully employed at these rates for the rest of the year, i.e., for about ten months, he could only make a maximum income of about Rs. 850 per year. Actually, it is more common for agricultural workers to find harvesting work only thirty or forty days a year and to remain idle for at least one or two months. The average laborer in the western part of the delta, therefore, probably earns a maximum of Rs. 600-700 per year. Yet, in the best case, laborers report virtually no improvement in real income over the last several years. Increases in daily cash wages even when combined with additional job opportunities simply do not yield any margin once rising prices are taken into account.

Nevertheless, like their counterparts in West Godavary, casual laborers in western Thanjavur have experienced substantial social and psychological benefits from the expansion of work opportunities. Customary attitudes of deference exhibited by laborers toward landowners are increasingly being shed in favor of an unprecedented self-assertiveness. Laborers who routinely worked eight or ten hours a day for Rs. 1 some years ago are now working five or six hours daily and demanding twice or three times the cash wage as payment. Landowners are the first to comment on this transformation. They report with some uneasiness that workers are now "conscious of their rights"; and they recognize in a matter of fact way that "times have changed."

In the most impoverished eastern part of the delta, the self-assertive attitudes of agricultural laborers have begun to shade over into open hostility and combativeness toward landowners. Actually, the agricultural economy of East Thanjavur as a whole gained very little from the operation of the I.A.D.P. Situated in the coastal region, much of the area is subject to submersion during the northeast monsoon. Consequently, it has proved especially difficult to convert single-cropped to double-cropped land. As a result, the benefits of agricultural modernization have come almost exclusively to large landowners, in the form of higher yields from the application of chemical fertilizer to the main *samba* crop, and from the substitution of ADT 27 for local varieties during the *kurvai* season on land that has always been double-cropped.

It is in contrast to the large landowners that the landless workers have experienced the greatest relative decline in their economic position. In some cases, moreover, negative

107

changes have added up to an absolute decline in the standard of living. There are three main reasons for this: (1) the
I.A.D.P. has generated very few new opportunities for employment, leaving most farm workers idle from three to six
months a year; (2) payments for harvesting, and even cash
rates for day labor have remained stationary in the face of
rising prices; and (3) the proportion of wages traditionally
paid in kind is shrinking as *mirasdars* substitute cash payments for a growing number of agricultural operations.
Thus, in 1967, laborers were still receiving the traditional
rate for harvesting of four litres per half bag. At an average
output of one and one-half bags per day per male worker,
an agricultural laborer earned twelve litres—the equivalent
of about Rs. 5—during the harvest season of about 40 days.
Daily wages were ostensibly also fixed in kind, the standard
rate being four litres—the equivalent of about Rs. 1.7—but
many *mirasdars* had begun to substitute cash for at least a
portion of this payment. At this rate, even if a farm worker
were idle only three months a year, his maximum earnings
in 1967 could not have been more than the equivalent of
Rs. 600. More important, his purchasing power was steadily
decreasing in the face of rising prices, and the propensity
of the *mirasdars* to substitute cash for paddy in making
wage payments. As a result, many laborers were forced
deeper and deeper into debt, subsisting for long periods of
time only by taking loans from *mirasdars* (against promises
to carry out future agricultural operations). Moreover, the
worsening economic condition of the landless workers occurred at the same time that the large landowners were increasing their cash income per acre by three times or more
from the substitution of ADT 27 for local varieties on double-cropped land. Added to the discontent caused by growing material deprivation, therefore, was a sense of injustice
at the inequitable distribution of benefits from the new

108

technology. Feelings of resentment were increased when the laborers, citing higher costs of living and rising levels of productivity, especially on large farms, asked the land-owners for higher wages, and were told in response that additional farm income was being absorbed in the squeeze between rising production costs and low government procurement prices for paddy. The strained situation was aggravated, when the landlords began to rely more heavily on migrant workers from poorer districts to the south, who were willing to work for the existing wages. Inevitably, the entry of additional farm workers on an already over-crowded job market reduced still more the bargaining power of local laborers, and added to the anger of the landless.

· VI ·

The potential political implications of the erosion of traditional status relationships and their replacement by contractual arrangements based on bargaining are already discernible in the eastern portion of the delta. In this area, the deteriorating economic position and growing discontent of agricultural laborers created new opportunities for Communist party workers to expand the base of their political support by organizing large numbers of the poorest peasantry for strikes against landlords over the issue of agricultural wages. Moreover, the year 1967 saw a number of political factors coalesce to favor the efforts of a political strategy based on peasant mobilization. First, the Congress party was defeated in Tamil Nadu during the 1967 elections. It was succeeded by a political coalition led by the D.M.K., the *Dravida Munnetra Kazhagam* or Dravidian Progressive Federation, a state party which not only promised to protect the regional language of Tamil against encroachments by the official national language of Hindi, but also made a strong populist appeal, including a pledge to

109

redistribute land. More important, the new government included the recently formed C.P.I. (Marxists) as a constituent member. Organized in Tamil Nadu after the 1964 split in the national C.P.I., the Marxists represented the left faction in the Party which rejected the more orthodox approach of trade union agitation and opted for a militant rural strategy, aimed at creating a mass movement among the landless. The results of the 1967 election in Tamil Nadu showed that the Marxists had inherited the larger share of the popular strength of the undivided C.P.I. Compared to a total of 7.7 percent of the popular vote polled by the C.P.I. in the state elections of 1962, the regular C.P.I. won only 1.6 percent in 1967. By contrast, the newly organized C.P.I.(M) won over 4 percent of the total vote.[33] The victory of the D.M.K.-led coalition was especially significant for Communist prospects in Tamil Nadu because it marked the end of long-standing curbs on Communist agitational activity imposed by previous Congress governments. For the first time since 1952, both the C.P.I. and the C.P.I.(M) were given free reign in organizing rural workers.

The Communists enjoyed special advantages in Thanjavur. Farm laborers had played an important part in the 1948 Communist-led agrarian uprising; although the earlier movement was ultimately suppressed by the police and army, many laborers retained their ideological affinity for the left. Further, in East Tanjore, the C.P.I.(M) was able to step into an almost complete political vacuum. The *Swatantra* (Freedom) party[34] was identified as the party of the

[33] *India Votes: A Source Book on Indian Elections*, 718.

[34] The Swatantra party was formed in June 1959. Organized and supported by Bombay industrialists and dissident elements of the Congress party, the founders immediately forged an alliance with the All-India Agriculturists Federation, an interest group dominated by large landowners. The major purpose of the new party was to offer a viable conservative alternative to the Congress party, and reverse the trend toward increasing state controls on private property and

110

Brahmin *mirasdars* and high-caste businessmen and professionals. The Congress party was distrusted by most farm laborers belonging to the Scheduled Castes as the spokesman of middle class, middle caste cultivating peasants. Even the D.M.K. which came closest to being a populist party drew most of its organizational strength in Thanjavur from small traders in the towns and petty merchants in the villages, both of whom were hostile to the economic and status aspirations of Harijans. In fact, in 1967 the only party to attempt systematic canvassing among members of the Scheduled Castes was the C.P.I.(M). These efforts were rewarded by the election results which showed that Marxist-supported candidates had defeated the Congress party in contests for four out of six assembly seats.[35]

Marxist workers immediately followed up these electoral victories by increasing their visits to the area with the purpose of organizing farm workers into unions. The advent of the new technology actually provided the party with an unexpected tactical advantage: any labor strike or agitation that delayed harvesting of the *kurvai* crop until the onset of the northeast monsoon meant serious yield losses to landowners from germination of ADT 27. The thrust of the organizational effort, therefore, was to establish a united front among farm laborers with respect to two major issues: (1) a refusal by all unionized workers to carry out agricultural operations until a minimum wage was agreed upon; and (2) a commitment by all unionized workers to obstruct the landlords in any attempt at importing laborers from neighboring districts who were willing to work at lower rates.

---

investment in both the industrial and agricultural sectors. For an analysis of the factors leading to the formation of the party, see Howard L. Erdman, *The Swatantra Party and Indian Conservatism* (Cambridge University Press, 1967), 65-81.

[35] Under the terms of the electoral alliance, three of the four victorious candidates ran on the D.M.K. ticket; the fourth was a member of the Praja Socialist Party.

111

Starting in the summer of 1967, these tactics were put into action: large parties of Marxist-led farm workers began to enter the paddy fields of recalcitrant landowners to prevent farm operations from being carried out by imported laborers or local laborers who remained loyal to the landowners.

The immediate victory went to the farm workers. Two factors were largely responsible: the landowners' concern over large yield losses in the event of prolonged delays in farm operations; and perhaps more important, the failure of the police under the D.M.K. government to take firm action against trespassers. For example, the manager of a 600 acre estate in Valivalam village, Kaivalur Block, recalled that during *kharif* 1967 a Marxist M.L.A. from the neighboring district took the lead in organizing local laborers for the purpose of obstructing the employment of outside workers. The manager's dilemma, as he explained it was that, "Our laborers [in the village] are communist. They want to create a loss. If they are engaged for work they adopt go-slow policy and will not harvest the entire produce. Then if we try to get outside laborers the local laborers obstruct them. Our laborers won't work and they won't let others work." In mid-August 1967, tensions between the estate manager and the laborers over the use of imported labor reached a peak. Five hundred farm workers led by the Marxist M.L.A. *gheraoed* (surrounded) the manager in a courtyard outside his house and demanded an assurance that no more outside workers would be permitted to enter the village. Although the farm workers shouted death threats and carried an effigy of the manager's "corpse" over which they wept elaborately, the local police superintendent and the district collector, both of whom arrived on the scene along with a detachment of police, "just sat there and watched." The result was, as the manager recalled not without some humor, that "the police were also *gheraoed*." In this particular incident, the laborers dispersed voluntarily

112

and violence was averted. In nearby villages, similar incidents reportedly ended in bloodshed.

The outcome of the 1967 agitations was a state imposed settlement called the Mannargudi Agreement under which rates paid for harvesting were increased from four litres to 4 1/2 litres per half bag. At the rate of three bags per worker per day, the settlement represented a rise in the cash value of wages from about Rs. 5 to Rs. 5.6. Simultaneously, wages for daily labor were increased from the traditional rate of about Rs. 1.7 or four litres to Rs. 2.5; only a small fraction could be paid in cash, amounting to about one-third of a rupee, with five litres accounting for the bulk of the payment. In return for these concessions, the landowners' right to import laborers from other districts was confirmed—subject to the requirement that workers in the home village and neighboring locality must first be fully employed.

The 1967 agitations proved to be only the first round of a prolonged and increasingly violent confrontation between the laborers and landowners of East Thanjavur. The next two years saw the steady acceleration of labor demands, and a growing attitude of intransigence on the part of the landowners. Actually, from the beginning, the large landowners believed the labor agitations involved much more serious issues than the limited demand for higher wages. They saw in them a prelude to a frontal attack on the entire system of property rights. Indeed, farm laborers participating in *gheraos* shouted the standard Marxist slogans of "the land belongs to labor," "land ownership should go," "let the landlord be put out." Moreover, after the police failed to offer adequate protection to victims of *gheraos* in 1967, the landlords concluded they would get no help from the D.M.K. government as long as it was in alliance with the Marxists. The landlords' solution to a growing sense of physical insecurity was to form the East Thanjavur

113

Mirasdars (Landowners) Association, both to pressure the government for adequate protection, and even more urgent, to organize their own security forces drawn mainly from non-Harijan farm workers. Subsequently, attempts were made to dissuade Harijan farm workers from joining Marxist-led unions, and these efforts were reported to include strong-arm methods such as abductions, beatings, and arson.[36] By 1968, moreover, even the ruling D.M.K., which had unexpectedly won an absolute majority in the State Assembly and did not need Marxist support in order to govern, became increasingly alarmed by the successes of Marxist-led unions, and the alienation of the landowning middle class. As a result, the police were no longer restrained in taking action against trespassing farm workers. On the contrary, local Marxist leaders denounced them for "unspeakable brutalities" against Harijan laborers in cooperation with landlords' "goondas," or thugs.[37]

By the time of the harvest in November 1968, a combination of *mirasdar* strong-arm methods and police harassment proved largely successful in suppressing the labor unions. Indirect evidence of the impact of these tactics was supplied by the decision of the Marxists to raise their own volunteer corps in Thanjavur district, citing police failure to protect the laborers from "attacks by *goondas* of the landlords.[38] In fact, only in Nagapattinam and Nannilam *taluks* of East Thanjavur did the Marxists feel strong enough to launch another agitation. Repudiating the Mannargudi Agreement of the previous season, they demanded an increase in wages for harvesting from 4 1/2 litres per half bag to 6 litres per half bag—or a raise in the cash value of average daily wages calculated on the basis of three bags harvested per day, from about Rs. 5.6 to Rs. 7.5. Applying the

[36] *New York Times*, January 15, 1969.
[37] *The Statesman*, November 8, 1968.
[38] *Ibid.*

same tactics that had been successful the year before, Marxist workers attempted to obstruct the *mirasdars* from using nonunion or imported labor by entering paddy fields and preventing harvest operations. This time, however, the political situation was much less favorable. The Tamil Nadu government announced that the Mannargudi Agreement reached the previous season must be honored; and the police were ordered to arrest any trespassers who interfered with harvesting. In addition, the landlords now had their own security forces which could be mobilized against trespassing farm workers. By December, numerous beatings, abductions, incidents of arson, and even murder, were reported on both sides. Finally, on the night of December 25 accumulating hostilities exploded. In the village of Kilvenmani, 25 huts of Harijan farm workers were set afire; inside one hut, 43 persons, mainly the wives and children of striking laborers, were burned alive. Among the 200 attackers reportedly involved were some of the richest landowners in East Thanjavur.

The immediate circumstances leading to the attack on the Harijans of Kilvenmani are uncertain. According to one version, laborers imported from nearby villages for harvest operations were returning from work on the evening of December 25 when they were waylaid and attacked by local laborers. Their leader was taken to Kilvenmani and stabbed to death. Two hours later, the landlords led loyal workers in a retaliatory raid, and set fire to the huts in the *Harijan* quarter.[39] According to a second account, fighting broke out between Harijan laborers of Kilvenmani and laborers loyal to the landowners after the latter had abducted a *Harijan* leader in order to coerce striking laborers to abandon their agitation. On December 25, the Harijans attacked the landlords' camp and succeeded in forcing the release of their leader. In the fighting, however, a loyal laborer was killed

[39] *The Statesman*, December 27, 1968.

115

and his body was taken to Kilvenmani. That evening, the landlords retaliated. Leading a large band of workers, they entered Kilvenmani, fired a few shots, and then put torches to the huts of the *Harijans*.[40]

Whatever the immediate precipitating factors, however, it is clear that the tragedy of Kilvenmani had much deeper roots in the progressive polarization between landowners and laborers that started as early as the first Communist-led agitations in 1948. At issue was much more than the low level of agricultural wages. Rather, the confrontation represented a direct attack on the legitimacy of the traditional village system under which harmony was preserved by the mutual acceptance of ascriptive inequalities sanctified by the religious myths of caste.

Whatever the underlying social significance of the confrontation in East Thanjavur, however, the state government chose to consider the incident as a law and order problem. Shortly after, over 100 persons were arrested, including a number of prominent landlords from the area.[41] A one-man judicial commission was appointed to make recommendations for resolving the labor dispute in the affected villages. The settlement recommended was an increase in wages for harvesting from 4 1/2 litres per half bag to 5 1/2 litres per half bag—or a raise in the value of daily wages calculated on the basis of three bags harvested per day from about Rs. 6.2 to Rs. 6.9. Daily wages were also increased from Rs. 2.5 to Rs. 3, of which three-quarters of a rupee might be paid in cash, and the remainder in kind amounting to 6 litres.

Yet, given the changing nature of the confrontation between landlords and laborers, from a limited conflict over the question of wages to a broad attack on traditional social and economic patterns, any settlement based on principles

[40] *New York Times*, January 15, 1969.
[41] *The Statesman*, January 5, 1969.

116

of accommodation or compromise was bound to be temporary. Not surprisingly, therefore, the conflict in East Thanjavur continued. During the *kharif* season, 1969, many *mirasdars* ignored the new government-fixed minimum wage for harvesting, and refused to pay more than the rate set by the Mannargudi Agreement of 1967. Similarly, they rejected government guidelines in apportioning cash and kind components of daily wages; compared to an upper limit of one-fourth the total amount permitted as payment in cash under the 1968 award, *mirasdars* commonly gave one-half the daily wage in cash. At the same time, the East Thanjavur Mirasdars Association, meeting in early June, took a hard line on the importation of outside workers, threatening to leave their fields fallow during the *kurvai* season unless the government assured the security of the *mirasdars*. In a further effort to limit their dependence on local farm workers, the largest *mirasdars* began to purchase tractors with the aim of reducing the requirement for hired labor during the sowing season. This tactic apparently did have some negative effect on local employment opportunities. It was immediately countered by a Marxist-led anti-tractor agitation. But as in 1968, the police quickly moved to arrest all trespassers and almost 300 farm laborers were jailed.[42]

No matter how effective the suppression of Marxist farm workers may appear in the short run, however, the enduring reality in East Thanjavur is the collapse of the traditional self-enforcing mechanisms of social control based on caste, and a widespread breakdown of law and order. Abductions, arson, beatings, and murder are becoming a common feature of rural life. Relations between landowners and laborers have settled into a permanent adversary pattern, and the growing hostility between the two groups has found organizational expression in the rival private armies

[42] *Ibid.*, August 17, 1969.

117

or "volunteer" forces now commanded by both sides. In Thanjavur, the increasing polarization between the landless and the large landowners is all the more bitter—and explosive—because the new cleavage now being drawn on the basis of class largely coincides with the traditional division rooted in caste. In East Thanjavur, the landless farm worker is most commonly also a Harijan. In the *mirasdar* he confronts not only a landlord, but also a Brahmin, the age-old symbol of the Harijan's inferiority and degradation.

Still, the bulk of the farm laborers in Thanjavur remain quiescent. Even in East Thanjavur, the state administration is essentially correct in saying that

> we are at the very beginning of trouble yet. Although the political parties are trying to capitalize on grievances, they have not been successful in organizing agricultural labor as a whole. Government wants to prevent serious trouble from developing and the revenue machinery is trying to bring the parties together and to reach an accommodation between landlords and laborers. It will be some time before the outcome is clear.[43]

By contrast, in states where Marxist-dominated United Front governments came to power, few institutional brakes were applied to prevent an acceleration of rural violence. Instead, the boundaries of social conflict were systematically broadened in order to increase the number of confrontations between landless Harijan castes and landowning middle and upper castes, and create a new form of political awareness among the poorest peasantry based on growing recognition of common class interests.

[43] Interview with Secretary, Land Revenue Board, Madras, April 10, 1969.

5. Palghat, Kerala

Situated in central Kerala, Palghat is an area of great natural diversity. The lowlands, a narrow coastal strip on the western boundary at the edge of the Arabian Sea is a region of lagoons and coconut palms, and fields cultivated under paddy. The midlands, an extensive area of plains and valleys to the east is more agriculturally diversified, having substantial acreage under pepper vine, arecanut, coconut, and a variety of other commercial crops in addition to paddy. The highlands, a hilly expanse of forests, jungles, and mountains stretching to the border with Tamil Nadu, is bounded by the Western Ghats, long celebrated as the "chief glory of the District." Indeed, the high mountain peaks impart a splendor to the Palghat countryside that is absent from the lives of the people who labor there.

Despite the appearance of tropical abundance, in 1960 Palghat supported a population of over 1.7 million persons on a limited area of less than 2,000 square miles, and had one of the highest population densities in the rice belt, 897 persons per square mile. Fully 90 percent of the total population lived in rural areas.[1] Heavy labor pressure on land resulting from an agricultural work force of approximately 170,000 and a net sown area of about 600,000 acres put the availability of land per adult worker at about 3.5 acres.[2] Moreover, opportunities for industrial employment were extremely limited. The district could boast of only seven

---

[1] *District Census Handbook 3 Palghat 1965*, 29, 45, 47.
[2] Intensive Agricultural District Program, *Second Report (1960-65)*, 330.

towns and a rate of urbanization over the decade 1951-61 of less than one percent.[3] Factory jobs numbered under 27,000 and were concentrated in small-scale industries, such as production of rice and flour and handloom weaving, which operated with outmoded techniques and offered little beyond subsistence wages to workers.[4]

The major untapped resource of the district was the abilities of its population. Despite the very low level of urban development, about 34 percent of all persons were classified as literate in 1961.[5] Indeed, in rural areas, a majority of villages reported over 40 percent of males with reading and writing skills.[6] The outstanding exception to this pattern occurred in the case of persons belonging to the Scheduled Castes. Accounting for some 13 percent of the rural population, they had an illiteracy rate as high as 90 percent.[7]

Literacy was one important advantage when the I.A.D.P. was started in Palghat during 1962-63. Another was the high potential for increasing productivity as revealed in demonstrations with the recommended package of practices. Even with local varieties, yields on demonstration plots were 41 to 46 percent higher than on control plots in *kharif*; and about 38 percent higher in *rabi*. The economics of modern practices also seemed attractive: for each additional rupee expended on modern inputs, the return was Rs. 2.37 to Rs. 2.56.[8]

Yet, Palghat could not realize its potential. The largest yield increases were achieved in the first years of the program. Between 1962-63 and 1964-65 average yields for the *kharif* and *rabi* crops combined increased by approximately 15 percent, from 1,372 pounds to 1,575 pounds per acre.

[3] *District Census Handbook 3 Palghat*, 45.
[4] *Ibid.*, 33. [5] *Ibid.*, 52.
[6] *Ibid.*, 53. [7] *Ibid.*, 201.
[8] Intensive Agricultural District Program, *Second Report* (*1960-65*), 335.

This upward trend was reversed in the drought year of 1965-66 when yields fell below 1,500 pounds and subsequently stabilized at somewhat higher levels. A similar pattern characterized the progress in production during this period. After a spurt in output from 293,849 tons in 1962-63 to 343,940 tons in 1964-65, there was a modest decline and then incomplete recovery. Average yield rates and production of rice in Palghat district between 1962-63 and 1967-68 are shown in Table 6. The same unsteady perform-

TABLE 6

Average Yield and Production of Rice in Palghat District
1962-63 to 1967-68

Year	Combined yield (kharif and rabi) in pounds per acre	Indices of yield rate taking prepackage rates as base	Total production of rice	Indices of production figures taking prepackage figures as base
Prepackage period (Average of 1959-60 to 1961-62)	1390	100.0	295,262	100.0
1962-63	1372	98.7	293,849	99.3
1963-64	1513	108.9	327,506	110.7
1964-65	1575	113.8	343,940	116.3
1965-66	1434	103.2	320,120	108.2
1966-67	1540	110.8	340,978	115.3
1967-68	1513	108.9	332,807	112.5

SOURCE: I.A.D.P.-Palghat, *Progress Report, 1961-62 to 1967-68.* 10-11. Mimeo.

ance characterized the progress in offtake of fertilizers. Between 1962-63 and 1966-67, consumption of nitrogenous fertilizers increased from 6,480 metric tons to a peak of 18,922 metric tons, and then slipped back the following year to 14,898 metric tons. During the same period, there was a

121

slight decline in the use of superphosphate and a modest rise in the consumption of potash.[9]

As in other parts of the rice belt, the indifferent performance of Palghat is intimately connected with the problem of water. The main obstacle is not inadequate supply—the annual rainfall averages between 60 and 80 inches—but inefficient utilization of available sources. Altogether, Palghat district accounts for about 250,000 acres of paddy land, most of which is double-cropped. The *kharif* or *Viruppu* crop, cultivated from May to September covers 250,000 acres and the *rabi* or *Mundakan* crop, extending from September to February, about 208,000 acres. Together with a small *Punja* or summer crop extending over some 12,000 acres, the gross cropped area under paddy is about 470,000 acres. Yet, less than one-half the net sown area under paddy, 115,000 acres, is served by canal irrigation from medium projects. Moreover, virtually all of the irrigation projects are located in one-half the district, known as the Palghat Revenue Division. The larger part of the area under paddy is cultivated under rain fed conditions in Ottappalam Revenue Division, where the area covered by minor irrigation projects, representing mainly lift irrigation schemes, is only some 4,000 acres.

Actually, agricultural operations in both Palghat and Ottappalam Divisions are heavily dependent on the monsoons. While the southwest monsoon rarely fails completely, the rains in the *kharif* season are often delayed. As a result, even in areas with canal irrigation, cultivators cannot always be certain of having adequate water at the time of transplantation. Consequently, many do not plant any seedlings for the first crop, sowing according to broadcast methods. While this practice significantly reduces the yield per acre of *kharif* paddy, it nevertheless protects farmers from losses they would sustain on expenditures for nurser-

[9] I.A.D.P.-Palghat, *Progress Report, 1961-62 to 1967-68*, 2.

ies if water shortage at the time of transplantation caused extensive damage to yields. With the second *rabi* crop, the normal practice is to wait until rainfall and/or irrigation is assured to plant nurseries and transplant. But in some years, the northeast monsoon arrives too late to make a second crop feasible; or, after a good start, the rains fail, causing serious losses in output. In fact, the low-yield trend in Palghat district after 1964-65 is officially blamed on unfavorable weather conditions: "The unprecedented drought witnessed during the second crop of the year 1965-66 was so severe that the yield rate could not regain its original trend thereafter. In each of the successive years the climatic conditions were not at all satisfactory. Either the first crop suffered from heavy rains or the second crop withered away in the drought."[10]

Yet, this is by no means an inevitable feature of the agricultural economy of Palghat. On the contrary, given such plentiful rainfall, a massive construction program of minor irrigation works—especially tanks to store water, and pumpsets to lift it—could transform the production potential of the District. Cultivators could not only increase their yields from the *kharif* crop, substituting nurseries and transplantation for broadcast sowing, but would also be assured of full yields during the *rabi* crop. Indeed, many would find it possible to raise a third, short duration *Punja* or summer paddy crop. Even more striking, Palghat does not face the obstacle of an early northeast monsoon in adopting the short-duration high-yielding varieties during the *kharif* season. In fact, given supplementary water facilities, it would become feasible to double-crop paddy lands with I.R. 8. Actually, with the recent development of culture-28 or Annapurna, a new, short-duration, high-yielding dwarf hybrid (representing a cross between PTB-10, a local short-term strain and Taichung Native I), it is now tech-

[10] *Ibid.*, 10.

123

nically possible—assuming supplementary water from a well or tank—to take three crops of high-yielding paddy varieties annually.

The increase in returns to management from three crops of high-yielding varieties compared to two crops of local varieties is striking. Gains under field conditions have been estimated at about 80 percent, or a difference in net profit per acre of Rs. 3,170 and Rs. 1,750, respectively.[11]

Yet, as in West Godavary, the inescapable precondition of the introduction of the new technology is supplementary water from a well or tank. In the case of I.R. 8, it is especially necessary to be sure of having adequate water supplies since the variety must be sown as seedlings first and then transplanted to achieve normal yields. Of course, cultivators can wait until water is released from the irrigation project (if there is one) or for the first rains, but there is still no assurance that the monsoon will continue in sufficient force to provide adequate water at crucial stages in the plant cycle. For example, I.R. 8 must have sufficient water at the time of transplantation, i.e., on the 21st day after the seedling is planted in order to achieve maximum potential yields; otherwise the plant flowers early and yields are reduced. Since production costs for I.R. 8 range between Rs. 550 and Rs. 600 per acre (compared to maximum costs of Rs. 350 and Rs. 400 for local varieties—usually much less in the case of farmers who do not use optimum inputs), the dimensions of loss resulting from water shortage would be so large that no farmer would consider adopting I.R. 8 without supplementary water facilities.

Notwithstanding the potential gain, the average cultivator finds it virtually impossible to solve the immediate problem of finding from Rs. 6,000 to 8,000 to finance a well or

[11] These estimates presuppose the use of optimum practices for both traditional and high-yielding varieties, and are taken from the records of a progressive farmer, Shri T. G. Narayanaswamy, in Palathully village, Coyallamannam block, Palghat.

tank and pumpset. As in West Godavary, the agroeconomic pattern and the tenurial system are both so unfavorable that the overwhelming majority of cultivators cannot hope to accumulate the large capital surpluses necessary to participate in the benefits of the new technology. In Palghat, as in West Godavary, the success of the package program has been confined to the irrigated portions of the district "where the bulk of the cultivators with size of holding greater than 10 acres is concentrated."[12]

· I ·

According to agroeconomic surveys conducted in Palghat district in 1962-63, 55 percent of all cultivators had holdings of less than 5 acres. Five to 10 acre holdings accounted for another 22 percent, and an almost equal proportion of 23 percent represented farms of 10 acres or above. As in West Godavary and other parts of the rice belt, however, the majority of the cultivated *area*, over 60 percent, was operated in holdings of 10 acres or more; an additional 23 percent of the area was farmed in holdings of 5 to 10 acres. By contrast, holdings of less than 5 acres accounted for only 15 percent of the cultivated land. Table 7 shows the distribution of cultivators and cultivated area according to size of holdings.

The estimates of the Joint Director of the I.A.D.P. in Palghat suggest a more unfavorable distribution of operational holdings. His judgment is that over 80 percent of all cultivators operate holdings of 5 acres or less, and account for as much as 45 percent of the area under paddy. Estimates supplied in the villages visited tend to support these higher figures. For example, in Kuthanoor village, 67 percent of all cultivating families operated holdings of 5 acres or less and accounted for 42 percent of the land; in Mathur village, 84 percent of cultivating households had holdings

[12] I.A.D.P.-Palghat, *Progress Report, 1961-62 to 1967-68,* 4.

125

INDIA'S GREEN REVOLUTION

TABLE 7
Distribution of Cultivators and Cultivated Areas
in Palghat District by Size of Holdings

Item	Holding size			
	Less than 2.5 acres	2.5 acres to 4.9 acres	5 acres to 9.9 acres	10 acres and above
Percentage of cultivators in the group to the total sampled	34	21	22	23
Average size in acres	1.1	3.6	7.4	19.6
Percentage of the cultivated area for the group to the total	5	10	23	62

SOURCE: Intensive Agricultural District Program, *Second Report* (1960-65), 339.

of 5 acres or less, accounting for 48 percent of the land; in Mannarghat village, fully 95 percent of all cultivators operated holdings of 5 acres or less, accounting for 65 percent of the land. In any case, if one accepts the estimate of the Joint Director that 5 acres of irrigated land is the minimum necessary for an economic holding in the district, it is clear that the overwhelming majority of cultivators cannot be included in this category.

In fact, it is precisely this assessment of the majority of farmers, as uneconomic, that has guided the I.A.D.P. staff in formulating its field approach to intensive development in the district. Assuming that the majority of cultivators operate either at a loss or with only marginal surpluses, the development staff has made virtually no effort to bring small farmers into active participation in the Package Program or the High Yielding Varieties Program. In essence, the I.A.D.P. has operated only through the minority of large farmers. Virtually no extension effort has been made to in-

126

struct small farmers in proper cultivation practices for the high-yielding varieties. As a result, even if some cultivators were willing to take the financial risk of participation, they would still not have access to good technical advice, e.g., how to cope successfully with the serious problem of plant disease.

Unfortunately, the I.A.D.P. staff's assessment of the majority of farmers as incapable of participating in programs of agricultural modernization is well founded. Apart from the tiny size of most farms, which is in itself a crippling limitation, most small farmers are also handicapped in accumulating surpluses for investment by deductions from net returns representing payments of rent under a pervasive system of tenancy.

The land tenure system found in Palghat district is distinct from those in other parts of the south.[13] The origins of the land system in Kerala as a whole are shrouded in myth. According to one legend favored by the landed castes, an incarnation of Lord Vishnu raised Kerala from the Arabian Sea and presented the land to a class of Namboodri and Malayalee Brahmins or *jenmies* as their permanent birthright (*jenmom*). In fact, prior to independence, the major portion of the land in the areas now comprising Kerala, i.e., the erstwhile states of Travancore and Cochin and the district of Malabar (formerly administered by the British as part of the Madras Presidency), was owned by a tiny class of *jenmies*.

Actually, the *jenmom* right was enjoyed by three different categories of owners: individual Brahmins, Hindu temples, and major chieftains, warriors, and captains of the Kings in the princely states, belonging mainly to the upper-caste Nair community. The *jenmies* rarely cultivated the land, leasing out some 99 percent of their holdings.

[13] A summary of the history of the land tenure system in Palghat district is available in the *District Census Handbook, 3, Palghat.*

Palghat district is located in the ex-Malabar region; i.e., the part of Kerala that was formerly administered as a portion of the Madras Presidency. However, the agrarian pattern in Palghat closely resembled arrangements in other parts of Kerala, namely Travancore and Cochin. In all these areas, it had become the practice for *jenmies* to transfer a part of their interest in the land to a tenant, in return for the payment of a lump sum in money or in kind, and an additional nominal payment of rent, and other customary fees and dues. Such transactions were duly recorded in registered leases. In such cases, the tenant, known as *kanomdar* acquired the right, *kanom*, of holding the property for a period of twelve years, after which the contract might be renewed at the pleasure of the *jenmi*. The tenant was legally liable to eviction at the expiry of the contract period, but in practice, *kanom* rights were usually hereditary, and passed on from one generation to the next.

When the first Congress ministry came to power in Madras in 1937, one of the land reforms it carried out was to confer hereditary tenancy on *kanomdars*, relieving them of the necessity of renewing these leases every twelve years. After independence, new land reform laws passed in the states of Travancore and Cochin also gave occupancy rights to *kanom* tenants and fixed the amount due annually to *jenmies* on a permanent basis. Recently, the rights of the *jenmies* were completely extinguished in Travancore by the Jenmi Kanom Compensation Abolition Act which provided for the payment of a lump sum to the *jenmies* in compensation for the loss of any remaining rights in the land. A similar reform is in progress in Cochin. As a result, in both areas, *kanomdars* are now full proprietors and enjoy the status of *ryotwari* tenure, coming into direct relationship with the state. *Jenmies* still exist in the ex-Malabar region, including Palghat, but *kanom* tenants are in almost as favorable a position as their counterparts in Travancore

128

and Cochin, paying only some 5 percent of the total produce as rent annually, and enjoying the right to transfer their interests in the land.

All of these reforms, however, frequently failed to have any impact on the status of the actual tiller of the soil. Many of the *kanomdars* had become intermediaries, leasing out portions of their land to cultivating tenants known as *verompattomdars*. Legally, the *verompattomdars* were tenants at will. Again, however, in many instances, they came to enjoy hereditary rights by the "custom of the locality." Even though the *verompattomdar* was required to renew his lease after a fixed period and could be evicted at the will of the landlord, customary relationships between landlords and tenants extending over two or three generations became common. By contrast, there has always been a residual category of cultivating *verompattomdars* who do not have hereditary rights and cultivate the land only for limited periods at the will of the landowner.

In Palghat district, the overwhelming majority of cultivators are customary *verompattomdars*. In the villages visited, 75 percent to 95 percent of all cultivating households operated holdings on *verompattom* tenure. On the whole, it is estimated that about 60 percent to 70 percent of the land in the district is currently cultivated by *verompattom* tenants.

The permanent rights of *verompattom* tenants were strengthened under the Kerala Land Reforms Act of 1964, which conferred security of tenure on all tenants and prohibited evictions except in the case of a court order showing adequate cause, usually nonpayment of rent. The 1964 Act also included a schedule which laid down principles according to which "fair rent" should be fixed for all leased land. The Act further provided that the tenant could file an application with the Land Revenue Tribunal, composed of officers of the judiciary, to have the "fair rent" fixed.

129

The provisions of the 1964 Act prohibiting eviction of tenants are generally enforced in the case of customary *verompattomdars*. Such cultivators usually have proof of possession, including in many cases, receipts for rent. Also, there are now relatively accurate land records at the headquarters office of the revenue village, constructed over the last few years to implement the state government's program of procurement of food grains through a levy of paddy on all holdings above 2 acres. (However, there is still a category of tenants cultivating on oral lease who are excluded from these records; and at present, it is impossible to make any estimate of their numbers.)

The 1964 Act has been less successful in ensuring cultivators the fair rent. Although an increasing number of *verompattomdars* have applied to the Land Tribunals over the last few years, most tenants are still inhibited from claiming their rights because the court procedure involved is time-consuming, costly, and complicated, and more important, because they fear to damage their "good relationship" with the landlord. While landowners do not share any of the costs of cultivation, still, in cases where good relations exist, the landlord may advance interest-free production loans and other facilities to the tenant in time of need. Since the tenants have so far been unable to find any institutional support for such purposes, many have preferred to conciliate the landlord by neglecting to apply for fixation of fair rent. For their part, the landlords have been content to receive the customary rates, and have not tried to raise rentals. One result is that the burden of tenancy falls unevenly among cultivators. For example, a *verompattomdar* having access to irrigation can increase his yields by higher applications of chemical fertilizers, and in the process reduce the relative proportion of the crop paid as rent to as little as one-fourth of the total produce. However, in the case of cultivators without assured water and/or without

130

adequate finances to invest in modern inputs, the burden of rent at customary rates—assuming static yields—can be as high as 60 percent.

Notwithstanding these handicaps, many cultivators in Palghat district have experienced some improvements in yields, ranging from about 25 percent to 50 percent over the last five years. Mainly, this has come about as a result of the application of chemical fertilizers and pesticides and the adoption of more labor-intensive techniques. While some of these gains have been absorbed by rising costs for fertilizers and higher wages for labor, cultivators report some modest improvement in their standard of living, mainly in the quality and quantity of food and clothing consumed. Others have managed some margin for the construction of cattle sheds, or tile roofing of houses, or buying of gold ornaments, or purchase of working bullocks or buffalo for milk selling. Yet, as a group, this great majority of *verompattom* tenants have not been able to accumulate any surplus for investment in land improvement, especially minor irrigation. As a result, they report that cultivation of the high-yielding varieties is much too risky, and they have no plans to try them.

· II ·

Although credit cooperatives in Palghat district are considered the most successful in the state, still they offer only modest help to the majority of small farmers. About 80 percent of all cultivating families are members of primary agricultural credit societies; but only 50 percent to 60 percent of the members actually take loans[14] and most small farmers do not borrow up to their maximum borrowing limit.

[14] Estimate supplied by the secretary of the Palghat Central Cooperative Bank. Information on the operation of the crop loan system as presented in the following paragraphs was gathered during interviews with the chairman and secretary of the Palghat Central Cooperative Bank and from written and mimeographed statements furnished by them.

131

The Palghat Central Cooperative Bank operates under the crop loan system. The scale of finance for paddy per acre is fixed both for cultivation of local varieties and high-yielding varieties. In each case, it is divided into cash and kind components. For the cultivation of local varieties, each member is entitled to production credit of Rs. 350 per acre, which is divided into three portions: Part A, of Rs. 175 cash; Part B, of the recommended fertilizer dose valued at Rs. 200; and Part C, of an optional cash loan of Rs. 100 to meet the labor costs associated with the application of fertilizer. Under the high-yielding varieties program, these amounts are increased to a total of Rs. 475, composed of cash, kind, and supplemental cash components valued at Rs. 175, Rs. 200, and Rs. 100, respectively. Of the approximately 200 primary agricultural credit societies that are members of the Palghat Central Cooperative Bank, about 50 percent have established individual maximum borrowing limits for short-term and medium-term credit of Rs. 5,000; and an equal number have doubled this amount to Rs. 10,000 with the division between short-term and medium-term advances left to individual societies.

The scale of production credit now established seems adequate to meet the cultivation costs of paddy, especially of locally improved varieties on which no more than Rs. 350 or Rs. 400 is normally expended, even with optimum practices. For the high-yielding varieties, the scale is less satisfactory, the total loan available in cash and kind amounting to Rs. 475, compared to estimated production costs of Rs. 550 to 600 per acre. Nevertheless, those small farmers who belong to the cooperatives rarely draw the maximum limit. There are many reasons for this: small farmers are afraid of incurring large debts to the cooperative society which they may not be able to repay. In fact, some have already become defaulters and are no longer eligible for loans. Moreover, since small farmers cannot afford minor irrigation facilities, and are particularly vulnerable to the vagaries of the monsoon, they hesitate to make large investments on fertilizer. This is reflected in the experience of the Palghat Cooperative Bank, which used to insist that members draw all three components of the crop loan, but now permits cultivators to draw the Part A cash portion only, in recognition that many farmers do not want to use chemical fertilizers in the prescribed proportions. Since the cooperatives are the only distribution agent for fertilizer in Kerala, the poor offtake is a direct measure of the small farmers' unwillingness to risk heavy outlays on modern inputs as long as there is no assurance of adequate water. In fact, with crop failures a common occurrence, small farmers try as far as possible to remain out of debt entirely, or to take very small production loans only when absolutely necessary. There is an additional constraint: most farmers need consumption loans sometime during the year. This can only be provided by private sources, in many cases from moneylenders who charge 30 to 40 percent interest on the loans advanced. The first charge on the crop is therefore debt repayment to private lenders, and this further diminishes the small cultivator's capacity to repay loans from the cooperatives.

It is true that between 1964-65 and 1968-69, short-term production credit advanced by the Palghat Central Cooperative Bank increased from almost Rs. 40 lakhs to over Rs. 80 lakhs. But inability to make the majority of small farmers active participants in the new technology is indicated by the growing disparity between package loans sanctioned and package loans actually issued during the same period. In 1964-65, when farm plans were still drawn up mainly for large farmers, package loans of over Rs. 50 lakhs were sanctioned, and almost Rs. 40 lakhs were issued. In 1968-69, when coverage was extended to include a larger proportion of small cultivators, the corresponding figures

133

were Rs. 148 lakhs and Rs. 80 lakhs.[15] Moreover, in 1968-69 total overdues on package loans amounted to about 26 percent.[16] The failure of the Palghat Central Cooperative Bank to find methods of reaching the small farmer is also clearly revealed in the fact that offtake of short-term loans declined from Rs. 191 lakhs in 1967-68 to Rs. 80 lakhs in 1968-69, and that like the rest of the Central Cooperative Banks in Kerala, Palghat had more funds to lend than could be absorbed. In 1968-69, the borrowing reserve of the Palghat Central Cooperative Bank was Rs. 417 lakhs; by contrast, the total of short-term and medium-term loans advanced was Rs. 93 lakhs.[17]

· III ·

The largest proportion of the agricultural population in Palghat district—about 55 percent—are farm laborers. They are drawn mainly from the substantial Muslim community in the district and the backward and Scheduled Castes. Most laborers still maintain a permanent working relationship with one landowner; in some cases, they are also permitted to seek casual labor during the slack season when work is not available on the home farm. One factor reinforcing such traditional ties is the general oversupply of agricultural labor in Palghat. In striking contrast to Ludhiana, and even to West Godavary, farm laborers face serious problems of underemployment. As a result, laborers are reluctant to break permanent ties with landowners which are a source of job security and also of fringe benefits that would be lost if they took casual work. One effect of this unwillingness to openly challenge the landowners is that the new wage rates prescribed for agricultural laborers by the Agricultural Minimum Wages Act of 1969 are gen-

[15] I.A.D.P.-Palghat, *Progress Report, 1961-62 to 1967-68*, 8.
[16] *Ibid.*, 9.
[17] From a statement prepared by the Additional Registrar, Cooperation, Kerala State, Trivandrum.

erally not enforced. According to the Act cash wages for day labor are set at Rs. 4.5 per day for men and Rs. 3 for women. Payments in kind for harvesting have also been raised from one share in ten to one in eight. However, laborers commonly report lower wages than the legal minimum for casual day work, and many also receive lower rates for harvest.

Over the last five years, agricultural laborers have experienced very meager improvements in their standard of living, amounting to some modest increases in the quantity of food consumed or clothing. Some laborers report no improvement at all, or a deterioration in their standard of living due to rising prices. A major problem is that employment opportunities have not significantly increased over the last five years. Laborers report they find agricultural work for only 180 to 200 days a year. It is true that over the last five years wages for day workers have increased from about Rs. 1.5 to Rs. 3 for men; and from Rs. 1.25 to Rs. 2 for women, payable either in cash or kind at the worker's preference. In some cases, workers are also receiving the higher rates for harvesting operations, i.e., a share of one-eighth instead of one-tenth, valued at about Rs. 3 per day. But on the average, an agricultural laborer in Palghat district probably does not make more than Rs. 600 to Rs. 700 per annum. Possibly the rise in cash wages has been sufficient to keep pace with the rise in the cost of living. But the lack of alternative employment opportunities and the subsistence standard at which most laborers live keep them dependent on the landowner for extra concessions to tide them over the lean times of unemployment. For example, laborers report they receive interest-free loans from their employers, some clothing at the end of the year, gifts at marriages or festivals, medical care, and perhaps an extra bonus payment of paddy annually. One is inclined to conclude it is these marginal additions to income that make the difference in the

135

laborer's capacity to maintain even his present low level of subsistence.

· IV ·

All this does not mean that Palghat presents a picture of unrelieved agricultural backwardness. On the contrary, from the very beginning of the I.A.D.P. there were striking gains in yields from higher applications of modern inputs in irrigated areas. Taking the district as a whole, the indices of increase in yield rate in 1967-68 over the base period 1959-60 to 1961-62, were only about 14 percent for the *kharif* or *Viruppu* crop, and no more than one percent for the *rabi* or *Mundakan* crop; but in blocks having canal irrigation, the increase was as high as 57 percent for *Viruppu* and 30 percent for *Mundakan*.[18] Moreover, starting in 1965-66, farmers in the irrigated areas took advantage of generous state subsidies for the installation of minor irrigation works, at the rate of 25 percent for electric engines and 50 percent for diesel engines. In the district as a whole, the number of pumpsets distributed rose from 79 in 1964-65 to 1,592 in 1967-68, and in the latter year demand exceeded supply by about 1,000. Similarly, demand for tractors more than trebled between 1965-66 and 1967-68, bringing the total number in the district to 377.[19] Once again, nonavailability, and not lack of demand, was the limiting factor in the distribution of more machines.

All of these gains however were concentrated among a small minority of cultivators, those who already enjoyed a broad array of other advantages: holdings in the irrigated areas of the district, economic units of operation, and *jenmom* or *kanom* rights in the land. Inevitably, it was this group of farmers that also benefited most from the intro-

[18] I.A.D.P.-Palghat, *Progress Report, 1961-62 to 1967-68*, 12.
[19] *Ibid.*, 5.

duction of the high-yielding varieties. When Tainan-3 was first taken up in 1965-66, threshing difficulties and the glutinous quality of the strain caused cultivators to reject it. But in 1966-67, I.R. 8 was introduced and found acceptable. In addition, the Kerala Agriculture Department developed the new hybrid Annapurna, with a yield level of over 4,100 pounds per acre and greater resistance to disease. Since then, the adoption of the high-yielding varieties in Palghat district has slowly expanded. By 1968-69, 17,441 acres were covered under the *Viruppu* crop (about 6 percent of the total acreage), and 28,977 under *Mundakan* (about 13 percent). Altogether, about one-tenth of the gross-cropped land, almost 46,500 acres, has so far come under the high-yielding varieties.[20] The *Progress Report* for 1967-68 confirms that cultivators who have adopted these strains are almost exclusively the small minority with 10 acres or more:

The Package Program has been highly successful in increasing the income of the cultivating households as is evident from the increased demand for tractors and pumpsets. But this success is confined to the blocks in the Palghat Revenue Division where all the major irrigation schemes are situated, and also where the bulk of cultivators with size of holding greater than ten acres is concentrated. With the advent of the high-yielding varieties of paddy, the income of the cultivating households has considerably increased and this additional income is now being invested in capital investments. The purchase of large numbers of tractors and pumpsets and the utilization of large amounts of money for conspicuous consumption such as construction of new houses go to show that the cultivators in the ayacut areas of major irrigation schemes have benefitted considerably from the implementation of the package program.[21]

[20] *Ibid.*, 9.   [21] *Ibid.*, 4.

137

· V ·

In terms of numbers, the cultivators involved in the green revolution of Palghat district represent a small minority of all farmers. Yet, with respect to cultivated area, they account for the majority of acreage under paddy. It is precisely this disproportion between numbers of cultivators with holdings of 10 acres or more, and the percentage of cultivated area operated by them that provides the economic rationale for a development strategy based on private investment by the large farmer. The advent of the high-yielding varieties increases the feasibility of such an approach. Indeed, in Kerala State as a whole, after nearly ten years of static production at levels of 900,000 to 1,100,000 tons of paddy per year, output jumped from 1,120,000 tons in 1967-68 to 1,409,000 tons in 1968-69,[22] largely as the result of the introduction of I.R. 8 over approximately one-fourth of the gross-cropped area. State officials believe that if 50 percent of the gross area could be covered by I.R. 8 and other high-yielding varieties by the end of the Fourth Plan, Kerala's food deficit would be eliminated.

At the same time, the social costs of relying on a small minority of large farmers to spearhead the process of agricultural modernization are nowhere more obvious than in Kerala. In fact, the situation in Kerala suggests that while it may be economically advantageous to adopt an agricultural strategy based on the large farmer, in some areas at least, it is no longer socially desirable or politically prudent to do so. Although it would be an exaggeration to claim a causal relationship between the green revolution and rural conflict, growing income disparities associated with application of the new technology can have a catalytic effect in accelerating the rate at which social tension is transformed

[22] Production estimates supplied by the Office of the Director, Agriculture, Kerala State, Trivandrum.

into violence, particularly when other factors are also present. As the situation in East Thanjavur demonstrates, the most important of these is the presence of a well-organized Communist party, and an active propaganda campaign to explain the deprivations created by increasing disparities in terms of class exploitation and conflict. The prospects of harnessing social discontent for class struggle actions are further enhanced when a Communist dominated United Front Government is already in power. In such cases, the major agencies of social control and coercion, including local police and administration, are generally restrained from intervening on behalf of landowners in clashes with landless laborers and tenants, and the peasantry is emboldened to demand immediate redress of grievances. Indeed, under United Front regimes, a deliberate effort may be made to increase the incidence of direct confrontations between the landless and the propertied castes as one means of promoting the class consciousness of the peasantry.

In striking contrast to the Punjab, and even to Andhra Pradesh and Tamil Nadu, all of these factors are present in the political setting of Kerala. Ever since the linguistic reorganization of States in 1956, and the creation of Kerala State out of the former Travancore-Cochin State and the Malabar region of Madras, the Communist party has rivaled the Congress party in its share of the popular vote.[23] In 1957, the Communist party polled 35.2 percent of the votes cast in the state elections compared to 38 percent received by the Congress party. Indeed, with the help of postelection political alliances, the C.P.I. succeeded in forming the first Communist-led State Ministry in India. In

[23] For a detailed review of the comparative strength of the Congress party, the undivided C.P.I. and the C.P.I.(Marxists) in the state elections of 1957, 1960, and 1965, see Bashiruddin Ahmed, "Communist and Congress Prospects in Kerala," in *Party System and Election Studies*, Center for the Study of Developing Societies, Occasional Papers: Number 1 (Bombay: Allied Publishers, 1967).

1960, even after a Congress-dominated coalition succeeded in toppling the Communist Ministry and forcing President's Rule on the State, the C.P.I. was able to win 40 percent of the popular vote against a united opposition in the mid-term election—although it was prevented from returning to power by substantial losses of assembly seats to the combined opposition. In 1965, when the Communists' strength was badly drained by a split into feuding right and left wings, the combined vote of the C.P.I. and the newly organized C.P.I.(Marxists), was still almost 30 percent of the total. Finally, in 1967, after yet another period of political instability and President's Rule, the C.P.I.(Marxists), were able to come to power as the leader of a United Front alliance against the Congress party. In the 1967 election, the combined vote of the C.P.I.(M) and the C.P.I. was 32 percent of the total, while the Congress party and a newly formed splinter group, the Kerala Congress won 35.4 percent.

The most salient political fact about the relative strength of the Communist parties and the Congress party in Kerala, however, is not the rough equality in the percentage of the popular vote they attract, but the different social characteristics of the groups that give each party their support. The Communists have been most active in the rural areas, concentrating their political work among the landless laborers, most of whom belong to the Muslim minority or the backward and Scheduled Castes. By contrast, the Congress party has made little effort to develop direct organizational links with the poor peasantry. On the contrary, in the rural areas, the party is heavily dependent on alliances with Brahmin and Nair landlords and owner-cultivators to deliver the votes of low-caste client groups, including tenants and agricultural laborers. In addition, the Congress party compensates for weakness in the countryside, by arranging alliances with urban-based factions and organiza-

140

tions, enjoying a long-standing association with the substantial Christian community in the state.

These broad differences in voter support for the Communist and Congress parties is evident from an analysis of political preferences in state elections since 1957. According to data prepared by K. G. Krishna Murthy and G. Lakshmana Rao, the Congress party enjoys few reliable strongholds outside of the larger towns. In the rural areas, moreover, Congress voter turnout improves in direct proportion as the ratio of cultivators to laborers rises. By contrast, popular support for the C.P.I. and the C.P.I.(M) has fluctuated widely in urban areas from one election to the next, with the maximum concentration of Communist votes coming from factory workers in small and middle-size towns. More striking, the Communist parties have shown consistent strength in rural areas. The data shows that in rural constituencies, "in all the elections the C.P.I. has secured maximum voter turnout in heavy labor pressure areas and its lowest voter turnout from cultivator dominating areas and low labor pressure areas . . . the C.P.I. derives its strength primarily from labor pressure areas."[24]

The most reliable Communist strongholds are in the Malabar region where there are an estimated 1,046 agricultural laborers for every 1,000 cultivators compared to the ratio of 831 to 1,000 for the state as a whole. Indeed, the Communists' hold on Malabar is so strong that they were able to maintain their lead in the area even in 1965, the year that the leftist parties suffered substantial losses in all other parts of the state.[25] Within Malabar, moreover, Palghat early became a Communist stronghold. The C.P.I. won eight of fourteen assembly seats in 1957; and they dupli-

[24] K. G. Krishna Murthy and G. Lakshmana Rao, *Political Preferences in Kerala* (New Delhi: Radhakrishna Prakashan, 1968), 72.
[25] Bashiruddin Ahmed, "Communist and Congress Prospects in Kerala," 247.

141

cated this record three years later in the mid-term election of 1960.[26]

· VI ·

It is clear that by the time the I.A.D.P. was started in Palghat district, the Communists already had a strong grassroots political organization. Indeed, the election results indicate that they enjoyed the sympathy and active support of more than half the agricultural population. Yet, the political setting was generally ignored in introducing the new approach, partly because social tensions were obscured by the persistence of traditional ties. Labor's poor bargaining position combined with the paternalistic attitude of the landowning castes tended to minimize the incidents of open confrontation. Even so, there had already been scattered eruptions of labor "indiscipline" dating to the period of the first United Front Government. A typical instance in the late 1950's was the one related by a district administrative officer: workers who occupied huts on his land under a customary arrangement providing they would be on permanent call for agricultural and other work began to refuse to come when the time was inconvenient. In addition, they took to large-scale stealing of the landowner's coconuts which they sold on the market. Ultimately, a group of landlords who were having similar trouble joined together, and adopting a tactic foreshadowing the tragedy in Thanjavur, burned the laborers' huts, thereby forcing them to leave.

However, labor indiscipline was just beginning. The formation of the C.P.I.(Marxists) in 1964 proved to be a turning point for agrarian relationships in the state. The Kerala C.P.I. leader and General-Secretary of the national C.P.I., E.M.S. Namboodripad, had been trying since 1962 to com-

26 R. Chandidas et al., ed., *India Votes: A Source Book on Indian Elections* (New York: Humanities Press, 1968), 430.

142

mit the Party's National Council to a more militant program. In particular, he wanted the Communists to go beyond a parliamentary approach and adopt a revolutionary strategy involving the creation of a mass movement among the poorest sections of the peasantry. When this position was defeated in the Central Executive Committee of the National Council in April 1964, Namboodripad led his faction—amounting to about one-third of the national leadership, but more than one-half of the local cadres—out of the C.P.I. to form an independent party, the C.P.I.(Marxists).[27] In Kerala, Marxist cadres concentrated on organizing a statewide network of district and *taluk* party branches, including village cells wherever possible. The village units were headed by younger agricultural workers, many of whom used their new prestige as political cadres to assert their personal independence of the landowners. Like their counterparts in West Godavary and Thanjavur, they began to work shorter hours for higher cash wages and to insist on perquisites like rest periods, coffee, and lunch. As one Marxist farm worker interviewed in Kuthanoor village put it: "I wanted to feel independent, I wanted to feel free. That's why I stopped working as a permanent laborer even though there was some sacrifice in earnings. When I have money in my pocket, I don't work. Maybe I will work three days a week. If I run out of money, then I work. Otherwise, I go to the movies, or I take up political activities."

It is true that most laborers in Palghat were more cautious. They did not join the local branch of the C.P.I.(M) or Marxist sponsored workers unions that organized agitations for better wages and working conditions. Nevertheless, by the mid-1960's, the landowners were convinced of

[27] See John B. Wood, "Observations on the Indian Communist Party Split," *Pacific Affairs* (Spring 1965), for an analysis of all the factors leading to the break.

the laborers' sympathy for Communist ideology, and believed they refrained from joining rural agitations only for fear of the consequences. Some laborers candidly agreed, saying if they lost the perquisites supplied by landowners— as retaliation for participation in Marxist-led strikes—"who will help us when we starve?"

The election of 1967 provided the Marxists with a major opportunity to convert silent sympathy into open support. This time, a prime target of propaganda in Palghat district was the tenant-cultivator. The Marxists made their strongest appeal in local elections with the slogan "land to the tiller." Although cultivating peasants had previously been hostile to the Communists, by 1967 they were ready to listen. Indeed, ever since eviction of customary *verompattam* tenants had been legally prohibited by the Kerala Land Reforms Act of 1964, relations between tenants and landowners (whether *jenmies* or *kanomdars*) sharply deteriorated. Landlords tended to react by immediately withdrawing all customary facilities from tenants, including advances for production and other loans in times of emergency, illness, or marriage. Embittered tenants responded by refusing to recognize any right of the landlord beyond that of collecting rent. For example, they ignored the landowner's advice about proper cultivation practices; some even went to the extent of prohibiting the landlord from visiting his field.

The Marxists' success in exploiting social tension as a vehicle for enhancing political support is apparent from the results of the 1967 elections. In Palghat (which had been divided into the two parliamentary constituencies of Palghat and Ponnani in 1962) the C.P.I.(M) won five out of seven assembly seats in the new, smaller Palghat constituency, and six out of seven in Ponnani.[28] Moreover, with the formation of the Marxist-dominated United Front Min-

[28] *India Votes: A Source Book on Indian Elections,* 566.

144

istry in March 1967, the Marxists were in a position to consolidate and expand their gains in rural areas by measures designed to appeal to the most impoverished sections of the population. An additional factor contributed to the increased rate of peasant mobilization after 1967. The Marxists and their coalition partners, the C.P.I., were locked in bitter competition for popular support among the most numerous elements of the agricultural population, the tenants, and landless laborers. They tended to outbid one another in their promises of benefits to these groups, not only contributing to a sharp acceleration in the aspirations and demands of the landless, but also creating a climate of resentment and insecurity among the large farmers on whom the major burden of agricultural modernization had been placed.

The atmosphere of strain was immediately intensified by the introduction of the Kerala Land Reforms (Amendment) Bill in 1968. An omnibus bill, it lowered the upper limit on landownership from 25 acres to 20 acres per family; vested ownership rights to housesites in tenants; and provided that on a date to be designated by the Government all intermediary rights in land, including those enjoyed by Hindu temples and *kanomdars* would vest in the Government, subject to compensation at sixteen times the fair rent. Subsequently, rights of ownership were to be assigned to cultivating tenants; and rents payable to the landlord would be collected by the State and adjusted toward the purchase of land.[29]

As always, some stress can be alleviated by evasion. Reports are current of landowners coming to private agreements with *verompattom* tenants, giving them outright one or two acres in exchange for voluntary surrender by the tenant of rights in any remaining land in his possession.

[29] See the Kerala Land Reforms (Amendment) Bill, 1968 (L.A. Bill No. 35 of 1968), (Trivandrum: Government Press, 1968).

Nevertheless, given the existence of relatively accurate records of *verompattom* tenures in Kerala, the Land Reforms Act stands a good chance of achieving its main aim of transferring ownership rights to the large majority of cultivators. In Palghat, at least, both the landowners and tenants generally believe that full ownership rights over leased land will ultimately be vested in the tenants. Yet, such a reform is not expected to transform small farmers into economic producers. Unless the State Government intervenes with a massive program of financial and other support for the small farmer (which is highly doubtful given the precarious budgetary position) the new owners will find themselves the proprietors of uneconomic holdings of 2 or 3 acres with no capital to invest in land improvement and modern methods. The task of agricultural innovation would still fall mainly to large farmers.

While this class might not be unduly deterred from agricultural modernization by tenancy reform alone—largely because the size of the home farm is unaffected—some would surely be cautious about making large investments in land improvement as long as the wider question of property rights has again been raised. Much more immediately frightening to this class, however, is the marked deterioration in relations between landowners and laborers in many parts of the state over the last couple of years.

Ever since the formation of the Marxist-dominated United Front Ministry in 1967 and intensified organizational activities in rural areas, incidents of labor indiscipline have increased. But the most unnerving change to many landowners is the psychological transformation in the workers' attitudes. Most simply put, "the fear is gone." Large farmers now believe that despite the long history of "good relations" in Palghat district, laborers will not long resist Marxist propaganda that "the land you work with your hands is yours; tomorrow you can live in the big house of the landlord." Indeed, in anticipation of any agitation for implementation of the Agricultural Minimum Wages Act, landlords are already thinking in terms of stopping traditional bonus payments of paddy and other articles in kind at the time of festivals or other religious occasions, and of withdrawing any other facilities like loans and advances. Some have said that they will keep their land out of cultivation entirely if an effort to enforce higher wages is made. Others see a remedy in mechanization. By 1968-69 there were already 430 tractors in the district,[30] and the Joint Director estimated he could immediately dispose of an additional 1,000 without any subsidy, the major source of attraction being not greater efficiency in farm operations but the opportunity to be rid of the laborers. No doubt the sense of urgency was increased by the first instances of direct confrontation between landowners and Marxist-led farm workers in 1968. In Chittor village, a laborer loyal to a local landlord was murdered when Marxist-led agricultural workers attempted to prevent the landowner from transplanting paddy with nonunionized workers. Again in June 1969, two separate clashes over the issue of agricultural wages occurred between farmers and laborers, each side armed with sticks and knives.[31]

Moreover, while Palghat remains relatively quiet, the large farmers are acutely aware of the sharp polarization between landowners and laborers that has already emerged in the second I.A.D.P. District of Alleppey. In Alleppey, which accounts for one-tenth of the gross-cropped acreage under paddy in the state, the rivalry of the C.P.I.(M) and the C.P.I. in organizing farm workers has been especially sharp. The police have often had to intervene to halt interparty clashes. The C.P.I. has charged that under the Marxist-dominated United Front Ministry, Marxist organizers

[30] Estimate of the Joint Director, I.A.D.P., Palghat.
[31] *The Statesman,* June 15, 1969.

147

were generally favored by such intervention. Whatever the truth of such charges, it does seem clear that the police were not used to protect the landowners from *gheraos* organized by unionized workers. In one incident, the police chief and his deputy were suspended when the local Marxist party leader complained to the state Minister that policemen were ordered to carry out a *lathi* charge against laborers who refused to remove paddy for threshing to the landowner's house, and then surrounded the field to prevent other workers from carrying on farm operations. Subsequently, the two officers were reinstated, but only after winning a stay order from the High Court. The local judiciary also failed to offer any protection to landowners. Those who refused to cultivate their fields in the absence of adequate police protection were served with land utilization orders requiring them to put the land under crops or suffer confiscation of their property. Once again, only a High Court stay order came to their rescue.

As state officials readily concede, the difficulties in Kerala have progressed much beyond the troubles in Thanjavur. Constant agitation among farm laborers by rival leftist groups have inflated union demands to an extravagant level, and created an unwillingness to bargain seriously on realistic terms. For example, in Alleppey, some groups of agricultural laborers refused to harvest the crop and/or divide the crop on the farmer's threshing floor unless they received one-fifth or even one-fourth of the crop as their share. Others engaged in work slowdowns that caused severe losses to the landowners: in April 1969 it was estimated that as a result of such tactics one-fourth to one-fifth of the standing crops would not be harvested.[32] Finally, laborers' unions have also "forbidden" the use of tractors for ploughing—which they argue displaces 40 men per acre during

---

[32] Estimate provided by the Office of the Director, Agriculture, Trivandrum.

148

the peak sowing season—and they have tried to enforce this dictum by surrounding tractors in the field and preventing owners from using them. Large farmers, overwhelmingly outnumbered, and fearful of their security in a situation where the police do not offer adequate protection, responded mainly by threatening not to cultivate their fields; many, in fact, left them entirely fallow. Others refused to plant a second crop in order to rob the laborers of their main advantage—the necessity for rapid harvesting—at the end of the *Viruppu* season. In response the laborers threatened to forcibly occupy the land and cultivate it themselves. Moreover, as in Thanjavur, the bitterness of the conflict is magnified by the superimposition of new lines of class cleavage over age-old divisions based on religion and caste. The agricultural workers of Alleppy are predominantly drawn from the Scheduled Castes and backward castes. Their opponents, the small landed elite, are mainly upper-caste Brahmins and Nairs.

· VII ·

The collapse of the United Front Government in October 1969 amid charges by the C.P.I. and other constituent members, that the Marxists had abused the police power and permitted widespread corruption in administration, did bring some immediate improvement in security for the rural areas. The successor Government, a leftist "mini-front" led by the C.P.I. proved much less reluctant to extend police protection to large landowners. Indeed, by November 1969, the Marxists were accusing the C.P.I. of using the police to carry out an "inhuman repression" of the agricultural workers "in the interests of the property owners." A. K. Gopalan, the State Secretary of the C.P.I.(M) charged that a "reign of terror" has been unleashed against the agricultural laborers of Alleppey and that the police and the Kerala Congress had been given "unfettered and

149

unbridled license . . . to oppress workers and agricultural laborers."[33]

Nevertheless, the C.P.I.(M) called for a statewide offensive against the Kerala Ministry with major emphasis on peasant mobilization. Charging that the "mini-front" Government could not be trusted to carry out the Land Reforms (Amendment) Act effectively, the Marxists announced they would lead agricultural workers in forcible occupation of private land held in excess of the reduced ceiling. In practice, the "land-grab" movement was largely confined to Alleppey, and headway was difficult because of swift intervention by the police and large-scale arrests of persons taking illegal possession of land.[34]

The Government also used the police to protect landowners during the harvesting season. In January 1970 when 5,000 Marxist-led agricultural workers demanded one-seventh of the paddy as wages, and attempted to enforce this rate by attacking landowners and the laborers loyal to them, the police were called in and ordered to fire, killing one worker and wounding another.[35] At the time of the second harvest in June, no further incidents were reported.

However, the mini-front Government proved no more than a temporary phenomenon. The Kerala Ministry, with a razor-thin majority of three or four votes operated in constant danger of collapse from defection by splinter groups or disgruntled individuals. By June 1970, the Communist Chief Minister announced he would call a mid-term election.

The elections, held in September 1970, confronted the C.P.I.(M) with a particularly difficult political situation. In November 1969, the Indian National Congress, the dominant party at the Center and in most states since Independence, had formally split into two rival Congress parties. This

[33] *The Statesman*, November 15, 1969.
[34] *Ibid.*, December 7, 18, 1969. Also January 3, 5, 1970.
[35] *Ibid.*, January 28, 1970.

outcome followed a long fight for control of the party machinery between two factions in the chief executive organ, the Working Committee, one led by the Prime Minister, Mrs. Indira Gandhi, and the other composed mainly of prominent state party leaders, headed by the President of the Congress party, S. Nijalingappa. In the aftermath of the split, Mrs. Gandhi's faction, subsequently known as the New Congress party, carried the majority of the undivided Congress party in Parliament as well as the majority of members in the key national executive body, the All-India Congress Committee (A.I.C.C.).[36] The political impact of the split was significantly heightened by Mrs. Gandhi's insistence that the crisis represented an ideological conflict "between those who are for Socialism, for change and for the fullest internal democracy and debate in the organization on the one hand, and those who are for the status quo, for conformism, and for less than full discussion inside the Congress."[37] Indeed, the factional division did visibly harden only in July 1969 after Mrs. Gandhi unexpectedly confronted the Working Committee with a new set of radical economic guidelines on the eve of the Bangalore A.I.C.C. session, and then went on to win the delegates' approval for the new programs. Among other economic initiatives, Mrs. Gandhi proposed the nationalization of major banks, the appointment of a Monopolies Commission, nationalization of the import of raw materials, and in the agricultural sector, speedy implementation of existing land reform laws, as well as new

[36] Apart from the Annual Congress Session, the All-India Congress Committee was the most representative of the national decision-making organs of the undivided Congress party. Its membership included all the Presidents of the State or Pradesh Congress Committees (P.C.C.'s), 1/8 of P.C.C. members elected from among themselves, the Leader of the Congress party in Parliament, 15 members elected by the Congress party in Parliament, and the Leaders of Congress parties in the state legislatures. One-third of the membership of the chief executive organ, the Working Committee, was elected by the A.I.C.C., with all other members appointed by the President.
[37] *The Statesman*, November 12, 1969.

151

legislation to lower ceilings on individual ownership of land. Moreover, after Bangalore, Mrs. Gandhi acted swiftly to give substance to her new radical image. Assuming the Finance portfolio from Morarji Desai, her conservative Finance Minister and party rival, the Prime Minister moved to have fourteen major Indian banks nationalized by Presidential ordinance. As a result of these actions, Mrs. Gandhi was branded a "dictator" and a Communist "fellow traveler" not only by the conservative Swatantra and Jan Sangh opposition parties, but by the Old Congress party, the organization formed by the Nijalingappa faction of the undivided Congress after the party officially split in November. Meanwhile, Mrs. Gandhi proved increasingly adept at turning such personal attacks into public popularity, emerging as the champion of the common man, prepared to do battle with all politicians wedded to the status quo and "powerful economic interests."[38]

In Kerala, the formation of Mrs. Gandhi's New Congress party had strong repercussions on the balance of political forces. On the eve of the mid-term elections, the New Congress party had inherited the bulk of the undivided party's organization in the state. Moreover, on the basis of a refurbished radical image, the New Congress party entered an electoral alliance with the C.P.I. led United Front[39] and set out to erode the political base of the Marxists in their traditional rural strongholds. As a result, the Marxist led Peoples Democratic Front[40] was confronted by a united opposition throughout the state;[41] in addition, Mrs. Gandhi personally

[38] Ibid.
[39] In addition to the C.P.I., the Front included the Muslim League, the Revolutionary Socialist Party and the Praja Socialist Party.
[40] The C.P.I.(M)'s Peoples Democratic Front included the Samyukta Socialist Party, Kerala Socialist Party, and the Indian Socialist Party.
[41] A third Democratic Front, composed of the Old Congress party, the Kerala Congress, Jan Sangh and Swatantra also contested the elections in 91 out of 134 constituencies, but it was too weak a politi-

campaigned for New Congress candidates in several Marxist constituencies.

On the whole, these tactics were successful. The political effectiveness of the Marxists' vote-getting power in the state was significantly reduced. Although the C.P.I.(M) actually improved its overall electoral performance between 1967 and 1970—increasing its share of the total popular vote from 22 percent to 30 percent—they were able to win only 34 seats in the 134 member state assembly, representing a loss of 17 seats over their 1967 total. Altogether, the C.P.I.(M) led Peoples Democratic Front accounted for just 47 seats in the new assembly.[42] Moreover, Mrs. Gandhi had been effective in her effort to reduce Marxist margins in several rural constituencies, and New Congress candidates actually defeated Marxists in a few of their strongholds. In Palghat, the C.P.I.(M) won only three out of seven seats in the Ponnani parliamentary constituency, compared to six out of seven in 1967; although it did maintain its position in the Palghat parliamentary constituency, winning five out of seven seats.[43] More important, the New Congress party, polling 1.4 million votes, or a little less than 20 percent of the total, managed to emerge as the second largest party in the state assembly with 32 seats. Together with the C.P.I led Front, which bagged a total of 37 seats, the united opposition commanded a bare majority sufficient to deny the Marxists a role in the new government.[44] A C.P.I. led coalition, again headed by Achutha Menon returned to power, with the New Congress party remaining outside the Ministry, but supporting the government in the state assembly.

Nevertheless, the Marxists can now use a number of levers in their competition with the C.P.I. and the New Congress

cal force to mount an effective challenge to the rival leftist Fronts in all but a handful of contests.

[42] *The Times of India*, September 20, 1970.
[43] *Ibid.*, September 19, 1970.   [44] *Ibid.*, September 20, 1970.

party to compensate for their loss of the official apparatus. Indeed, the Marxists now have a much stronger organizational machinery in rural areas than they commanded in 1967. The popular enthusiasm stimulated by tenancy reform under the Kerala Land Reforms (Amendment) Act and higher wages for laborers under the Agricultural Minimum Wages Act has been institutionalized at the village level through the creation of "popular" committees. In a growing number of villages, moreover, the Marxists have mounted private security forces, the newly created "red" volunteer force. Finally, the normal advantages of strong grassroots political organization will be magnified by the proposed decentralization of broad powers of government to popularly elected district councils.

Under a new pattern of local government adopted in 1969, jurisdiction over virtually all development activities, including agriculture, irrigation, health, communications, and education is to be vested in nine directly elected District Councils. More important, the power to collect revenue, which has traditionally resided in the office of the District Collector as the local representative of the State Land Revenue Board, is also to be transferred to the Councils. Apart from following broad state guidelines concerning the pattern of development outlay, the District Councils appear to be potentially autonomous in carrying out major governmental functions. In fact, official opinion in the capital of Trivandrum is that the new pattern of local self-government will leave the state with only "residuary" functions, i.e., law and order, administration of justice, preparation of the state budget, and liaison with the Center. The legislation, which is ostensibly "a response to a demand by the people from below for a larger share of political power" was pushed vigorously by local units of the C.P.I.(M) and the Marxist Minister of *Panchayats* (Councils), apparently in the belief that it would enhance the position of the party

154

in the state as a whole. This is consistent with the overall Marxist approach which seeks to give as much power as possible to "the people" and then to utilize "peoples institutions" as instruments of mass mobilization for political agitations. Moreover, inasmuch as Marxist strength varies from one district to the next, extreme decentralization of governmental powers and patronage will permit the party organization to consolidate their grip on areas like Palghat where the Marxists are strong. A key advantage of the new system under the present circumstances, is that it safeguards predominant Marxist influence in local politics through the control of popularly elected District Councils even when the C.P.I.(M) are not included as members of the state government.

On the whole, the case of Kerala calls attention to what may be an increasing constraint on the prospects of a capital-intensive agricultural modernization strategy, especially in the rice belt. That is the desire of radical parties to exploit the social discontents arising out of increasing economic disparities for political gains, rather than to develop the potentialities of modern technology for solving the problems of production. The leadership of the C.P.I.(M) has been notably frank in stating that under the present economic and political system, even United Front Governments can at best bring only marginal relief to the people. The primary goal must be to strengthen the radical forces for social revolution by creating new organizational channels for the mobilization of popular discontent.

Indeed, in Palghat and Alleppey, a major casualty of the leftist political strategy has been the development effort. Marxist propaganda stigmatizing senior administrative officers as "bourgeois" elitists and glorifying equality in the name of the "proletarian" clerks, peons, and even junior grade officers has so eroded the prestige of district administrators that they can no longer expect compliance from development staff even on routine matters. Only if there is a good "personal relationship" between senior officers and subordinates does some work get done. Even this tenuous authority, however, is undermined by political interference from above. Until recently, for example, both the Joint Director and Collector played a large part in determining the opportunities for promotion or transfer of district and block development officers through confidential evaluation reports which weighed heavily in personnel decisions taken by the State Revenue Department. Under the Marxists, however, the Revenue Minister issued instructions that such reports must be shown to the officers concerned. With the new system of local government, even this formality will be abandoned and the entire development staff will be responsible only to the elected members of the District Councils. Already, it is clear that the younger block officers are extremely careless about their duties. Community Development offices are left unattended for long periods except for a few clerks; few detailed work programs are prepared; and block extension officers are absent from work without explanation. An indication of the extent of demoralization that has already overtaken senior officers is their reluctance to inquire into unauthorized absences by subordinates: the absentee may turn out to have influential friends in one of the leftist political parties.

6. Burdwan, West Bengal

BURDWAN district shares many problems of areas singled out for intensive development on the basis of favorable agronomic features. A region of high annual rainfall and fertile alluvial soil located in the Gangetic plain of central West Bengal, in 1961 Burdwan supported a population of over three million persons on an area of 2,705 square miles and had one of the highest population densities in India: 1,139 persons per square mile. The overwhelming majority of persons, 83 percent, lived in rural areas.[1] Although Burdwan is a major rice producing district in the state, in 1961 there was little more than 2.5 acres of cultivated land for every adult employed directly in agriculture.[2] However, by contrast with other parts of the densely populated rice belt, Burdwan did enjoy a burgeoning industrial sector, consisting mainly of small-scale enterprises in tool making, manufacture of precision instruments, printing, brickmaking, and the more traditional crafts of spinning and leather working. Alternative job opportunities were also provided by the area's mines and quarries, and by the communications and transportation network centering in the capital of Calcutta to the south. Nevertheless, jobs requiring some education or specialized skill were outside the range of the majority

[1] Census 1961, West Bengal State, *District Census Handbook: Burdwan*, Vol. II, 23.
[2] During the period 1959-60 to 1961-62 the net area sown averaged 1.2 million acres. *I.A.D.P. Program, Second Report, 1960-65*, 452. The total agriculturist population, including cultivators and agricultural workers, numbered approximately 480,000. *District Census Handbook: Burdwan*, Vol. II, 23.

of the rural population; 72 percent of persons living in rural areas were illiterate, and this proportion rose to over 90 percent among the most impoverished class of landless laborers.[3] Over one-quarter of the rural population suffered under an additional handicap to social mobility—membership in the Scheduled Castes and Tribes.[4]

There were other reasons why the majority of agricultural families were unable to appreciate their good fortune of living in the "granary of West Bengal."

Less than 50 percent of the gross area of some 1.1 million acres under paddy is served by canal irrigation. The Damodar Valley Corporation (D.V.C.) supplies irrigation water to about 500,000 acres; the smaller Mor project to an additional 30,000 acres. However, the D.V.C. does not have a network of field channels for the regulation of irrigation water at farmers' fields: instead, the project supplies water through canals which operate according to a flood system. As a result, the level of standing water in farmers' fields, both in canal irrigated and rainfed areas, depends heavily on the strength of the monsoon. In normal years, when rainfall averages about 40 inches between June and September, fields in all parts of the district are flooded. In fact, under the D.V.C. system, a good deal of water is wasted for agricultural purposes. It is estimated that about 25 to 30 percent of irrigation water is annually allowed to run off into the Bay of Bengal. In years of particularly heavy monsoons, the standing water in the fields is sometimes so high that it does damage to the crops. By contrast, when the monsoon fails, the D.V.C. system, which itself depends on rainfall for irrigation water cannot meet the normal requirements of the main *Aman* winter paddy crop. For example, a serious failure of the monsoon both in 1965-66 and 1966-67, followed by a partial failure in 1967-68, led to the progressive reduction of total output, and in some parts of the district

[3] *Ibid.*, 55. [4] *Ibid.*, 304.

to "near famine conditions."[5] Another limitation of the D.V.C., deriving from its dependence on rainfall for irrigation water, is that it can supply adequate water for a second crop only over 25,000 acres, inasmuch as the annual incidence of rainfall in Burdwan during the rest of the year is normally no more than 10 or 15 inches. Traditionally, therefore, Burdwan district like the state as a whole has been a predominantly single-cropped paddy area.

The distinctive characteristics of the *Aman* crop represent an adaptation to the local topography and available supplies of water. Most of the *Aman* crop is cultivated on medium or low lying ground, while the amount of water that ultimately reaches the farmers' fields is not subject to regulation. In normal weather years therefore, standing water in the fields is so high that paddy is cultivated under flooded conditions over the major part of the area; conversely it is the peculiar feature of *Aman* paddy that it *must* be grown under flooded conditions to yield well.

The cropping pattern has also been adapted to the water supply. Sowing and transplantation begin during what is considered the middle of the *kharif* season in other parts of India, i.e., in July and August, and harvesting takes place during the middle of the *rabi* season, in mid-December or January. Usually, therefore, cultivators have no time to plant either a *kharif* crop prior to transplantation or a *rabi* crop after harvest. At the time of the introduction of the I.A.D.P. in 1962, only about 7 percent of the net sown area was double-cropped. Most of this represented upland areas where cultivators took either an *aus* variety of paddy—a photo-insensitive and quick maturing plant which could be sown by broadcast method in April or May and harvested in October—followed by a second crop of wheat; or jute, followed by potato. On slightly lower land, it was some-

[5] *A Short Note on the Progress of I.A.D.P., Burdwan, for the Year, 1968-69*, mimeo. p. 5.

159

times possible to take a transplanted variety of *aus* followed by wheat; or an early *Aman* variety—maturing one month sooner than normal *Aman*—or jute, followed by potato. Finally, there was very limited scope for a second summer or *boro* crop of paddy in medium or low-lying areas, having both abundant supplies of water and soils with good moisture retentive capacity.

The major achievements of the I.A.D.P. in Burdwan district between 1962-63 and 1968-69 were to increase the irrigation potential by about 100,000 acres during the main *Aman* season and by about 52,000 acres during the second or *rabi* season; and to expand the opportunities for double-cropping. Approximately one-third of the new irrigation potential (in both the *Aman* and *rabi* seasons) was created by government investments in medium irrigation projects. These included 182 deep tubewells installed by the State, each with a command area of about 150 acres during *Aman* and 75 acres during *rabi*; and 53 river-lift irrigation schemes, each commanding 200 acres during *Aman* and 100 acres during *rabi*. The balance of two-thirds of the new irrigation potential represented private investments by individual farmers in tanks, pumping sets, and shallow tubewells.[6] As a result, between 1962 and 1969, the total area under double-cropping increased from 7 percent to about 20 percent, raising the gross-cropped acreage from 1,258,000 acres to about 1,400,000 acres. Gross area under paddy also increased, from 1,080,000 acres to 1,130,000 acres, as some cultivators harvested a second summer or *boro* paddy crop; the remainder of the *rabi* area was brought under high-yielding varieties of wheat, potato, vegetables, pulses, and mustard.

Up to 1967-68, therefore, the greatest beneficiaries of the

[6] Progress in extending the irrigation potential of the district and the scope for multiple-cropping is summarized in *ibid.*, 4.

I.A.D.P. approach were those relatively few farmers whose holdings fell within the area covered by State-sponsored deep tubewell or lift irrigation schemes; and those individual cultivators who could afford to invest in supplementary irrigation facilities, especially tanks, pumpsets, and shallow tubewells. This latter class included farmers with compact holdings of 5 acres or more, who were eligible for the Department of Agriculture's loan and subsidy scheme, under which diesel and petrol driven pumps were made available at 30 percent subsidy, with the balance of the cost of the pump—some Rs. 3,000 to Rs. 4,000—repayable in five annual installments. The major benefits to farmers of additional irrigation facilities were higher yields from *Aman* paddy with increased dosages of chemical fertilizer and the ability to take a second crop of summer or *boro* paddy, or high-yielding wheat. During 1969-70, it was proposed to increase the irrigation potential by another 45,000 acres. In a special effort to distribute the benefits even more widely among small farmers, the State Government decided to extend loans for shallow tubewells to cultivators with as little as 2 acres of compact land, and on terms that did not require more than a down payment, or deposit, of Rs. 62— some 2 percent of the total value of the pumping sets.

Despite these achievements, however, the aggregate production of rice in Burdwan district between 1963-64 and 1967-68 actually declined somewhat, from about 658,000 tons to 621,000 tons; this was at least partly due to poor rains during three successive seasons, beginning with 1965-66. The yield rate of rice per acre also showed a steady decline during this entire period. With the introduction of the high-yielding paddy varieties in 1968-69 on some 110,000 acres (and the benefit of a good weather year), the production of rice did increase to 725,000 tons. Yields per acre also rose, but not to levels significantly higher than

161

those previously achieved in 1963-64. The record of rice production between 1963-64 and 1968-69 is presented in Table 8.

TABLE 8
Progress in Production of Rice in Burdwan District
1963-64 to 1968-69

Year	Area '000 acres	Production in '000 tons	Yield rate in pounds per acre
1963-64	1055.1	658.7	1386
1964-65	1137.8	681.4	1320
1965-66	1107.3	646.9	1304
1966-67	1078.0	588.0	1214
1967-68	*N.A.	621.0	1222
1968-69	*N.A.	725.0	1427

* Not available.

SOURCES: Government of West Bengal, Department of Agriculture and Community Development, *A Short Note on the Progress During 1962-63 to 1967-68*, Intensive Agricultural District Program (Package Program) Burdwan, 16.
A Short Note on the Progress of the Intensive Agricultural District Program, Burdwan for the Year 1968-69. 5. Mimeo.

Unfortunately, there are a number of serious obstacles to the widespread cultivation of the high-yielding paddy varieties in Burdwan district. First, the topography of the land is generally unsuitable during the main *Aman* season. With most of the area at medium or low levels of elevation, and no means of regulating the flow of water at farmers' fields, the standing water in fully three-fourths of the area planted under rice would be too high for the dwarf varieties, and the plants would be submerged. At most, about 300,000 acres would escape this difficulty. Second, in addition to adequate water, the high-yielding paddy varieties need about 12 to 13 hours of sunlight daily to produce optimum yields. However, during the main *Aman* season cultivation occurs under the heavy cloud cover of the monsoon. Even when adequate drainage facilities are available, therefore, yields from the high-yielding varieties are reduced below the optimum for want of sunlight—although they may still be somewhat better than levels achieved with local varieties. For many cultivators this advantage is cancelled out by the higher costs of cultivation and the greater incidence of plant diseases. Actually, under the conditions of Burdwan district, the best period to grow I.R. 8 is during the dry and sunny summer season as a *boro* crop. But while sunlight conditions are optimal, most cultivators do not have the supplementary minor irrigation facilities that are necessary to take a second paddy crop.

Once all these limitations are taken into account, the major advantage of the high-yielding varieties in Burdwan district can be summarized as follows. Where the topography is suitable, i.e., over a maximum of 300,000 acres, shorter-duration, high-yielding strains can be substituted for local varieties to convert a portion of the single-cropped area into double-cropped land. This possibility arises from the opportunity to harvest I.R. 8 approximately one month earlier than traditional *Aman* varieties, and to use the water thus saved for a second crop of either wheat, potato, or vegetables, or pulses and mustard, which can be grown with residual moisture in the soil.

Nevertheless, given the constraints imposed by topography and the irrigation system, the main opportunity for increasing yields and output in Burdwan remains the greater utilization of modern inputs, especially fertilizers and pesticides, on local varieties during the main *Aman* season. Looked at from this perspective, and taking into account the poor performance of the I.A.D.P. over the last six years, the major obstacles to agricultural modernization appear to lie less with unsuitable topography or inefficient utilization of water, serious as these problems are, than with an extremely unfavorable agroeconomic pattern. Uneconomic farms, often cultivated in several tiny fragments, combined

163

with very high rates of rental for leased land have left the majority of agriculturists with neither the means nor the incentives to invest in modern methods of production.

· I ·

Available agroeconomic data for Burdwan district are incomplete. According to the 1961 census, almost 50 percent of all cultivating households operated holdings of less than 5 acres.[7] Yet, village records in the three blocks visited suggest that the distribution of operational holdings is much more unfavorable. In Jamulpur block, a canal irrigated area having a relatively high incidence of double-cropping, 4 acres of land is considered the minimum size for an economic holding sufficient to maintain an average family of five or six persons. By contrast, in the three villages selected, the majority of agricultural families, ranging from 51 percent in Ruppore village to 54 percent in Selimabad village to 58 percent in Habashpur village were either landless or had holdings of less than one acre. An additional 26 percent, 29 percent, and 22 percent, respectively, had farms of 1 to 3 acres. The remainder, ranging from 23 percent in Ruppore to 17 percent in Selimabad and 20 percent in Habashpur had holdings of 3 acres or more. In Selimabad, the only village for which data was available on acreage cultivated under each size of holding, about 70 percent of the land was cultivated in farms of 3 acres or less; 14 percent in holdings of 3 to 5 acres; and only 2 percent in farms of 8 to 10 acres.

In Galsi-II block where irrigation is generally sufficient to assure one crop only—the typical situation in the district —and a 6-acre holding is considered the minimum size necessary for an economic unit, data on the distribution of operational holdings for the three villages visited (Babla, Saral, and Bardighi) reveal a larger number of economic

[7] *District Census Handbook: Burdwan*, Vol. II, 221.

holdings, but also a greater degree of concentration of land. Available data for each village is given in Table 9.

TABLE 9

Distribution of Agricultural Workers and Cultivated Area in Three Villages of Galsi-II Block by Size of Landholding

Distribution of Landholdings	Number of families	Percent	Area (acres)	Percent
BABLA VILLAGE				
Landless laborers	25	20	—	—
Landless sharecroppers	24	19	95	20
1-3 acres	35	27	70	15
3-6 acres	27	21	135	29
6-12 acres	12	10	108	23
12-20 acres	4	3	64	13
Total	127	100	472	100
SARAL VILLAGE				
Landless laborers	67	38	—	—
Landless sharecroppers	25	14	149	21
1-3 acres	30	17	75	10
3-6 acres	20	11	100	14
6-12 acres	20	11	200	27
12-20 acres	16	9	201	28
Total	178	100	725	100
BARDIGHI VILLAGE				
Landless laborers	58	53	—	—
Landless sharecroppers	15	14	30	11
1-3 acres	12	11	25	9
3-6 acres	8	7	40	15
6-12 acres	10	9	75	28
12-20 acres	4	3	55	20
above 20 acres	3	3	45	18
Total	110	100	270	100

In Ausgram-II block, where 90 percent of the paddy area is cultivated under rain-fed conditions, and even one crop is not assured, 15 acres is considered the minimum neces-

165

sary to maintain an average family of six persons. Data on the distribution of landholdings in the two villages of Kalikapur and Mongolpur visited show that only 2 or 3 percent of all families actually operated holdings of this size. Data for the two villages is given in Table 10.

TABLE 10

Distribution of Agricultural Workers and Cultivated Area in Two Villages of Ausgram-II Block by Size of Landholding

Distribution of Landholdings	Number of families	Percent	Area (acres)	Percent
KALIKAPUR VILLAGE				
Landless laborers	52	52	—	—
Landless sharecroppers	7	7	144	39
1-3 acres	25	25	75	20
3-6 acres	8	8	44	12
6-12 acres	5	5	52	14
12-20 acres	3	3	54	15
Total	100	100	369	100
MONGOLPUR VILLAGE				
Landless laborers	16	18	—	—
Landless sharecroppers	28	31	77	26
1-3 acres	16	18	15	5
3-6 acres	18	20	90	30
6-12 acres	10	11	80	27
12-20 acres	2	2	36	12
Total	90	100	298	100

The Project Officer and I.A.D.P. staff support the general conclusion suggested by this data that the overwhelming majority of farm families in Burdwan district are either completely landless or operate uneconomic holdings of less than 3 acres. They estimate that about one-third of all agricultural households are pure labor families. Of the two-thirds who are cultivators, approximately 50 percent take some land on crop share. Current estimates are that about

166

50 percent of the land is cultivated under sharecropping arrangements.

Yet, while the West Bengal Land Reforms Act provides that the sharecropper or *bargardar* who supplies his own bullocks and other inputs should receive 60 percent of the total produce, this provision appears to be universally ignored. In practice, there are a variety of arrangements governing the terms of crop sharing. In some cases, the annual rent is set in fixed terms, i.e., regardless of output, at about 15 maunds of paddy per acre. In a very good year, the *bargardar* may realize some 35 maunds of paddy per acre; his rental will therefore absorb only some 45 percent of the produce. Yet, in the more likely event of a smaller crop, e.g., 30 maunds, it will rise above 52 percent. Moreover, all the costs of cultivation, including water cess, are borne by the tenant. Under proportional sharecropping arrangements, when the *bargardar* supplies his own bullocks and inputs, the division of the crop between the landowner and the cultivator is usually fixed in a ratio of 50:50. However, in the poorest, unirrigated areas of the district, the *bargardar* frequently does not own any bullocks, and he is also dependent on the landlord for inputs. In such cases, the rental is normally fixed at a proportional rate of 66:34 in favor of the landlord. In practice, however, the sharecropper commonly receives much less of the crop than this formal arrangement implies. Throughout the year, the *bargardar* is dependent on advances from the landlord for payments to agricultural laborers—which are not met by landowners—and for consumption loans for food, clothes, medicine, or other family emergencies. At the end of the crop season, these advances are deducted from the sharecropper's one-third of the produce as the first charge on the crop. After allowing for such deductions, it is not unusual for sharecroppers to be left with 12 percent to 15 percent of the total output, about 4 or 5 maunds per acre. One sharecropper interviewed reported that he had received no paddy at all during the previous year, after "adjustments" for all loans had been made against his crop share. Such cultivators survive mainly by taking even larger loans, thus falling into a state of perpetual indebtedness and by taking up some additional employment, when it is available—as farm laborers or construction workers. A few have been able to double-crop a fragment of their holdings with wheat or vegetables and add marginally to their consumption, or to earn a little cash by putting a fraction of an acre under sugarcane.

The sharecropping system as it is practiced in Burdwan district is particularly unfavorable for investment in improved practices. Most landowners are not interested in sharing the cost of modern inputs. Many landlords are actually absentees, living in other villages or in Calcutta; they have other occupations and consider their income from rent simply as supplemental income. Moreover, many landowners are not wealthy men. They may belong to the lower-middle or middle class; or even be factory workers who hope sometime to come back to the land. It is common to hear of landlords with 5 and 10 acre holdings who have leased out plots of 2 and 3 acres on crop-share.

If the landowner lacks the ability or interest to invest in modern inputs, the sharecropper plainly finds it impossible to do so. In fact, over the last five years, sharecroppers report that their economic situation has considerably deteriorated. Partly, this is the result of the political climate created by long-standing government commitment to land reform. Many landowners are afraid that leased land will ultimately vest in the sharecroppers. They not only refuse to have the names of sharecroppers entered in village records (as presumptive evidence of possession), and change sharecroppers every other year, but recently, they have also

168

resorted to forcible eviction in order to take up direct cultivation or cultivation through hired labor. As a result, many
sharecroppers are now cultivating smaller holdings than in
previous years; and in extreme cases, they have been reduced entirely to work as agricultural laborers. Even those
who have managed to retain roughly the same size of holding report deterioration in their economic position with the
rise in prices of essential commodities. Almost none of the
sharecroppers interviewed were currently members of primary agricultural credit cooperatives; a few had been, but
then defaulted on loans. Landlords and local businessmen,
charging rates of interest of up to 36 percent per year were
their main source of production credit. As a result, sharecroppers rarely used any chemical fertilizers, or only small
doses. They reported no increase in crop yields with local
varieties over the last five years. None had tried the high-
yielding varieties, even though some parts of their holdings
were topographically suitable, because of the high production costs involved. As subsistence farmers, they had no
surplus to sell, and could not benefit from rising prices for
food grains. On the contrary, confronted by higher prices
for essential consumer items, and in many cases, with ex-
panding families to support, they experienced a definite
deterioration in all aspects of their economic life.

The circumstances of farmers with ownership holdings
of less than 3 acres were only moderately better than those
of sharecroppers. Generally, they achieved some increase
in yields, about 25 to 30 percent over the last five or six
years from the use of small doses of chemical fertilizer. But
at most, this permitted them to maintain their existing
standard of living in the face of rising prices for farm inputs and essential commodities. They reported no improvements and virtually no adoption of the high-yielding
varieties.

169

· II ·

The vast majority of agriculturists in Burdwan district, i.e., sharecroppers and small farmers with holdings of less than 3 acres, have received very little help from the co-operatives. The Burdwan Cooperative Bank, which serves four out of six subdivisions of Burdwan district, covers 37 percent of the agricultural population. It includes 750 primary agricultural credit societies, each serving an average of three or four villages. Two hundred of these societies are actually defunct, and the Central Bank extends credit to only 500 societies.[8]

Until three years ago, credit was extended to members only on the basis of land offered as security for loans. In 1966-67, with the Reserve Bank's insistence on a production oriented crop-loan system, lending procedures were formally amended to give some appearance of conformity to the Reserve Bank's directives; in practice, however, most loans are still sanctioned only against land as security.

Nevertheless, each year, just before the *rabi* season in November or December, there is a field workers' conference to set down scales of finance per acre based on the production costs of each major crop, using both traditional and improved methods. As a result, the Cooperative Bank now has no less than four different scales of finance for the cultivation of paddy alone. Farmers using traditional methods in nonirrigated areas may receive Rs. 200 per acre, of which Rs. 150 is given in cash, and the remainder in fertilizers and pesticides—although cultivators are not compelled to accept the kind component as a condition of receiving the cash part of the loan. On irrigated land, the scale of finance is higher, amounting to Rs. 300, of which Rs. 200 is given in cash and Rs. 70 in kind. In this case, cultivators are required to accept the kind component of the loan as a condi-

[8] Figures supplied by the Secretary of the Burdwan Central Cooperative Bank.

tion of receiving the cash portion, but they are also eligible for an additional loan of Rs. 30 to meet expenditures arising out of the application of fertilizers. There are also two scales of finance for the high-yielding varieties of paddy. Cultivators growing an indigenous indica variety, NC 678, are eligible to receive Rs. 350 per acre, of which Rs. 200 is in cash, Rs. 100 in kind (compulsory), and an additional Rs. 50 in cash (optional). For I.R. 8, the scale is higher: the total loan is Rs. 450 per acre, of which Rs. 200 is extended in cash, Rs. 175 in kind (compulsory), and Rs. 75 in cash (optional).

Despite these very elaborate formulas, however, bank officials freely concede that small farmers do not ask for the maximum credit limits provided, and that the amount actually sanctioned as production loan for any member is in any case determined according to the value of land offered as security. The only exception to this rule is that all members, including sharecroppers, can receive personal surety loans up to Rs. 300 per year on the guarantee of two members of the primary agricultural credit society, both of whom are landowners. But for loans in excess of Rs. 300 the Central Bank requires members to execute a land mortgage deed in favor of the primary society. This requirement has generally inhibited small farmers from joining the cooperatives; they are afraid of losing their lands in case of default.

Despite (or because of) these restrictions, the Burdwan Central Cooperative Bank is in an extremely weak financial position. Owned funds, the bulk of which come from contributions to share capital by member societies, have remained stagnant at about Rs. 30 to Rs. 31 lakhs for the last three years. A very high incidence of overdues has normally placed the Bank in C Audit Class, which restricts its capacity to borrow from the Reserve Bank to two times its owned funds. In 1967-68, however, overdues jumped to 58 percent of all loans outstanding; and the Central Bank could not

171

meet the Reserve Bank's minimum requirement of a 50 percent nonoverdue cover to qualify for further loans. Nevertheless, inasmuch as Burdwan is an I.A.D.P. District, the Reserve Bank waived this requirement, and actually agreed to sanction loans amounting to three times the owned funds of the Bank, i.e., Rs. 90 lakhs; a similar accommodation was also extended in 1968-69. Together with deposits, which have shown a modest increase from about Rs. 136 lakhs to Rs. 144 lakhs over the last three years, these loans helped raise the Bank's working capital to some Rs. 241-49 lakhs. Yet, the Reserve Bank's generosity has been wasted. In practice, the Cooperative Bank has been able to utilize only some 50 to 60 percent of the loans sanctioned. Because of heavy defaults at the village level, the total volume of short-term credit advanced over the last three years has declined from about Rs. 106 lakhs to Rs. 84 lakhs.[9] The Bank's record on medium-term loans is little better. Over the last three years, advances have remained static at about Rs. 5.5 lakhs, with the overwhelming majority of loans sanctioned for the purchase of buffalos and bullocks.

It is clear that the bulk of the credit needs of the majority of cultivators continue to be met by local moneylenders— either village landlords and traders charging an average of 36 percent interest per year, or by cold storage merchants who advance credit against the delivery of the potato and jute crops. The State Government is now thinking that three to five-year loans should be given to privately indebted persons to enable them to liquidate outstanding loans and join the local cooperatives. But unless this class as a whole can find some subsidiary sources of income that permit them to repay loans from cooperatives in time, it is doubtful that even such a program could permanently increase the repayment capacity of the majority of agriculturists.

[9] Written statement provided by the Secretary of the Burdwan Central Cooperative Bank.

172

· III ·

It is only when one comes to the upper one-fourth or one-third of rural families, and these in the irrigated areas of the district, that any signs of tangible improvement appear. Farmers with 3 to 6 irrigated acres report some increase in yields ranging from 40 to 60 percent as the result of higher applications of fertilizers and pesticides. Although production costs have also increased, this class has benefited somewhat from rising prices for paddy. Overall, they have experienced modest additions to net income that have been used to improve consumption. There is greater expenditure on clothing, on education for sons, and occasionally on the purchase of consumer durables, such as a transistor or cycle. In addition, some farmers have used the opportunity provided by higher yields of paddy to diversify their cropping pattern and provide a more varied diet for home consumption, including wheat, potatoes, or vegetables. A few farmers have enjoyed more substantial improvement, and some report the introduction of intensive cropping either as a result of additional water becoming available under the D.V.C. system or the acquisition of a hand tubewell with the help of a government subsidy. For example, one particularly fortunate 3-acre cultivator was able to take two paddy crops, *Aman* and *boro*, on one acre over the last two years as a result of additional water supplied by the D.V.C.; and he was also able to introduce a second potato crop on one acre of *aus* land by installing a hand tubewell purchased under the government subsidy program. His additional income was being used not only to improve consumption, i.e., for better housing, a private drinking water tap, transistor, and education, but also for further investment in modern inputs, including a moldboard plough and seed drill.

This is, however, still a rare case. Generally, it is only

173

among the small minority of cultivators with ownership holdings of 6 acres or more that such gains are found. Farmers with 8 or 10 acres have increased their yields from ordinary *Aman* varieties by 30 to 60 percent over the past five years. On that portion of their output that is marketed, rising prices have increased their cash income by as much as five or six times per acre of paddy. Most important, they have increased their net returns to management from the introduction of intensive cropping, at least on a portion of their holding. Sinking tubewells with the help of government subsidy, some farmers have managed to bring 1 or 2 acres under double or triple-cropping, taking an *aus* and potato crop; and/or an early *Aman* and *boro* paddy crop; and/or jute, early *Aman* and wheat. They then pyramid their gains further by the introduction of high-yielding wheat varieties and I.R. 8 on suitable areas under *Aman* and during the *boro* season. Much of the additional income thus generated goes for consumption: clothing, children's education, electrification, private drinking taps, watches, transistors, and cycles. But at least a few cultivators among this size class are also able to accumulate some surplus for further investment in land improvement, including shallow tubewells and some improved implements.

However, the greatest gains by far have come to resident farmers in the largest size category; i.e., those with holdings between 12 and 20 acres. It is among this class of cultivators that privately owned minor irrigation works are most common, either shallow tubewells or tanks and pumpsets for lift irrigation. Improved implements—moldboard ploughs, seed drills, and sprayers—are also much more in evidence. Over the last five years or so, they have increased their yields from local varieties by 30 to 60 percent, and their cash income per acre by five to six times. With supplementary water facilities, they have put a larger proportion of their holding under double and triple-cropping. Those hav-

174

ing land suitable for the cultivation of I.R. 8 are introducing it during the *Aman* season: they expect to double their yields and almost double their net profit per acre on these portions of their holding. Additional income among this group also tends to be spent on consumption: home improvement, consumer durables, and education. But, in addition, large farmers are using their profits to carry out further land improvements; purchase improved implements; and initiate new enterprises, including fisheries, dairies, grocery shops, and even rice-husking mills.

· IV ·

One-third of all agricultural families in Burdwan district are agricultural laborers, of whom over 40 percent belong to the Scheduled Castes. Permanent relationships between landowners and laborers still persist; they are particularly common in parts of the district dominated by larger holdings. In fact, with the introduction of intensive cropping, the necessity of having assured labor at peak cultivation periods has actually tended to strengthen the system of permanent landowner-laborer relations.

There are two major categories of permanent laborer—*Mahinder* and *Nagare*—with local variations based on custom. The *Mahinders* are employed according to a traditional arrangement by which agricultural labor families are permanently attached to the family of a landowner, usually from one generation to the next. *Mahinders* are employed by larger landowners at the rate of one man for each plough unit, and are on permanent call by the employer, e.g., a *Mahinder* may be requested to come in the night with no additional payment. Although the exact terms vary in different parts of the district, *Mahinders* receive payments both in cash and kind. Those interviewed reported cash payments ranging from Rs. 110 to Rs. 150 annually; and varying amounts of paddy, averaging six to seven

175

maunds a year. In addition, they ordinarily receive two or three meals a day of rice or pudding, and during the year, three or four lengths of cloth for *dhotis*, two towels, one shirt, one woolen wrapper, oil, *beedi*, and paddy straw for thatching their houses. These are customary terms, and have not varied over the past few years, the single improvement being that the market value of rice has appreciated. However, with static cash earnings, and rising prices for essential commodities, *Mahinders* generally report a deterioration in their economic situation over the last few years.

Nagares, the second category of permanent laborer in Burdwan district, also have a customary relationship with only one landowner, but the obligations on both sides are more limited. *Nagares* will not work for any other landowner, and if a *Nagare* appears for work, the landowner must give him first preference. But *Nagares* are paid according to the task performed at rates set down for casual labor, except that they also receive a lump payment of paddy of some 10 to 12 maunds a year. Except for loans they do not get any other facility from the landowner. At the same time, the *Nagares* are not on permanent call.

Rates for casual labor—including work done by *Nagares* —are essentially determined by supply and demand conditions in Burdwan district. In turn, these are controlled by the annual migration into Burdwan of laborers from the western districts of West Bengal and the eastern districts of Bihar. After the migratory workers arrive, just before the peak season begins in July, the laborers meet with the landowners and bargain over the season's rate, citing rises in prices to justify an increase in wages. Nevertheless, with an abundant supply of migratory workers, local laborers are not in a good bargaining position and there has been little change in wage rates over the last few years. During the peak season, lasting three months, *Nagares* receive Rs. 1.50 to Rs. 2 in cash, plus 1.25 kg. of rice, oil, and *beedi*, equivalent to about Rs. 3.50 or Rs. 4. In addition, migratory workers also get pulses, spices, oil, salt, vegetables, fuel, *beedi*, and kerosene—but no advances against their wages from the landowners. Off-season rates go down to Rs. 1 or Rs. 1.25 plus 1.25 kg. of rice, oil, and *beedi*. Altogether, *Nagares* and casual laborers report that they find work for six to seven months a year from all sources—agricultural as well as construction and other odd jobs in the slack season. This represents an improvement over previous years, when, with less intensive cropping, work was available only about four months a year. Nevertheless, any additions to cash income generated by new opportunities for employment tend to be cancelled out by rising costs of essential commodities. Apart from some minimal improvement in clothing, *Nagares*, especially those with growing families, report either no improvement or a deterioration in their economic condition over the last few years. However, they are so dependent on "good relations" with the larger landowners for assurance of even this minimal subsistence level—as long as laborers are easily imported from outside—that efforts to organize the agricultural workers in Burdwan have so far largely failed.

· V ·

Actually, until the mid-1960's, the most depressed sections of the rural population, sharecroppers and laborers, were generally ignored by the major political parties. They accepted the prevailing view that the peasantry of West Bengal was deeply conservative and inert, strongly committed to the traditional social hierarchy of caste, and largely reconciled to their impoverished condition. The following description by an American scholar was typical of this assessment.

177

The vast majority of the peasants and rural cultivators have imbibed very little education at all, much less a Westernized education that would inculcate a belief in the legitimacy or necessity of egalitarian or class forms of social organization. Most peasant cultivators remain deeply committed to a hierarchical social system in which authority relationships between individuals and classes are well defined; in which the area of legitimate individual ambitions and aspirations is carefully circumscribed; and in which the weight of almost all symbols of authority is on the side of obedience to caste, family and village superiors. These factors are in turn reinforced by the wide economic gap that exists between the peasant-cultivator low castes and the non-cultivating high castes. The existing man/land ratio and the short supply of land in relationship to demand reinforce an economy of high rent and a high rate of tenancy, and encourage attitudes of acquiescence on the part of the landless and tenant farmers.[10]

A number of historical factors peculiar to West Bengal also reinforced an urban-centered strategy of party organization.[11] Ever since the end of the nineteenth century, the city of Calcutta, as the first political and administrative capital of British India, and the foremost commercial, trading, and industrial center in the eastern region, served as a magnet for rural migrants. The opportunity to acquire an English education and thus employment in government service, the professions, and business, early attracted members of the landed castes who found their incomes from rentals dwindling as multiple layers of intermediaries acquired rent-collecting rights in land, while productivity re-

[10] Marcus F. Franda, "West Bengal" in Myron Weiner, ed., *State Politics in India* (Princeton University Press, 1968), 268.
[11] See *ibid.* for a general analysis of the social, economic, and political development of West Bengal since the British period.

mained static. At the same time, villagers from the Bengali hinterland (and neighboring Bihar, Orissa, and Uttar Pradesh) also surged toward the city, seeking employment as laborers and factory workers to supplement the meager earnings of their families who stayed behind on the land. When new opportunities for employment began to lag far behind demand, it was the urbanized and Westernized Bengali middle class who provided the leadership for opposition movements to British rule, which ranged the whole political spectrum, from terrorist associations to Communist and Marxist revolutionary parties and to the moderate Bengali unit of the Congress party.

After independence in 1947, this pattern of political recruitment was slow to change. On the eve of the first national elections in 1952, the Congress party leaned heavily on urban groups and factions, assigning key importance to the financial support of big business elements in Calcutta. Little effort was made to establish an independent organizational base in the rural areas. Instead, the state leadership rested its support on a series of ad hoc alliances with large landowners, traditional patrons who acted as brokers between small-scale village communities and the political system, rallying their kin groups, caste fellows, and clients, including sharecroppers and agricultural laborers, behind the Congress party in return for access to official patronage.

Like the Congress party, the Communist party of India (C.P.I.) and other Marxist political parties active in West Bengal failed to build effective peasant organizations. The Russian oriented C.P.I. remained wedded to the orthodox Marxist approach of militant trade union organization and agitation to tap the revolutionary potential of the growing numbers of urban workers and educated unemployed crowding Calcutta and smaller towns. Indeed, the failure of the Communist parties to create direct linkages with the peasantry, combined with their inability to mobilize popular support by proxies, i.e., through alliances with traditional landowning patrons in the constituencies, indirectly strengthened the position of the Congress party in the countryside by limiting the scale of the electoral effort that could be made by the left opposition.

During the first decade of electoral politics, the growing success of the Congress party reinforced the general impression of a conservative and tradition-bound peasantry. In the three general elections of 1952, 1957, and 1962, the Congress party won more than 60 percent of the seats in the legislative assembly. Moreover, its share of the total popular vote steadily increased from 38.9 percent in 1952 to 46.1 percent in 1957 and to 47.2 percent in 1962.

In 1967, however, there was a striking shift. The Congress party for the first time since independence failed to win a majority of seats in the state legislative assembly. At the same time, its share in the total popular vote declined from 47.2 percent in 1962 to 41.1 percent in 1967. The victors in the 1967 general election were two Communist-dominated electoral fronts, the Peoples United Left Front, led by the regular C.P.I., and the United Left Front led by the newly formed C.P.I.(Marxists). It is true that the constituents of the electoral fronts managed to win only a bare majority of the popular vote, and they had to arrange ad hoc alliances with members of all other minor opposition parties to secure a one seat majority in the state legislative assembly. Nevertheless, in March 1967, the first Communist-dominated United Front government succeeded in coming to power in West Bengal. Predictably, internal dissension brought the tenuous majority of the United Front ministry into public question after only seven months, and after an abortive attempt by the governor to install a Congress-led successor government, President's Rule was imposed on the state.

The 1967 defeat of the Congress party in West Bengal could be attributed to skillful electoral tactics by the combined opposition rather than to any significant change in the distribution of popular preferences for revolutionary and moderate parties. Severe factionalism within the Congress party leading to the defection of large numbers of active members into a new political organization, the Bangla Congress, and the participation of the new party in the C.P.I. led Peoples United Left Front, played a pivotal role in the election outcome. Indeed, Congress losses, both with respect to the popular vote and numbers of seats won in the legislative assembly were made good mainly by the Bangla Congress, rather than the Communists.

A similar pattern was evident in the mid-term elections of 1969, when a twelve-party United Front electoral coalition, again including the Bangla Congress, won almost 50 percent of the popular vote, while the Congress party's poll declined somewhat to little over 40 percent. This time, however, the United Front delivered a decisive defeat to the Congress party in the legislative assembly as well, winning 214 out of 280 seats.

Nevertheless, a comparative analysis of voting preferences in West Bengal from 1952 to 1969 indicates that recent Communist victories cannot be adequately explained by citing their successful effort at building united electoral coalitions. Indeed, the most salient fact about Communist gains in West Bengal is that they have been steadily increasing. The undivided C.P.I. was able to improve its popular vote from 10.7 percent in 1952 to 17.8 percent in 1957 and to 24.9 percent in 1962. The combined strength of leftist electoral fronts also increased during this decade from almost 20 percent of the popular vote in 1952, to 25 percent in 1957 and to 34 percent in 1962. Even in a state where the proportion of urban to rural population is relatively high

181

(24.4 percent in 1961), these figures reveal growing support for the Communist party and Marxist-left groups in rural areas.[12]

Significantly, the spurt in leftist strength beginning in the mid-1960's coincided with the 1964 split in the C.P.I. An immediate issue was the future of party ideology and program in the face of strong nationalist attacks on the patriotism of the C.P.I. after the Chinese invasion of India. The Rightist faction, in an effort to demonstrate unqualified loyalty to the Indian Constitution inclined toward parliamentary tactics and peaceful social reform. By contrast, the Leftists, in an attempt to define a revolutionary strategy that was at once differentiated from the "bourgeois nationalism" of the Congress party, and the international expansionism of Chinese Communism, turned to the idea of mounting an indigenous mass movement in the Indian countryside. This change in approach was formally explored by the Kerala Marxist leader and theoretician, E.M.S. Namboodripad as early as 1962, when he argued that the "essentials of a correct strategic approach, according to me, are . . . with the rural people against the urban monopolists; and above all, with the peasantry and other sections of the working people against the ruling classes as a whole."[13] As in Kerala, the Leftists of West Bengal carried most of the membership with them. In the state elections of 1967, the newly organized C.P.I.(Marxist) won 18.1 percent of the popular vote while the C.P.I. polled 6.5 percent.

Reinforcing the strategic shift in West Bengal were tactical considerations. The tenuous legislative majority of the first United Front Government foreshadowed rapid collapse of the Ministry and the likelihood of new elections.

---

[12] For a comparative analysis of election results in West Bengal see Marcus F. Franda, "Electoral Politics in West Bengal: The Growth of the United Front," *Pacific Affairs*, XLII (Fall 1969).

[13] Cited in John B. Wood, "Observations on the Indian Communist Party Split," *Pacific Affairs* (Spring 1965).

Both Communist parties rapidly became convinced of the practical necessity to widen the base of their popular support by penetrating the rural areas. Moreover, both the C.P.I. and the C.P.I.(M) considered the major agricultural development programs, especially the I.A.D.P. and the High-Yielding Varieties Program, essentially "rich men's schemes." The first United Front Ministry gave only passive support to the propagation of the new technology. Instead, the major constituents set out to exploit the political opportunities provided by increasing economic disparities. Unlike the Communists in Kerala, who had long been active in rural areas and commanded strong grassroots political organizations for harnessing social discontent, the Communists of West Bengal had to pave the way for the creation of peasants associations by articulating popular grievances in terms of class conflict ideology. The main target of Leftist agitation was the sharecroppers, the group that had already experienced the greatest absolute deterioration in their economic position, and were facing the bleak prospect of even further deprivation with an upward trend in evictions.

Prior to the 1969 mid-term elections, the Marxists' primary appeal was to the landless. Party workers approached sharecroppers and agricultural laborers with simple but effective propaganda, emphasizing that "you have been working the land for long years, your families have been working it for generations, yet the man who does not even recognize which plot of land is his, gets all the profits and you remain oppressed." The implication of such arguments was clear—the land belongs to the tiller. Grassroots response was immediate. For the first time since independence, the Leftist electoral fronts easily contested almost all constituencies in the state. Of 280 assembly seats, the Marxists and C.P.I. led alliances won 155. Moreover, the Marxists alone won 80 seats, emerging as the largest single party in the assembly and the dominant partner in the United Front

183

ministry. The key to Marxist success could be found in the political transformation of rural districts like Burdwan. As late as 1967, the Congress party won 14 out of 25 assembly seats in Burdwan district; the C.P.I. (M), 7. In 1969, the Congress party barely managed to survive, winning only 2 seats; the C.P.I.(M) won 17.[14]

After the 1969 elections, the Marxists increasingly followed a rural strategy. At the village level, they concentrated on organizing sharecroppers and landless laborers into *Krishak Sabhas* (Peasants Associations). In Burdwan, the immediate program of the *Krishak Sabhas* was one of amelioration—higher wages for agricultural laborers and a 50:50 division of crops between landlords and sharecroppers, with landowners paying one-half of all production costs. In other parts of the state, particularly in the most impoverished southern districts, the Marxists used the *Krishak Sabhas* as the organizational arm of a rural movement to seize *benami* land, i.e., land which had been illegally retained by owners in defiance of the state's ceiling legislation which established an upper limit on landholding of 25 acres. By June 1969, the *Krishak Sabhas* were estimated to have a membership of about 480,000 (out of a total landless population of over 15 million),[15] and in a few of the south Bengal districts, the incidents of forcible seizure of land increased sharply. During the first few months of 1969, a total of 30,000 to 35,000 acres of land were occupied by laborers.[16] A report of the West Bengal *Krishak Sabha* issued in June 1969 announced that a total of over 100,000 acres of *benami* land had already been identified, largely through the efforts of organized peasants, implying that another 65,000 acres or so were marked for immediate seizure.[17] As in Kerala, more-

[14] *Hindustan Times*, February 23, 1969.
[15] *The Statesman*, June 5, 1969.
[16] Estimate provided by the Land Revenue Department, Government of West Bengal, Calcutta.
[17] *The Statesman*, June 5, 1969.

184

over, the Marxist-led Home Ministry was reluctant to use its control over the police in order to protect landowners against illegal occupation of their land. The general attitude of the Marxist administration was that while it is illegal for landless workers to seize *benami* land, it is not immoral. Therefore, the powers of the state should not be used against them except in extreme cases that threaten the complete collapse of law and order in rural areas. Not surprisingly, incidents of arson, kidnapping, and even murder rapidly multiplied as *jotedars* (large landowners) sought to prevent landless peasants from occupying their lands, and frustrated sharecroppers and workers retaliated in mob attacks against large landowners.[18] As in Kerala, moreover, interparty rivalry between the two major parties in the United Front, the C.P.I.(M) and the C.P.I., tended to intensify the atmosphere of insecurity in rural areas as rival *Kisan Sabhas* clashed over the distribution of occupied land, and the police were accused of intervening in favor of Marxist partisans.

Marxist agitation among sharecroppers further increased the level of social tension. They encouraged the *bargardars* to withhold the owners portion of the crop, and/or to refuse to divide the crop on the landowner's threshing floor. Violent confrontations over these issues occurred in several parts of West Bengal. On balance, the sharecroppers suffered most as a result of these tactics, with landowners becoming more determined than ever to use forcible means of eviction in order to protect their property rights. In the process, however, it is likely that sharecroppers only became more embittered and radicalized, as well as more convinced of the Marxists' political propaganda that fundamental social change can only be accomplished by the complete overturn of the existing property system.

[18] See *ibid.*, July 18, 1969 and July 29, 1969 for reports of typical instances.

185

Indeed, recent political developments in West Bengal suggest that the Marxists will be increasingly forced into a direct attack on all propertied groups simply to maintain their popular support. The Marxist leadership is already facing pressure from below from the most militant cadres in the *Kisan Sabhas* for an expanded attack against middle and small landowners. In addition, they have to contend with the potential mass appeal of the revolutionary (Maoist) splinter group, the *Naxalites*, which broke off from the Bengal C.P.I.(M) in 1967 after the state leadership refused to support an immediate program of agrarian revolution based on systematic terror and forceful expropriation of all *jotedars*.[19] Moreover, despite the fact that the official tactical line stresses the need for solidarity among landless peasants with small and medium landowners against the *jotedars*, interparty competition between the C.P.I.(M) and other Leftist parties is forcing a pattern of popular mobilization based on the creation of rival volunteer forces that are likely to prove difficult to control. By August 1969, the Marxists reported that 22,000 volunteers had already

[19] The *Naxalites* take their name from the Naxalbari area of West Bengal in the northernmost part of the state where C.P.I.(M) cadres in the Darjeeling District Committee launched an abortive agrarian revolution in 1967 aimed at seizing political power through forcible expropriation of the landowning class. Openly announcing their political commitment to a Maoist model for India, and receiving enthusiastic support from Peking, the activities of the *Naxalites* threatened to jeopardize the electoral gains of the C.P.I.(M) by branding them an antinationalist party. In August 1967 the Marxists' Central Committee formally denounced the Chinese Communist party for violating "every Marxist-Leninist tenet of assessing a given political situation" by their support of armed revolution in Naxalbari. The action precipitated the defection of Marxist revolutionaries in West Bengal; they were subsequently joined by other activists from party units in Bihar, Andhra Pradesh, Kerala, Uttar Pradesh, Punjab, and Tamil Nadu. The total strength of the various *Naxalite* groups has been estimated at anywhere between 8,000 and 20,000. The most recent attempt to bring the *Naxalite* factions under a central political command occurred with the formation of the Communist Party (Marxist-Leninist) in May 1969. For a brief summary of *Naxalite* activities, see *The Times of India Magazine*, May 18, 1969.

186

been trained, and by the end of the year, this number jumped to 50,000.[20] A volunteer force formed by another United Front constituent, the Forward Bloc in 1969, claimed a membership of 25,000 by early 1970.[21] The oldest volunteer army, the Peoples Service Corps, organized by the C.P.I. in 1964, was believed to command an estimated 25,000 to 30,000 members.[22]

Whether or not such cadres have been directly responsible for acts of political intimidation as claimed by rival parties, the fact remains that by the end of 1969, the law and order situation in West Bengal had seriously deteriorated. Indeed, by October 1969, the Chief Minister, Ajoy Mukherjee, head of the Bangla Congress, the major non-Marxist constituent of the United Front, took the unprecedented step of supporting his party in a formal resolution charging that "disruption in every sphere of life . . . has taken place in the first seven months of UF rule in the State."[23] Two months later, Mukherjee was sufficiently alarmed to undertake a three-day fast against his Communist colleagues in the United Front ministry to call attention to the rise in interparty clashes, political murders, forcible collection of paddy by sharecroppers, illegal seizure of land by laborers, the inaction of the police, and a generally mounting atmosphere of insecurity in the state. According to Mukherjee, the life and property of people in West Bengal were no longer being protected by the government. Dramatically asserting that "there is no precedent for this state of affairs in the civilized world," Mukherjee went on to paint this picture of the law and order situation in some rural areas of Bengal: "Not to speak of improvement in the law and order situation, murders, violent clashes, looting,

[20] *The Statesman*, August 25, 1967; November 20, 1969.
[21] Hiranmay Karlekar, "Growing Cult of Militancy to Increase Party Influence," *ibid.*, January 21, 1970.
[22] *Ibid.*   [23] *Ibid.*, October 9, 1969.

187

gherao, and forcible occupation of land have become the order of the day in West Bengal. There is no denying the fact that people, particularly in the rural areas have become panicky, and in many places, a sense of insecurity of life and property has gripped the population."[24]

As the harvesting season approached, the situation grew even more tense. Frequent clashes were reported between supporters of the C.P.I.(M) and the Bangla Congress: agricultural laborers attempting to forcibly harvest paddy on *benami* land were met with armed resistance from the *jotedars.* The Chief Minister, accusing the Marxist Home Minister of failing to provide adequate police protection for landowners, threatened to take the Bangla Congress out of the United Front government and topple the Ministry. The response of the Marxists was to countercharge that "vested interests" were determined to oust the United Front Ministry before the end of the harvest season in order to prevent the landless from occupying plots of land that were rightfully their own.[25] Indeed, by early 1970, the Marxist Land and Land Revenue Minister was claiming that more than 300,000 acres of land had been distributed to the landless and poor cultivators, mainly as a result of forcible occupation.[26]

On March 16, 1970, Ajoy Mukherjee finally submitted his resignation as Chief Minister, publicly charging the C.P.I.(M) with establishing a "reign of terror" in the state. President's Rule was imposed on West Bengal a few days later. It brought little immediate improvement in the law and order situation. Non-Communist opposition leaders complained that the administrative machinery had been infiltrated by the Marxists, and that the police were still in-

[24] *Ibid.,* November 11, 1969.
[25] *Ibid.,* December 4, 1969.
[26] Hiranmay Karlekar, "Land Distribution During U.F. Rule: Facts and Fiction," *ibid.,* May 20, 1970.

active in protecting *jotedars* against attacks by landless workers. Even more alarming, *Naxalite* groups bent on violent overthrow of the existing regime, sharply increased their terrorist activities. These ranged from murders of political opponents and *jotedars* in rural areas to bomb attacks on urban educational institutions and printing presses, as symbols of the "bourgeois-oriented educational system."[27]

Large-scale arrests of over 1,600 political extremists in the first half of 1970 proved inadequate to halt inter-party clashes between the C.P.I.(M) and the Naxalites, or to prevent Naxalite attacks on the police, Government officers and educational institutions. Nevertheless, the imposition of President's Rule did give the central government an opportunity to take direct initiatives in an effort to reduce the level of violence in West Bengal. By November 1970, the Cabinet advanced a two-pronged approach that was accepted by the Consultative Committee of Parliament for West Bengal and subsequently enacted by the President. As a short-term expedient for improving the law and order situation, a Prevention of Violent Activities Bill was promulgated that allowed the use of preventive detention in cases of known extremists. Of more long-range significance, a new West Bengal Land Reforms (Amendment) Bill was prepared with the aim of providing legal remedies for agrarian discontent that would minimize incentives for *bargardars* and landless workers to take the law into their own hands. The Bill attempted to meet the *bargardars'* grievances through a temporary stay of all eviction proceedings, and by provisions increasing the *bargardar's* share of the crop from 60 percent to 75 percent in cases where the cultivator supplies bullocks and other inputs; and from 60 percent to 70 percent in other cases; establishing the *bargardars'* cultivation rights as heritable; and permitting the *bargardar* to store and thresh paddy at a place of his own choosing as

[27] *Ibid.*, April 27, 1970.

long as the landowner retained reasonable access to inspect storage and threshing. In addition, a serious effort was made to ameliorate the plight of the landless by reducing the ownership ceiling on agricultural land from 25 acres per individual to 15 acres per family (husband, wife, and minor children) for irrigated land and 20 acres for unirrigated land.

Most important, during the harvesting season of December 1970, the local revenue administration was activated to enforce the new provisions. Camp courts were set up in rural areas to hold on the spot enquiries and take immediate action in the case of disputes arising between *bargardars* and landowners over the division of the crop. As a result, despite the announced intention of the C.P.I.(M) to mount large-scale agitations during the harvest season, the incidence of violent clashes in the rural areas significantly decreased from about 1,600 reported conflicts in 1969 to about 1,000 in 1970.[28] The Naxalites, deprived, at least temporarily, of a ready-made rural constituency, increasingly concentrated their energies on terrorist attacks in Calcutta and other urban centers.

[28] *The Statesman*, January 23, 1971.

7. Conclusions

It is always dubious to make broad generalizations about economic and social change on the basis of a few, selected district studies. It is all the more risky with respect to India, where conditions differ not only from district to district but block to block and even village to village. Nevertheless, the case studies presented here gain some credibility as a mirror of emerging relationships between agricultural modernization and social change from the strong resemblances they reflect of the impact of modern technology on rural income distribution and socioeconomic relations over widely separated parts of the country.

At least the following points seem clear. As a result of the I.A.D.P. approach, almost all classes of cultivators have experienced some improvement in income and yields from the introduction of modern methods of agriculture. This is particularly true in the wheat-growing region of Ludhiana where the cultivation of fertilizer-responsive dwarf varieties has been almost universally recognized as more profitable than the traditional techniques. In the rice-growing areas, the spread of the high-yielding varieties is still rather limited because of unfavorable agro-climatic conditions. Nevertheless, even in the rice areas, the introduction of fertilizers, pesticides, and other modern practices has produced a steady, if modest, increase in yields of local varieties over the last ten years.

The second major point, which also appears certain, is that the gains of the new technology have been very unevenly distributed. In Ludhiana, where the majority of

191

cultivators have economic holdings of 15 or 20 acres or more, and have accumulated surpluses from savings, or raised capital through loans, for investment in minor irrigation and improved equipment, the benefits of the new technology have been most widely, albeit still unevenly, shared. Probably only the bottom 20 percent of all farmers, i.e., those with holdings of 10 acres or less, have experienced a serious relative deterioration in their economic position for want of sufficient capital to invest in indivisible inputs (especially minor irrigation works) necessary for the profitable adoption of the new techniques. Yet, Ludhiana is atypical even for the Punjab, and much more so for large parts of the wheat-growing belt. For example, in Bihar and Uttar Pradesh, both major wheat-growing areas, *over 80 percent of all cultivating households operate farms of less than 8 acres.* It is therefore not unreasonable to assume that the relative percentages of cultivators who have received significant benefits from the new technology compared to those who have been left out are almost exactly the reverse in these areas than they are in Ludhiana.

Certainly, this has so far been the case in the rice-growing region. There, the majority of cultivators have uneconomic holdings of 2 and 3 acres. Such farmers have managed to increase per acre yields from the application of small doses of fertilizer, but aggregate gains in output have been insufficient to create capital surpluses for investment in land development. At best, they have permitted small farmers to stabilize their standard of living in the face of rising costs. In cases where small farmers also lease part of their holdings, or are pure tenants, rising rentals in recent years (in response to the sharp spurt in land values), and/or the tendency of landowners to resume land for personal cultivation with the introduction of more profitable techniques, have actually led to an absolute deterioration

192

in the economic condition of the small owner-cum-tenant cultivator class.

Farmers with ownership holdings between 5 and 10 acres have done better: they have experienced some improvement in net income that has permitted them to realize an overall increase in their standard of consumption. But it appears that only the small minority of cultivators with holdings of 10 acres or more have been in a position to mobilize surplus capital for investment in land development, especially minor irrigation, as an essential precondition for the efficient utilization of modern inputs. Moreover, this class has pyramided its gains by using increased profits to buy more land, improve land already under cultivation, and purchase modern equipment. Farmers with 20 acres or more have made the greatest absolute and relative gains, partly by mechanizing farm operations to take up double or multiple cropping, but also by diversifying their cropping pattern to include more profitable commercial crops. All of these innovations together—installation of private tubewells and other minor irrigation works, the introduction of double and triple-cropping, the cultivation of more profitable commercial crops, the purchase of more land, and the use of agricultural machinery to enhance farm efficiency—have substantially increased the lead of large farmers over small farmers, if not in terms of yields per acre, then certainly with respect to aggregate production. The majority of farmers—probably as many as 75 percent to 80 percent in the rice belt—have experienced a relative decline in their economic positions. Some proportion, representing unprotected tenants cultivating under oral lease, has suffered an absolute deterioration in living standards.

It is clear that the High-Yielding Varieties Program is being introduced into a setting where economic disparities have already been substantially sharpened by the differen-

193

tial capacity of small and large farmers, and tenants and landowners, to sustain the capital outlays on land development, especially minor irrigation, and other modern equipment that are necessary to realize the full benefits of the new technology. Given the much higher cultivation costs of the new varieties, and an even greater premium on timely agricultural operations—including a rigid schedule for the application of fixed amounts of water to achieve maximum potential yields—the economic disparities between the minority of cultivators who can finance land improvements and the majority who cannot are bound to widen further. In fact, in areas where the high-yielding varieties of rice have been successfully introduced, this tendency toward economic polarization between large farmers on the one hand, and the majority of small owners, owner-cum-tenant cultivators, and sharecroppers on the other, has already begun.

There has, of course, been increasing recognition on the part of the government that "the small farmers have not benefited in proportion either to their numbers or their needs from the various programs of rural development which have been under implementation during the three Plans."[1] There is even a commitment in the Fourth Plan to ensure that small farmers are enabled to "participate in development and share its benefits."[2] The difficulty is that the main programs under consideration are likely to fall very much short of the requirement. The Small Farmer Development Agency envisaged for the Fourth Plan is expected to reach a maximum of 2,000,000 farmers within the next five years; and this Agency will be concerned only with expediting arrangements for credit, irrigation, inputs, and technical advice for small farmers by "mak[ing] the fullest use

[1] *Report of the All-India Rural Credit Review Committee* (Bombay: Reserve Bank of India, 1969), 537.
[2] *Fourth Five-Year Plan*, 120.

194

of the existing institutions and authorities and also the funds already available otherwise."[3] Moreover, the definition of "small farmer" to include only those "who can be developed into surplus farmers if they adopt improved techniques on the basis of support in terms of supplies, irrigation, services of machinery, etc."[4] explicitly removes sub-marginal cultivators from the scope of the Agency's jurisdiction. The only other major program mentioned in the Fourth Plan is an allocation by the States of some Rs. 500 crores for community tanks, tubewells, and river pumping projects from which small farmers particularly are supposed to benefit.

Certainly these programs represent measures aimed in the right direction and deserve maximum support from State and local development administrations. Yet, the scale on which they are being mounted suggests that the "small farmer" is still being treated as if he belonged to a residual or marginal category. Unfortunately, the opposite is true. Once all the disabilities of the average cultivator are taken into account, and these only in the irrigated areas of the country, the majority of agriculturists actually fall into the "small farmer" category in the sense of lacking both the means and the incentive to participate in the new technology.

At present, it is virtually impossible to say how many of the majority of marginal farmers could be made viable. What is certain, however, is that the major programs now being advanced will reach only a small fraction of the total. Indeed, their potentialities are further reduced by the failure to take account of the tenurial situation in most parts of the rice belt (and for that matter in part of the wheat area, especially Bihar), where a large proportion of cultivators operate holdings under oral lease with no legal proof of

[3] *Report of the All-India Rural Credit Review Committee*, 580.
[4] *Ibid.*, 579.

possession. Yet, to qualify for assistance by the Small Farmer Development Agency a tenant will first have to produce evidence that he is in cultivating possession of the land. Even when this is not an obstacle, moreover, it is doubtful that more than a handful of small farmers will be able to find significant benefit from the adoption of the high-yielding varieties unless the central government is prepared to help the states finance a much more massive development program in minor and medium irrigation designed specifically to help small landowners. In fact, unless such a massive effort is made, the small farmers will continue of their own choice to ignore new opportunities to obtain larger production loans from cooperatives for cultivation of high-yielding varieties out of fear that crop failures in bad weather years will involve them in such heavy losses that they may have to sell their land in order to repay debts.

There is another serious—perhaps more serious—limitation to programs such as the Small Farmer Development Agency as an instrument for helping all classes of agricultural workers to participate in the benefits of the new technology. Not only are submarginal farmers explicitly excluded from the range of its concerns, but the landless, laborers as well as sharecroppers, are entirely passed over. While this may be considered sensible from an economic point of view, i.e., from the perspective of achieving maximum gains in production, it may prove shortsighted with respect to the social and political goals of development. Indeed, while small landowners are apt to experience a relative decline in economic position as a result of agricultural modernization, they are also likely to remain a conservative social force. Small landowners still respect traditional criteria of status and tend to identify with the larger landowners. But this is less true of sharecroppers and laborers who have been increasingly liberated from the old authority patterns by the erosion of customary patron-client ties.

196

Indeed, the introduction of modern technology under the intensive areas and the high-yielding varieties programs has not only quickened the process of economic polarization in the rural areas, but it has also contributed to increasing social antagonism between landlords and tenants, and landowners and laborers. In all areas, the introduction of modern methods of production has accelerated the transformation of the rural economy from a subsistence way of life to a profitable set of business activities. Landowners are now more likely to be influenced by rough calculations of opportunity costs in determining whether or not to lease out part of their land, or cultivate directly, than by traditional sentiments of personal obligation to customary tenants. Certainly, they do not hesitate to raise rentals in line with appreciating land values and/or to evict even tenants having long-standing cultivating possession of the land. Moreover, the land reform laws in all States, while largely abortive, have caused landowners to view tenants as potential adversaries, and this has further contributed to the breakdown of permanent patron-client relationships. As one observer has pointed out, the advent of the new technology confronts the small owner-cum-tenant cultivator with the bleak prospect not only of increasing economic disparity, but also of "an agonizing change from *security* in the midst of poverty to growing *insecurity* along with poverty."[5] Obviously, tenants who are shifted from plot to plot, and cultivate always in fear of losing some part of their holding to the landlord or another tenant, also quickly slough off traditional feelings of deference and obligation toward the landlord.

The same tendency toward erosion in traditional attitudes of mutual dependence and obligation is also apparent in relations between landowners and laborers. The impact of the I.A.D.P. and the High-Yielding Varieties Program on

[5] P. C. Joshi, "A Review Article," *Seminar* (May 1970), 32.

landless laborers usually looks favorable at first glance. With more intensive cropping and diversification of the cropping pattern, laborers tend to find more work. Moreover, during the past several years, the level of cash wages has also increased. Nevertheless, in the face of rising prices, laborers are generally left with little improvement in real income, and in some cases, they actually report deterioration over previous years. Paradoxically, their main hope of sharing equally in the benefits of the new technology is to maintain the traditional system of proportional payments in kind for major agricultural operations. Yet, the landowners, calculating that their own economic interests lie in converting all kind payments to cash, are denouncing the traditional system as exploitative and moving to introduce a cash wage for all kinds of farm work. Where mechanization is feasible, large farmers are anxious to buy machinery as quickly as possible to reduce their dependence on labor. Once again, there is not only growing economic disparity but social polarization between landowners and laborers. As impersonal bargaining arrangements replace customary patron-client relationships in the recruitment of farm labor, old ideas of reciprocal (albeit unequal) obligation give way to new notions of opposing economic or class interests.

In sum, therefore, the rapid progress of agricultural modernization tends to undermine traditional norms of agrarian relationships based on the exchange of mutual, if noncomparable, benefits and services that have historically provided a justification for inequalities between the propertied upper and middle castes, and the landless low castes and Harijans. As traditional landowning patrons increase their advantages by striking margins, yet neglect to fulfill their previous function of providing security to client groups, the legitimacy of existing—and growing—disparities is increasingly called into question. The potential impact on rural stability is all the more serious because radical parties

198

openly proclaim their intention of transforming social tension into political conflict between the minority of prosperous landowners and the large numbers of sharecroppers and landless laborers. Indeed, by the summer of 1970, both the C.P.I. and the C.P.I.(Marxists) had announced plans for a nationwide "agrarian struggle."[6] "Land-grab" agitations were started in Punjab, Uttar Pradesh, Rajasthan, Andhra Pradesh, Tamil Nadu, and Kerala. At the same time, *Naxalite* groups were reported to be gaining ground among "landless peasants and youth" in the rice-growing coastal areas of Andhra Pradesh, Kerala, West Bengal, and Orissa.[7] The Home Ministry in June found it necessary to formally caution six states—West Bengal, Bihar, Punjab, Orissa, Uttar Pradesh, and Kerala—about the activities of *Naxalites* who were said to be planning a "new, democratic" revolution on Maoist lines involving extensive class violence in rural areas.[8]

Yet, the assessment of state officials with respect to Thanjavur is essentially correct for the country as a whole. India is still "at the very beginning of trouble." Successes of radical political parties in mobilizing peasants for agrarian agitations are localized. Class-struggle actions, including "land-grab" movements, are sporadic. Local cadres of revolutionary parties have difficulty sustaining popular enthusiasm and support in areas where government makes a strong police response.

Whether or not peasant resentments will be effectively mobilized by radical parties for a mass revolutionary movement still very much depends on how existing governments tackle the phenomenon of rising rural tension. There are, of course, limits on what government can do. Certainly, the highly unfavorable land-man ratio in the most fertile rice areas of the country reduces possibilities for soothing agrar-

6 *The Statesman*, May 10, 1970.   7 *Ibid.*, May 11, 1970.
8 *Ibid.*, June 29, 1970.

ian discontent with a large-scale program for redistribution of land. However, within limits, and within limits that can be expanded, it is possible to narrow the advantages of the large landowners on the one hand, and increase the opportunities for the small farmer, the tenant, and landless laborer on the other. What is required in such an effort is renewed priority for the social and political goals of planning.

· I ·

So long as India was faced with the imminent danger of severe food scarcities, it was natural that planners should give exclusive attention to the problem of increasing production. Moreover, in the early stages of the new agricultural strategy, distribution problems were minimized by the coincidence that the areas of greatest immediate promise were those with the least severe agroeconomic problems. The new technology was most perfected with respect to wheat. In the Punjab and Haryana, which alone account for almost one-third the irrigated wheat acreage, the average size of ownership holding was large enough to permit most categories of cultivators to benefit from the introduction of modern methods. The prospect that large numbers of uneconomic farmers would be displaced did not have to be confronted, or could be projected into the future as a long-range problem that might solve itself with a general increase in alternative employment opportunities generated by a dynamic agricultural sector. In fact, this trend of development in districts like Ludhiana strengthened the rationale for a development strategy that emphasized the need to put production first, and deal with distribution problems afterwards.

Yet, the Ludhiana model cannot be applied over large parts of the country. It has limited applicability even to the 37 million acre wheat belt. It is almost totally inappropriate to the much larger area of 92 million acres under rice, where the small size of average holding and high incidence of tenancy exclude all but a minority from sharing in the gains of scientific agriculture. Moreover, while many large landowners have previously been content to remain absentees, some number are now resuming land for personal cultivation in order to benefit from more profitable techniques, thereby displacing (unrecorded and unprotected) tenants. Yet, the high percentage of landless workers to the total agricultural labor force in the rice areas makes it unlikely that displaced tenants can find alternative full-time employment even as farm laborers. Nor is it likely that over the next five to ten years the pace of industrialization will be so rapid as to absorb the overflow of unemployment from the agricultural sector. Indeed, the Fourth Plan started with a backlog of unemployment estimated at 9 to 10 million, of whom about three-fourths are already in the rural areas. According to 1966 projections, there will be a net addition of 23 million to the labor force during the period of the Fourth Plan, while the increase in employment opportunities outside agriculture is estimated at about 14 million and in agriculture at about 4.5 to 5 million. At the end of the Fourth Plan, therefore, the employment backlog will actually be greater than at the beginning by about 4 million persons.[9] Proposals for a rural works program as one way to close the gap offers only partial amelioration. Projected outlays are sufficient for State governments to provide employment for about 1.5 million persons during the slack agricultural season equivalent to 100 work days a year.[10]

Meanwhile, tendencies toward social polarization and class conflict have emerged much more quickly than originally anticipated. No doubt an important factor has been the demonstration effect of the new technology itself in creating awareness that modern methods can achieve spec-

[9] *Fourth Five-Year Plan 1969-74: Draft* (Delhi, 1969), 106, 108.
[10] *Ibid.*, 112.

tacular—and reliable—increases in productivity. For the first time, science is making the capricious world of the poor peasant amenable to prediction. Indeed, the new technology inadvertently challenges the underlying rationale of the traditional religious ethic of sacrifice and "renouncing all attachments to the fruits of action." Poverty and unrewarded effort are beginning to be perceived as remediable by man, and rooted in differential access to resources which are necessary for exploiting the opportunities created by modern science—opportunities which are objectively available to all men regardless of ritual ranking. It is precisely the social blindness of modern technology that is encouraging the most disadvantaged sections of the agricultural population to question the justice of inequalities that perpetually bar them from participating in gains that are otherwise within reach. It is the evenhandedness of the scientific method—the observable fact that high-yielding varieties, water, and fertilizer work as well on the small plot of the Harijan sharecropper as on the large estate of the Brahmin *mirasdar*—which gives rise to the notion that all castes and classes can *legitimately* claim a share in the new prosperity. Indeed, the rapid acceptance of Marxist ideology, with its emphasis on unjust capitalist expropriation of resources provided for common use, reflects the emotional, if unarticulated, response to the harsh reality of arbitrary exclusion increasingly imposing itself on the experience of the most disadvantaged sections of the peasantry.

It is probably impossible to prescribe an optimum balance between production and distribution goals in a successful development strategy. Certainly, an excessive emphasis on distribution may destroy the incentive and means to increase production. Yet, exclusive preoccupation with increasing production may ultimately bring about such severe social tension that the rural economy is disrupted.

Despite the difficulties, therefore, political prudence suggests that an appropriate balance should be sought.

· II ·

There are, in fact, a number of measures available to government for limiting the advantages of large farmers without destroying their incentive or ability to modernize. It is well known, for example, that State governments have never effectively enforced existing legislation imposing upper limits on land ownership. This is true even though ceilings in most states have been defined so generously that rigorous enforcement would yield only some two million acres of surplus land for redistribution.[11] Indeed, it is difficult to

[11] Existing state laws establish the ceiling on landownership as a multiple of the "family holding," defined as a fair employment unit for an average size family in local conditions. The leeway provided by this definition is very wide. The states have used this formula to define the family holding in terms of both "standard" and ordinary acres to compensate for regional differences in soil, irrigation, and other agronomic features. A "standard" acre is defined as a multiple or fraction of an ordinary acre with respect to some constant measure of value—either yield of principal crops, rental value, assessment rate, or market price. The size of an optimum family holding is first fixed in standard acres for each class of land, e.g., dry crop land, perennially irrigated land, or sandy, hilly land, and then converted into ordinary acres for the purposes of setting the ceiling. While this approach is basically sound in theory, the absence of reliable data has allowed most valuations to be made without reference to demonstrable economic yardsticks. Moreover, many states also rejected the Planning Commission's recommendation to limit landownership to three times the size of the family holding. As a result, the ceiling range in most states varies within rather high limits: 27 to 324 acres in Andhra Pradesh; 20 to 60 acres in Bihar; 19 to 132 acres in Gujerat; 25 to 75 acres in Madhya Pradesh; 24 to 120 acres in Tamil Nadu; 18 to 126 acres in Maharashtra; 27 to 216 in Mysore; 20 to 80 acres in Orissa, and 25 to 336 acres in Rajasthan. (India Planning Commission, *Progress of Land Reform* [Delhi, 1963], 65-67.) In 1966, the Planning Commission estimated that the application of ceilings to landownership would yield some two million acres of surplus land, although less than 500,000 acres had been actually taken over by the State governments for redistribution to landless workers. (*Statement to be laid on the Table of the Rajya Sabha in reply to Starred Question No. 475 on 17.8.1966*, prepared by the Land Reform Division of the Planning Commission, mimeo.)

203

argue that lowering the land ceiling even by substantial margins in most states would have a negative effect on opportunities for efficient farm management.

According to data collected by the National Sample Survey, Seventeenth Round, 1961-62, over 95 percent of all rural households owned holdings of less than 20 acres, and accounted for 64 percent of the total cultivated area. Less than 5 percent of rural households had ownership holdings of 20 acres and above, and controlled over 35 percent of the land. In absolute terms, 3.6 million rural households out of a total of 72.5 million owned over 111,000,000 acres of land out of an estimated owned area of 318,000,000 acres. Assuming a ceiling on land ownership averaging about 20 acres per rural household, it was possible in 1961 to find over 55 million acres of "surplus" land for redistribution. This can be measured against 8 million landless rural households, 24 million with holdings of less than 1 acre, and 11.5 million with holdings between 1 and 2.4 acres to see that redistribution even on this scale would not be sufficient to solve the problem of uneconomic holdings.[12] Yet, it could provide symbolic assurance of the commitment to greater equality; eliminate the most glaring rural disparities; and create a more favorable environment for voluntary cooperation among small farmers in pooling their resources to finance land development projects and/or to establish cooperative farms in order to form more viable units of production.

Even within the existing agrarian structure, however, there are palliatives available for preventing further increases in rural disparities. It is possible, for example, to prescribe ceilings on future acquisition of land in order to prevent greater concentration of ownership in the hands of a small minority of large farmers. Alternatively, large addi-

[12] *The National Sample Survey,* Number 140, Tables with Notes on Some Aspects of Landholdings in Rural Areas (State and All-India Estimates), Seventeenth Round, September 1961-July 1962 (Calcutta: Indian Statistical Institute, 1966), 11.

tions to farm income can be siphoned off through a graduated tax on agricultural income, or a wealth tax on agricultural property. It is also feasible to limit the gains of large farmers by adopting restrictive policies on the rate of mechanization, especially when the adoption of farm machinery is known to displace agricultural laborers.

At the same time that the advantages of large farmers are reduced, opportunities for the landless and owner-cum-tenant cultivators can be improved. Certainly, security of tenure and reduction in rents would help at least some marginal farmers to become economic cultivators. Effective implementation of minimum wage laws for agricultural laborers—where they exist—and efforts to organize farm workers for bargaining with landowners, especially if opportunities for mechanization are limited, can also have a significant effect in increasing labor's share of the new productivity.

All of these measures are, of course, well known to the Indian government. All of them have been actively considered. Almost all have been tried. Yet, most of them have so far failed. Difficulties in implementation persist in the political influence brought to bear at the state level by the dominant agricultural castes which still control local government bodies. The most recent proposals by the Prime Minister in September 1970 to lower the ceiling on land ownership were received without enthusiasm by the chief ministers of the states. Even the Prime Minister's urgent appeal for effective enforcement of existing land reform laws assuring security of tenure and fair rents to tenants has brought no apparent response. Moreover, the states have also proved unwilling to increase the burden of agricultural taxation, either by raising land revenue rates, irrigation levies, or agricultural income tax. Indeed, the central government's initiative in the 1970 budget in passing a new wealth tax on agricultural property was immediately challenged as

205

unconstitutional by several chief ministers. Court tests of the Center's authority were initiated both by the Punjab Government and a private landowner. In September 1970, a majority of the Punjab and Haryana High Court granted the writ petition filed by the landowner. The Court ruled that Parliament was prohibited from imposing any type of tax on agricultural land by provisions in the Constitution reserving this sphere of taxation to the State Legislatures. Meanwhile, large farmers in the Punjab are being favored still further by permissive policies on the part of both the central and state governments with respect to mechanization. A World Bank loan authorized in 1970 for a farm mechanization program in the state will make 8,000 imported tractors available. The Punjab State Industrial Development Corporation has also approved plans for the construction of a state-partnered factory with an annual capacity of 10,000 tractors to go into production by 1972. The first combines were introduced into the Punjab in 1970.

Yet, one thing is clear. Without at least some sign of good faith on the part of government, it cannot be expected that the mass of agriculturists and laborers will continue to passively accept their fate, or that government can continue to take for granted the fundamental requirement of any process of economic growth in the rural areas, conditions of "law and order." More than thirty-five years ago, Mahatma Gandhi first pleaded with the propertied castes to "read the signs of the time (and) revise their notion of God-given right to all they possess." His warning sounds all the more prophetic today: "There is no choice between voluntary surrender on the part of the capitalist of superfluities and consequent acquisition of the real happiness of all on the one hand, and on the other the impending chaos into which, if the capitalist does not wake up betimes, awakened but ignorant and famishing millions will plunge the country, and which, not even the armed force that a powerful government can bring into play can avert."[13] Certainly, it can be anticipated that in a growing number of areas, the dual objectives of increasing agricultural production and preserving social order will become incompatible unless a fundamental change occurs in the outlook of the propertied classes—if on no other ground than that of enlightened self-interest—so that the government of the day can ameliorate, if not remove, some of the most distressing inequalities that have so far accompanied the progress of agricultural modernization.

Finally, an effective response by existing governments to the rising level of agrarian tension requires full recognition that outbreaks of rural violence demand more than a law and order program. It is true that the police and army—in states where they have been freely used—are strong enough to snuff out local agrarian agitations. But unless a long-term strategy is devised, it seems unlikely that a brush-fire approach can indefinitely forestall more extensive conflagrations. Indeed, the real issues being raised are basic ones for any society. They involve nothing less than the criteria by which economic values, social standing, and power are to be allocated. The Harijans and other low-caste landless groups who have for so long been controlled by religious beliefs sanctifying impoverishment and powerlessness along with ascriptive inequalities in ritual status, are now making the first tentative distinctions between the secular and sacred spheres. Literacy, education, adult suffrage and, above all, the demonstrable liberative powers of modern technology and science have helped create a receptive environment for new slogans of economic and political equality raised by socialist and Marxist parties. It is doubtful that

[13] M. K. Gandhi, *Towards Non-Violent Socialism* (Ahmedabad, 1951), 144.

low-caste agricultural laborers or sharecroppers will long remain satisfied with their client status either in economic or political life. If only for this reason, vertical patterns of political mobilization are bound to undergo even more severe strain in the years ahead. The multicaste political faction led by traditional landowning patrons and constructed with support from families of low-status client groups, especially tenants and farm workers, will become more and more difficult to sustain as a viable political unit at the local level. The question is not whether the old pattern of clientelist politics can be put back together again, but how to fill the political vacuum developing in the rural areas as a result of its collapse.

Indeed, the outcome of the Fifth General Elections in March 1971 suggests that the ability of the traditional landowning patron to act as a broker between the poor peasantry and national political processes is already seriously eroded. Mrs. Gandhi's decision to go to the electorate one year earlier than mandated was undoubtedly prompted by the frustrations of political dependence on the C.P.I., the D.M.K., and Independents for parliamentary majorities after the 1969 split of the Indian National Congress reduced the New Congress party to a minority of 228 in a 520 member *Lok Sabha*. Nevertheless, the decision also grew out of a political gamble that local faction leaders could not hold the loyalty of Harijans and other low-status client groups if the question of redistribution was directly raised as the central issue of the campaign. This assumption was evident in Mrs. Gandhi's determination to separate the parliamentary elections from the State elections, and to minimize the opposition's advantage in mobilizing votes on the basis of local patronage networks put together by district and State party leaders and M.L.A.'s, as the local officials directly associated with allocations of government funds and services at the constituency level. This separation was achieved in all but three States. The exceptions were West Bengal and Orissa,[14] both under President's Rule, which opted for concurrent elections in an effort to find a new, stable majority, and Tamil Nadu, where the D.M.K. hoped to head off the growing challenge to its leadership from aggressive organization by the Old Congress party.

The "astonishing wins" nationwide that gave Mrs. Gandhi's New Congress party 350 seats in the 518 member *Lok Sabha*—a clear two-thirds majority—offer convincing evidence that previous patterns of clientelist politics did break down, not only in urban constituencies, but also in rural areas. Several aspects of the election point to this conclusion. First, the grass-roots organization of the New Congress party in 1971 was weaker than that of the undivided Congress in 1967, which then managed to win only 284 seats in the 520 member *Lok Sabha*, about 55 percent of the total. At the time of the party split in 1969, over 20 percent of the members of the Congress Parliamentary Party joined the Old Congress; and over one-third of the membership of the All-India Congress Committee opted for the Old Congress. In some states, notably Tamil Nadu, Mysore, and Gujerat, virtually the entire party apparatus of the undivided Congress remained with the Old Congress. As a result, in the 1971 General Elections, many New Congress candidates had to stand in constituencies where the Old Congress held sway over the patronage machinery through control of State Assembly seats as well as local government bodies. Second, either the Old Congress or opposition party coalitions commanded the State Governments of Uttar Pradesh, Bihar, Punjab, Gujerat, Mysore, and Tamil Nadu, suggesting that New Congress party candidates in these States were also often campaigning in constituencies where local patronage

---

[14] President's Rule was imposed on Orissa in January 1971 after the junior partner in the Swatantra-led coalition withdrew, and deprived the Government of a majority in the Legislative Assembly.

networks were led by members of opposition groups. Third, division of votes among the conservative opposition parties and the potential benefit to the New Congress was reduced by an electoral alliance among the Old Congress, Swatantra, and the Jan Sangh to support one candidate in some 300 constituencies.[15] Fourth, despite evident organizational weaknesses, the New Congress party paid little attention to strengthening the local party apparatus. On the contrary, its campaign strategy concentrated on projecting Mrs. Gandhi's personal image as a symbol of economic and social justice. Not only did millions of posters and badges carry Mrs. Gandhi's portrait into cities and small towns, but the Prime Minister undertook a national campaign tour aimed at marginal constituencies in key States, including rural areas. The message carried by the Prime Minister in person and through the media was simple. It explained the failure of government programs to improve the lives of the poor by the minority position of the New Congress party in Parliament which had to make compromises in order to survive. The appeal was direct. Mrs. Gandhi pleaded with the electorate to "strengthen my hands" against the vested economic interests by giving the New Congress party an absolute majority in the *Lok Sabha*. If the New Congress achieved a majority, Mrs. Gandhi promised, it would be possible to "put down poverty" and to provide more jobs for the unemployed, to place a ceiling on urban income and property, and to carry out effective land reforms, including a lower ceiling on land ownership.

Still, on the eve of the national elections, despite recognition that Mrs. Gandhi had "become a symbol of change for many" and had "a distinct appeal for the dispossessed and the poorer sections and a proportion of the young,"[16] in-

[15] The Samyukta Socialist Party also joined the Alliance in electoral adjustments.
[16] *The Statesman*, February 26, 1971.

formed observers, citing the organizational weakness of the party in several States, including Orissa, Bihar, West Bengal, Gujerat, Mysore, and Tamil Nadu, gave the New Congress little hope of winning an absolute majority. It was only after the electoral landslide that the experts realized where the projections had gone wrong. "The familiar pattern of local loyalties to specific leaders and of votes being determined by electoral alliances appears no longer to hold as good as it did in the past . . . established methods of wooing the voter—playing on local issues and loyalties and arrangements—have ceased to be valid."[17] In a similar vein, one commentator observed: "The estimates went wrong because no one anticipated that Mrs. Gandhi's simple message would get across to the bulk of the rural voters and compulsively superimpose itself on the caste, local, and regional factors. Not only did this message get across—obviously by word of mouth rather than through recognized channels of communication—but her appeal also momentarily swept away caste and regional prejudices."[18] Indeed, Mrs. Gandhi's sweep was not confined to the large cities of Delhi, Calcutta, and Bombay where relatively high rates of literacy and media exposure facilitated a direct appeal to voters. Striking victories were also won in the hinterlands of several States, including Uttar Pradesh, Mysore, Maharashtra, Bihar, Orissa, Punjab, and Haryana, lending substance to the assumption of a massive rural response cutting across regional, parochial, and caste lines.

Results in the three State elections, although complicated by local issues and regional party groups, also revealed a departure from previous patterns of vertical mobilization at the village and constituency levels. In Tamil Nadu, where the New Congress party agreed not to contest any State Assembly seats, but supported candidates endorsed by the

[17] *Ibid.*, March 13, 1971.
[18] S. Nihal Singh, "Mrs. Gandhi's Task of Redeeming Her Promises," *ibid.*, March 19, 1971.

211

Dravida Munnetra Kazhagam,[19] the D.M.K. was expected to have difficulty maintaining its majority after local elections to village and town panchayats gave the Old Congress party 46 percent of the seats compared to 34 percent for the D.M.K. Notwithstanding the alignments at the village level, however, the D.M.K. won a "sensational victory" in the State, increasing its dominant position in the 234 seat Legislative Assembly from 138 in 1967 to 184 in 1971. By contrast, the Old Congress party suffered a rout, declining to 15 seats from its previous total of 49. Analysis of available post-election data concluded that increased support for the D.M.K. came from "among the less affluent sections of society—that is to say among the predominant majority of the masses" in the rural and semi-urban areas.[20]

A similar phenomenon occurred in Orissa. In 1967, old patterns of vertical mobilization were sufficiently strong to make Swatantra the single largest party in the State Legislative Assembly. Based on its strength in the highlands areas, where the party was organized by former princely rulers commanding the loyalty of a predominantly tribal population, Swatantra was able to win 49 out of 140 seats, while the undivided Congress party, with 31 seats, was relegated to second position. Yet, in the 1971 elections, the New Congress party was able to reverse this relationship. Relying mainly on Mrs. Gandhi's pre-election visits to marginal constituencies, the New Congress won a total of 51 seats becoming the largest party in the Legislative Assembly, while Swatantra, with 36 seats, was reduced to second place. Moreover, the New Congress party also managed to turn back the challenge from the Utkal Congress in Orissa, which based its appeal on regional interests.

[19] This arrangement was made in return for an electoral adjustment with the D.M.K. to support New Congress candidates in 10 of 39 *Lok Sabha* constituencies.
[20] *The Statesman*, March 13, 1971.

Even in West Bengal where the Marxist-led United Left Front succeeded in winning 123 seats in the 277 member Legislative Assembly, and the Marxists emerged as the single largest party with 111 seats, the New Congress party was able to run a close second, winning a total of 105 seats. While a portion of this success can be explained by the heavy majorities for the New Congress in Calcutta, equally important were unprecedented victories in the rural constituencies of North Bengal, the target area for Mrs. Gandhi's personal campaign on the eve of the elections, where she once again stressed her commitment to eradicate poverty.

The 1971 Fifth General Elections gave unmistakable evidence of the direct participation of the poor and the young (there were 20,000,000 persons newly eligible to vote of whom the overwhelming majority necessarily are also poor) in a number of other ways. The Old Congress party, which was effectively attacked as the spokesman of vested economic interests, won only 16 seats compared to its previous strength of 56. The other major conservative party did worse: Swatantra managed to salvage only 8 seats as opposed to 42 in 1967. Only the Jan Sangh which had superimposed a populist program on its communalist appeal minimized its losses, winning 22 seats in 1971 compared to 35 in 1967. By contrast, although the Marxists suffered most from Mrs. Gandhi's promise to solve the problems of poverty without unleashing violence, they nevertheless managed a modest improvement in their position, winning 25 seats in 1971 compared to 19 in 1967, and emerging as the second largest party in the *Lok Sabha*. Together with the 23 seats won by the C.P.I. (the same number as in 1967) the two Communist parties improved their overall position, prompting talk about the possibilities of future reconciliation and a new United Front.

It may be that with the perspective of time, the 1971 General Elections will come to be seen as a watershed event in

213

Indian political development. The national leadership did succeed, possibly on a large scale, in eroding the strategic position of local factional leaders and intermediate elites as the political mobilizers of the poor peasantry. Some of the repercussions of this breakthrough are bound to be an enhanced political awareness among Harijans and other disadvantaged groups, and a growing desire and expectation for rapid improvement and change, especially inasmuch as Mrs. Gandhi's requirement of an absolute majority has been more than met. Moreover, the politicization of the peasantry, once begun, is likely to prove irreversible. It will inevitably bring in its wake proliferating demands for greater opportunities and services by large numbers of persons and groups formerly content with a passive or follower role in politics.

More immediately, Mrs. Gandhi's impressive electoral victory is significant in keeping open options for orderly change. It is, of course, possible that revolutionary parties will ultimately prevail, at least partly by default. Conversely, the propertied classes, frightened by the prospect of mass upheaval, may react with preemptive violence and establish a more authoritarian regime. Yet, given the broad mandate for peaceful reform now enjoyed by the New Congress party, there is still the possibility originally cherished by India's planners that the multiple economic and social aims of development can be achieved through the democratic structure. Indeed, with a two-thirds majority in the *Lok Sabha*, it is even feasible for the Government to think in terms of constitutional amendments that can weaken the fundamental guarantees for the right to property. Nevertheless, the crucial problem of implementation remains. Popularly elected national, state, and local governmental bodies can be made into effective legislative agencies for reform only if a strong party organization can institutionalize popular participation—and pressure—at the grass-roots level. A long-term strategy for peaceful change through the electoral process requires that the poor peasantry be educated in understanding their common interest and strength in cooperating through such organizations at all levels of government. It requires democratic parties to actively compete with the radical left in organizing the most disadvantaged sections of the rural population for direct participation in the political process. It requires a willingness by politicians to risk alienation of the prosperous landowning castes which still occupy key decision-making roles in local government and administration. Above all, it requires a genuine commitment to social reform. The response of the democratic parties to the growing challenge of agrarian unrest will weigh heavily in the option India finally chooses.

Glossary,
Appendix,
and
Index

Glossary

Agricultural Refinance Corporation	Public corporation established in 1963 to provide refinance facilities to State cooperative banks, central land mortgage banks, and commercial banks for schemes of agricultural development
Akali Dal	Literally Akali Party. Organized in 1920 by members of the Akali sect of Sikhism and dedicated to the establishment of a separate Sikh state within the Indian Union
aman	Main paddy crop of West Bengal cultivated between July-August and December-January
aus	Variety of paddy suitable for early sowing in West Bengal, cultivated between April-May and October
ayacut	Area served by a major irrigation project
bargardar	Sharecropper in West Bengal
beedi	Locally grown tobacco, hand-rolled into cigarettes
benami land	Land illegally held by owners in violation of state laws establishing a ceiling on land ownership

219

Bharatiya Jan Sangh	Literally Indian Peoples Party; the major spokesman of Hindu nationalism, advocating Hinduization of the Muslim minority, Hindi as the official working language, higher expenditures on defense, and economic self-sufficiency
Block	Basic unit of development planning and administration under the Community Development Program, typically covering 100 villages and 65,000 persons, and headed by a Government official called the Block Development Officer
boro	Summer paddy crop grown in West Bengal between March and June
Bose plough	Indigenous agricultural implement locally manufactured in Thanjavur and especially suitable for efficient preparation of paddy fields
Brahmin	Class assigned highest ritual ranking in the sacred Hindu texts; traditionally serving as priests
Burmese Satoon	Improved agricultural implement for puddling wet land adapted from a device used in Burma
Communist Party of India	Organized in the 1920's with help from the Soviet Union; generally following a United Front electoral strategy to win political power
Communist Party of India (Marxist)	Formed in 1964 by secession of the leftist faction of the Communist Party of India; committed to building a

mass movement among the poor peasantry in alliance with the workers as a strategy of coming to power

Community Development Program — Central scheme for rural development adopted in the five year plans, involving a coordinated attack on all problems associated with low agricultural productivity

dhoti — Cloth wrapped around the waist by male Hindus to fashion a long loincloth

Dravida Munnetra Kazakham — Literally Dravidian Progressive Association; an anti-Brahmin, populist party in Tamil Nadu committed to the protection of Tamil as the regional language, and social and economic reform

filter point — Shallow tubewell suitable to coastal and deltaic areas where the substrata soil is soft and groundwater plentiful

goonda — Strong-arm man or thug

gherao — Coercive tactic adopted by striking workers of surrounding landowners, factory managers, or government officers until demands are met

Harijan — Word coined by Gandhi for untouchable castes meaning "Children of God"

Indian National Congress — Mass-based political movement organized by Gandhi to lead the Independence struggle; until local election defeats in 1967, the ruling party both

	at the Center and in the states, committed to secularism, socialism, and democracy
jenmies	Hindu temples and individual Brahmins and Nairs enjoying full ownership rights in land under the traditional agrarian system of Kerala
jenmom	Full ownership rights in land enjoyed by the jenmies of Kerala
jotedar	Large landowner in West Bengal cultivating with the help of hired labor or through sharecroppers
kanom	Occupancy rights in land purchased by a tenant from a jenmie in Kerala
kanomdar	Tenant who has purchased occupancy rights in land from a jenmie in Kerala
kharif	Crop season beginning at the onset of the Southwest monsoon between May and July and ending between September-October
Krishak Sabha	Peasants Association
kurvai	Kharif paddy crop in Tamil Nadu
lathi	Long stick used as a riot control weapon
mahinder	Permanent laborer in West Bengal whose family is attached to the household of one landowner from generation to generation
maistry	Leader of a team of agricultural laborers; traditionally designated to

negotiate with landowners on wages in Andhra Pradesh

mirasdar	Large landowner in Tamil Nadu cultivating either with hired labor or through sharecroppers
mundakan	Rabi paddy crop in Kerala
nagare	Laborer in West Bengal enjoying a permanent working arrangement with one landowner
National Extension Service	Nationwide administrative apparatus operating at the district, block, and village levels to implement the Community Development Program
Naxalites	Revolutionary groups splintering off from the state units of the Communist Party of India (Marxists) to follow a Maoist strategy of class struggle in the countryside and terrorist tactics in the cities
New Congress	Political party formed by the Prime Minister, Mrs. Gandhi, and the majority faction of the Congress Party in Parliament and the party organization, after the Indian National Congress split in November 1969.
Old Congress	Political party formed by the minority faction in the Congress Parliamentary Party and the party organization after the Indian National Congress split in November 1969.
President's Rule	Provision under the Indian Constitu-

tion allowing the President of India to proclaim the existence of an emergency which prevents a State Government from exercising its powers under the Constitution, and to order that the powers of the State Legislature be exercised by the President in conjunction with Parliament, provided such a proclamation is ratified by both Houses of Parliament within two months

puddler

Agricultural implement designed to soften the soil in preparation for the transplantation of paddy seedlings

Punjabi Subah

Slogan demanding a separate state for Punjabi-speaking persons

rabi

Crops sown at the beginning of cold weather between October and December and harvested between February and May

ryotwari tenure

Land system in which the peasant pays revenue directly to the state rather than a landlord and enjoys full rights of ownership

Scheduled Castes

Lists of former untouchables drawn up by the Central Government and appended to the Constitution under provisions for reserved seats in Parliament and the Legislative Assemblies of the states for members of untouchable castes in proportion to their population

Sikhs	The followers of Guru Nanak (1469-1538) who separated from orthodox Hinduism and developed their own language, sacred book, ritual, and social organization; centering mainly in the Punjab
Swatantra Party	Literally Freedom Party. Organized in 1959 to provide a conservative alternative to the Indian National Congress in promoting national policies favoring private investment and ownership
panchayat	Village council elected by popular vote
Panchayati raj	Three-tiered system of local government usually organized on the basis of directly elected village councils and indirectly elected councils at the Block and district levels
punja	Summer paddy crop grown in Kerala between March and May
taluk	Administrative subdivision of a district generally including 100,000 people
thaladi	Rabi paddy crop grown in Tamil Nadu
tubewell	Deep bore drilled into the ground for the purpose of tapping groundwater through several permeable layers of water-bearing soil
samba	Main paddy crop grown in Tamil Nadu between August-September and January-February

225

United Punjab
Janta Party

Literally United Punjab Peoples Party; splinter group defecting from the United Front Government of Punjab in 1967 and ruling as a minority Government with Congress support until declaration of President's Rule in November 1968

verompattomdar

Tenant-at-will in Kerala

viruppu

Kharif paddy crop in Kerala

Appendix A

Conversion Ratios for Indian Currency,
Weights and Measures

CURRENCY

Rs. 1	= $0.13
Rs. 7.5	= $1.00
Rs. 1 lakh = Rs. 100,000	= $13,333
Rs. 1 crore = Rs. 10,000,000	= $1,333,333

WEIGHTS AND MEASURES

1 litre	= 1.05 quarts
1 kilogram	= 2.2 pounds
1 Madras measure = 1.22 kilograms	= 2.7 pounds
1 bag of paddy (West Godavary)	= 165 pounds
1 bag of paddy (Thanjavur)	= 125 pounds
1 quintal	= 220 pounds
1 maund	= 82 pounds
1 ton	= 2,000 pounds
1 metric ton	= 2,204 pounds

Index

agrarian conflict: causes and nature of, 9-10, 45, 111-18, 142-43, 146-49, 185, 187-90; land-grab movement, 150, 184, 188, 199; volunteer forces, 114-18, 153, 186-87. *See also* name of district

Ahmed, Bashiruddin, 139n, 141n

Akali Dal, 41-45

All-India Coordinated Rice Improvement Project, 7

Andhra Pradesh, 139, 186n, 199; state politics in, 74-79

Bangla Congress, 181, 187-88

Bihar, 45, 179, 186n, 192, 199, 209, 211

Brahmins: and landownership, 118, 127, 140, 149, 202

Burdwan district, 11, 46, 157-89; agrarian conflict, 184-90; cooperatives, agricultural credit, 169-72; cropping pattern, 159-60; distribution of holdings, 164-66; election results, 184; Harijans, 158, 175; High Yielding Varieties Program, 161-63; I.A.D.P., 159-63; income disparities, 168-69, 173-77; irrigation projects, 158-59; land reforms, evasion of, 168-69; social setting, 157-60; tenancy, incidence of, 166-67; tubewells and adoption of high-yielding varieties, 160-61

Communist Party of India: Andhra Pradesh, 74-77; Fifth General Elections, 213; Kerala, 139-44; 147, 149, 152-53; nationwide land-grab move-

ment, 199; parliament, 208; Punjab, 41, 43; Tamil Nadu, 109-10; West Bengal, 179-87

Communist Party of India (Marxists): Fifth General Elections, 213; Kerala, 140-50, 152-55; nationwide land-grab movement, 199; Punjab, 43; Tamil Nadu, 110-18; West Godavary, 75-76; West Bengal, 180, 182-90

Communist Party (Marxist-Leninist), 186n

community development program, 3, 4; in Kerala, 156

community projects, 3

cooperatives, agricultural credit, 4, 11, 20, 28-29, 66-68, 89, 96-98, 131-34, 169-72, 196. *See also* name of district

Desai, Morarji, 152

Dravida Munnetra Kazhagam, 109, 113, 208-09, 212

East Thanjavur Mirasdars Association, 113-14, 117

Erdman, Howard L., 111n

Fifth General Elections, 208-11, 213-14

Food Corporation of India, 91

Ford Foundation, 5, 91

Fourth Plan: High Yielding Varieties Program, 6; rural works, 201; Small Farmer Development Agency, 194; States' irrigation programs, 195; unemployment, backlog of, 201

Franda, Marcus F., 178n, 182n

229

231

Varieties Program, 90-92; I.A.D.P., 84-85; income disparities, 99-107; irrigation projects, 81-82; Land Mortgage Banks, 95; social setting, 82; tenancy, incidence of, 87-88, 98; supplementary irrigation water and advantages for adoption of high-yielding varieties, 94
Third Plan, 5

United Front governments: in Kerala, 139, 146, 149-50, 153; in Punjab, 42; in West Bengal, 180, 182-85, 187-88
United Punjab Janta party, 42
Utkal Congress, 212
Uttar Pradesh, 45, 179, 186n, 192, 199, 209, 211

Weiner, Myron, 41n, 77n, 178n
West Bengal, 186n, 199, 209, 211; state politics in, 178-84, 213
West Godavary district, 11, 46, 47-80; cooperatives, agricultural credit, 66-68; cropping pattern, 52-53; distribution of holdings, 61; election results, 75-76; Harijans, 48, 74, 77-79; High Yielding Varieties Program, 49-50; I.A.D.P., 48-49; income disparities, 64-65, 70-73; irrigation projects, 54-55; Land Mortgage Banks, 58-60; social setting, 47-48; tenancy, incidence of, 61-65; supplementary irrigation water and the adoption of high-yielding varieties, 53
Wood, John B., 143n, 182n

BOOKS WRITTEN
UNDER THE AUSPICES OF THE
CENTER OF INTERNATIONAL STUDIES
PRINCETON UNIVERSITY

Gabriel A. Almond, *The Appeals of Communism* (Princeton University Press 1954)

William W. Kaufmann, ed., *Military Policy and National Security* (Princeton University Press 1956)

Klaus Knorr, *The War Potential of Nations* (Princeton University Press 1956)

Lucian W. Pye, *Guerrilla Communism in Malaya* (Princeton University Press 1956)

Charles De Visscher, *Theory and Reality in Public International Law*, trans. by P. E. Corbett (Princeton University Press 1957; rev. ed. 1968)

Bernard C. Cohen, *The Political Process and Foreign Policy: The Making of the Japanese Peace Settlement* (Princeton University Press 1959)

Myron Weiner, *Party Politics in India: The Development of a Multi-Party System* (Princeton University Press 1957)

Percy E. Corbett, *Law in Diplomacy* (Princeton University Press 1959)

Rolf Sannwald and Jacques Stohler, *Economic Integration: Theoretical Assumptions and Consequences of European Unification*, trans. by Herman Karreman (Princeton University Press 1959)

Klaus Knorr, ed., *NATO and American Security* (Princeton University Press 1959)

Gabriel A. Almond and James S. Coleman, eds., *The Politics of the Developing Areas* (Princeton University Press 1960)

Herman Kahn, *On Thermonuclear War* (Princeton University Press 1960)

Sidney Verba, *Small Groups and Political Behavior: A Study of Leadership* (Princeton University Press 1961)

Robert J. C. Butow, *Tojo and the Coming of the War* (Princeton University Press 1961)

Glenn H. Snyder, *Deterrence and Defense: Toward a Theory of National Security* (Princeton University Press 1961)

Klaus Knorr and Sidney Verba, eds., *The International System: Theoretical Essays* (Princeton University Press 1961)

Peter Paret and John W. Shy, *Guerrillas in the 1960's* (Praeger 1962)

George Modelski, *A Theory of Foreign Policy* (Praeger 1962)

Klaus Knorr and Thornton Read, eds., *Limited Strategic War* (Praeger 1963)

Frederick S. Dunn, *Peace-Making and the Settlement with Japan* (Princeton University Press 1963)

Arthur L. Burns and Nina Heathcote, *Peace-Keeping by United Nations Forces* (Praeger 1963)

Richard A. Falk, *Law, Morality, and War in the Contemporary World* (Praeger 1963)

James N. Rosenau, *National Leadership and Foreign Policy: A Case Study in the Mobilization of Public Support* (Princeton University Press 1963)

Gabriel A. Almond and Sidney Verba, *The Civic Culture: Political Attitudes and Democracy in Five Nations* (Princeton University Press 1963)

Bernard C. Cohen, *The Press and Foreign Policy* (Princeton University Press 1963)

Richard L. Sklar, *Nigerian Political Parties: Power in an Emergent African Nation* (Princeton University Press 1963)

Peter Paret, *French Revolutionary Warfare from Indochina to Algeria: The Analysis of a Political and Military Doctrine* (Praeger 1964)

Harry Eckstein, ed., *Internal War: Problems and Approaches* (Free Press 1964)

Cyril E. Black and Thomas P. Thornton, eds., *Communism and Revolution: The Strategic Uses of Political Violence* (Princeton University Press 1964)

Miriam Camps, *Britain and the European Community 1955-1963* (Princeton University Press 1964)

Thomas P. Thornton, ed., *The Third World in Soviet Perspective: Studies by Soviet Writers on the Developing Areas* (Princeton University Press 1964)

James N. Rosenau, ed., *International Aspects of Civil Strife* (Princeton University Press 1964)

Sidney I. Ploss, *Conflict and Decision-Making in Soviet Russia: A Case Study of Agricultural Policy, 1953-1963* (Princeton University Press 1965)

Richard A. Falk and Richard J. Barnet, eds., *Security in Disarmament* (Princeton University Press 1965)

Karl von Vorys, *Political Development in Pakistan* (Princeton University Press 1965)

Harold and Margaret Sprout, *The Ecological Perspective on Human Affairs, With Special Reference to International Politics* (Princeton University Press 1965)

Klaus Knorr, *On the Uses of Military Power in the Nuclear Age* (Princeton University Press 1966)

Harry Eckstein, *Division and Cohesion in Democracy: A Study of Norway* (Princeton University Press 1966)

Cyril E. Black, *The Dynamics of Modernization: A Study in Comparative History* (Harper and Row 1966)

Peter Kunstadter, ed., *Southeast Asian Tribes, Minorities, and Nations* (Princeton University Press 1967)

E. Victor Wolfenstein, *The Revolutionary Personality: Lenin, Trotsky, Gandhi* (Princeton University Press 1967)

Leon Gordenker, *The UN Secretary-General and the Maintenance of Peace* (Columbia University Press 1967)

Oran R. Young, *The Intermediaries: Third Parties in International Crises* (Princeton University Press 1967)

James N. Rosenau, ed., *Domestic Sources of Foreign Policy* (Free Press 1967)

Richard F. Hamilton, *Affluence and the French Worker in the Fourth Republic* (Princeton University Press 1967)

Linda B. Miller, *World Order and Local Disorder: The United Nations and Internal Conflicts* (Princeton University Press 1967)

Wolfram F. Hanrieder, *West German Foreign Policy, 1949-1963: International Pressures and Domestic Response* (Stanford University Press 1967)

Richard H. Ullman, *Britain and the Russian Civil War: November 1918-February 1920* (Princeton University Press 1968)

Robert Gilpin, *France in the Age of the Scientific State* (Princeton University Press 1968)

William B. Bader, *The United States and the Spread of Nuclear Weapons* (Pegasus 1968)

Richard A. Falk, *Legal Order in a Violent World* (Princeton University Press 1968)

Cyril E. Black, Richard A. Falk, Klaus Knorr, and Oran R. Young, *Neutralization and World Politics* (Princeton University Press 1968)

Oran R. Young, *The Politics of Force: Bargaining During International Crises* (Princeton University Press 1969)

Klaus Knorr and James N. Rosenau, eds., *Contending Approaches to International Politics* (Princeton University Press 1969)

James N. Rosenau, ed., *Linkage Politics: Essays on the Convergence of National and International Systems* (Free Press 1969)

John T. McAlister, Jr., *Viet Nam: The Origins of Revolution* (Knopf 1969)

Jean Edward Smith, *Germany Beyond the Wall: People, Politics and Prosperity* (Little, Brown 1969)

James Barros, *Betrayal from Within: Joseph Avenol, Secretary-General of the League of Nations, 1933-1940* (Yale University Press 1969)

Charles Hermann, *Crises in Foreign Policy: A Simulation Analysis* (Bobbs-Merrill 1969)

Robert C. Tucker, *The Marxian Revolutionary Idea: Essays on Marxist Thought and Its Impact on Radical Movements* (W. W. Norton 1969)

Harvey Waterman, *Political Change in Contemporary France: The Politics of an Industrial Democracy* (Charles E. Merrill 1969)

Richard A. Falk and Cyril E. Black, eds., *The Future of the International Legal Order*, Vol. I, *Trends and Patterns* (Princeton University Press 1969)

Ted Robert Gurr, *Why Men Rebel* (Princeton University Press 1969)

C. S. Whitaker, Jr., *The Politics of Tradition: Continuity and Change in Northern Nigeria, 1946-1966* (Princeton University Press 1970)

Richard A. Falk, *The Status of Law in International Society* (Princeton University Press 1970)

Henry Bienen, *Tanzania: Party Transformation and Economic Development* (Princeton University Press 1967, rev. edn. 1970)

Klaus Knorr, *Military Power and Potential* (D. C. Heath 1970)

Richard A. Falk and Cyril E. Black, eds., *The Future of the International Legal Order*, Vol. II, *Wealth and Resources* (Princeton University Press 1970)

Leon Gordenker, ed., *The United Nations and International Politics* (Princeton University Press 1971)

Cyril E. Black and Richard A. Falk, eds., *The Future of the International Legal Order*, Vol. III, *Conflict Management* (Princeton University Press 1971)

Harold and Margaret Sprout, *Toward a Politics of the Planet Earth* (Van Nostrand Reinhold Co. 1971)